"The location and interrelationship of various biblical doctrines is a needful aspect of study in the realm of theological reflection. Watson has produced a study brimming with such considerations, dealing specifically with catechesis, baptism, and entrance into the covenant community of the local church. Sweeping in scope, the author engages readers with a working taxonomy of various positions on the interrelationship of these three ecclesiological categories. This work will offer clarity on the kinds of positions that are taken within various church traditions, showcasing the theological underpinnings of such practical matters. Such reflection will be of great benefit to the church at large, as the author compels us to think theologically about these practices."

—**Jeremy M. Kimble,** associate professor of theology, Cedarville University

"With careful historical and theological precision, Jonathan Watson examines not only the presence of catechesis, baptism, and Communion in the life of the churches but also the relationship between them. Watson's model for navigating this matrix of meaning and practice has considerable explanatory power for the study of historical theology and theological reflection on contemporary practice. For scholars and pastors, this volume would be an excellent initiation into this strategic area of ecclesiology. Warmly recommended!"

—**Ched Spellman,** associate professor of biblical and theological studies, Cedarville University; author of *Toward a Canon-Conscious Reading of the Bible*

"In this well-researched and thought-provoking academic study, Jonathan Watson employs 'liturgical logic' to provide an insightful and scholarly analysis of how different church traditions relate baptism, catechism, and Communion to each other."

—**Joel R. Beeke,** president, Puritan Reformed Theological Seminary

T0366652

IN THE NAME *of* OUR LORD

Four Models of the Relationship between
Baptism, Catechesis, and Communion

IN THE NAME
of OUR LORD

Four Models of the Relationship between
Baptism, Catechesis, and Communion

JONATHAN D. WATSON

STUDIES IN HISTORICAL AND SYSTEMATIC THEOLOGY

LEXHAM
ACADEMIC

In the Name of Our Lord: Four Models of the Relationship between Baptism, Catechesis, and Communion
Studies in Historical and Systematic Theology

Lexham Academic, an imprint of Lexham Press
1313 Commercial St., Bellingham, WA 98225
LexhamPress.com

Print ISBN 9781683594918
Digital ISBN 9781683594925
Library of Congress Control Number 2021933811

Lexham Editorial: Todd Hains, Claire Brubaker, Danielle Thevenaz
Cover Design: Bryan Hintz, Brittany Schrock
Typesetting: Justin Marr

This book is dedicated to Karen,

my excellent wife, my love,

whose love, care, and faithfulness are nothing short of praiseworthy,

and to Emma, Abby, Nathan, and Jude,

precious gifts from the Lord,

and to my parents, Ron and Janis Watson,

whose love for the Lord and for his Word

led me to Christ and catechized me to walk in the truth (3 John 4)

CONTENTS

FOREWORD

—

HOPE FOR THE LOGIC OF LITURGY

The Spirit himself bears witness with our spirit that we are children of God, and if children, then heirs—heirs of God and fellow heirs with Christ, provided we suffer with him in order that we may also be glorified with him (Rom 8:16–17 ESV).

When thoughtful Christians from one tradition encounter other thoughtful Christians from other traditions, they experience spiritual unity alongside cognitive dissonance. The Holy Spirit—who gives new birth—is clearly evident, but important aspects of Christian theology and life are seen in apparently irreconcilable ways. This conundrum is notable among those who understand the administration of baptism in radically different ways vis-à-vis catechesis and Communion. It is also noticeable when individual traditions begin to surrender their own liturgical coherence.

Important questions begin to appear during the inevitable process of discovery once a maturing Christian begins to think on these matters: How did we arrive at this enigma of ecclesiological dissolution? What are the structures of thought which may enable genuine believers to worship again with integrity? How can we find a way through this tangle to reclaim Christian worship within and without? How might we simultaneously confirm the presence of the Spirit of God and Christ, whom we see in others, yet admit we do not share the same way of witnessing to his divine presence?

Having carefully read the perceptive theological and ecclesiological models offered by theologians like Ernst Troeltsch, Richard Niebuhr, and Avery Dulles, Jonathan Watson has crafted a new typology intended to enable us to begin, at the least, to see how various models of "liturgical logic" function in relation to Scripture and to one another. While I embrace what he describes as an interdependent prospective model of catechesis and baptism, Watson's typology assists any careful theologian to understand how those adopting various logics of Christian liturgy might arrive at their position with faithfulness.

Ecumenical understanding is not the only benefit of this study. Just as important are the many ways the author helps pastors within different traditions to step back and evaluate how their own logic of liturgy may have been distorted through the careless, indiscriminate, and unthinking integration of their particular model. Watson encourages the various traditions to consider how they might recall and reinforce their theological convictions. The ancient principle of *lex orandi, lex credendi* is employed to suggest the means by which leaders could recall the center of their way of worship.

Especially helpful is his call for pastoral theologians to listen carefully to the voices of God, the initiate, and the congregation. For instance, Watson believes the Baptist tradition, and similar low-church ones, have not rendered sufficient attention to the connections between the three elements of baptism, catechesis, and Communion. Baptists tend to treat these elements independently, forsaking their beneficial interdependence. We can individualize worship to the point that its covenantal aspects, which ground our relations to God and one another, have disappeared almost entirely. Watson thus intentionally speaks not only to academics but also to pastors.

Here is a real opportunity for both confessional and ecumenical theologians to advance their understanding of Christian initiation. He is not dropping on Christian theology a polemic, as was all the rage immediately following the Reformation. Nor is he offering a comprehensive solution to divisions in liturgy, as was the fashion in the twentieth century. Rather, what Watson offers is a means to craft a superior understanding of the underlying structures of theology that shape not only our various liturgies, but also our diverse doctrines and divergent practices. His work provides a way of clarification.

We must recognize that, in part, the suffering we bear now is experienced in our relationships with one another. Such suffering occurs both within our churches and between our traditions. Within our various churches, we sense anguish in how the ordinances of Jesus Christ no longer coinhere to improve the life of the church. Sadly, each model is capable of losing its heart. A reformation of life and practice should come as the logic of a liturgy is remembered.

Between the traditions, our anguish manifests itself in the cognitive and liturgical discord that we sense when encountering fellow heirs with Jesus Christ on this side of his second coming. While we desire unity in worship with all children of God, we find our witness impaired by our inability to affirm the way others worship. Our debilitation may not perhaps be overcome simply by recognizing our problems, but at least Watson has offered a better way to conceive them than anything available hitherto.

I look forward to the day when all believers shall manifest both coherent local worship and the very unity which Christ himself prayed the Father would institute among us (John 17:22–23). I believe the Lord will be pleased with Professor Watson's efforts to bring us closer to that day, not only in what he wrote, but in the spirit in which he wrote it. Pastors and theologians of differing theological traditions will find his typology helpful for increasing awareness of God, of self, and of others through reclaiming the logic of worship. May our love for God and for one another, both within and between Christ's churches, manifest itself as we display God's glory through the integrity of initiation.

Malcolm B. Yarnell III,
research professor of theology,
Southwestern Baptist Theological Seminary;
teaching pastor, Lakeside Baptist Church of Granbury, Texas;
Easter 2021

ACKNOWLEDGMENTS

—

It is humbling to consider all the means of nurture and support the Lord has provided along the way in bringing this work to completion. The book you hold in your hands is a revision of the dissertation I completed at Southwestern Baptist Theological Seminary (Fort Worth, Texas). Dr. Jason K. Lee, my supervisor, taught me as much outside of the classroom as a churchman and family man as he did in the classroom as a scholar. With regard to the latter, the rigor he exemplified in his own work and to which he challenged each of his students is something to which I aspire in my own teaching.

Other significant mentors along the way are deserving of mention. My childhood pastor, Randy Owens, modeled for me what a pastor-theologian looks like. Preben Vang, my first formal theology professor, impressed upon me the need to do theology for the church ("We do theology because we preach on Sunday!"), a value that I hope has been embodied in this work. Dr. Stan Norman deepened my passion for theology as much as any professor I've ever had. The Lord used him to help me see the passion he was giving me for deeper study of the Scriptures and for teaching. Many other professors (more than I can recount here) from my undergraduate days at Ouachita Baptist University through my graduate studies at New Orleans Baptist Theological Seminary and culminating in my doctoral work at SWBTS have made unique and lasting contributions to my scholarship and discipleship unto Christ through both their persistent encouragement and faithful wounds. I am especially grateful for the work of Dr. Jeffrey Bingham, whose 2012 Day-Higginbotham Lecture "The Relationship between Baptism and Doctrine in the Second Century" and personal conversations provided much of the impetus for the topic of the original dissertation.

The band of friends that faithfully encouraged me along the way is too numerous to recount here. Several co-travelers were especially significant in the writing of this work, namely, Madison Grace, Matt Millsap, and Ched Spellman. Some of the first breakthroughs were catalyzed by a unique blend of coffee, scholarly conversation, and blitz chess with Ched. Additionally, Ched provided proofreading and writing advice for each chapter. E. B. White famously wrote, "It is not often that someone comes along who is a true friend and a good writer." Ched Spellman is both. Many thanks are due to Billy Marsh whose friendship and guidance the Lord used to seek publication of this work through Lexham Press. Many thanks to Jamey Droddy and the LSUS BCM for their hospitality in granting me access to their prayer room for a significant amount of quiet writing and editing in the summer of 2019.

My colleagues in the College of Christian Studies at Charleston Southern University are a joy and privilege to serve beside. Drs. Ben Phillips, Peter Beck, Pete Link, Ed Gravely, Ross Parker, Ryan Gimple, Jonathan Denton, and Ron Harvell are true friends and scholars. Each in his own way has been instrumental to my growth in scholarship and teaching. The interdisciplinary discussions that regularly take place in the faculty break room with Drs. John Kukendall (history), Brian Miller (history), and Scott Yarbrough (English) have enriched my thinking as well. In fact, the produce of some of those conversations have made their way into this book.

All those who worked with me in the Housing Office at Southwestern Seminary during my PhD journey share a special place in this achievement. Special thanks are also due to Beth Hill for her review of my treatment of Eastern Orthodox theology. Any shortcomings in my presentation, however, remain my own. My family, both immediate and extended, is a blessing which I do not deserve. The publication of this, my first book, while joyous, pales in comparison with the joy of being a husband to Karen and father to Emma, Abby, Nathan, and Jude. I am blessed beyond measure to be your husband and father.

Jonathan D. Watson
Soli Deo Gloria
Summerville, South Carolina
February 2021

ABBREVIATIONS

—

BC	*The Book of Concord: The Confessions of the Evangelical Lutheran Church*
BCF	*Baptist Confessions of Faith*
CCC	*Catechism of the Catholic Church: With Modifications from the Editio Typica*
CCFCT	*Creeds and Confessions of Faith in the Christian Tradition*
CCT	*Catechism of the Council of Trent: For Parish Priests*
LW	*Luther's Works*
MWJB	*The Miscellaneous Works of John Bunyan*
NPNF[1]	*Nicene and Post-Nicene Fathers*, Series 1
NPNF[2]	*Nicene and Post-Nicene Fathers*, Series 2
PG	Patrologia Graeca [= *Patrologiae Cursus Completus: Series Graeca*]
RC	*Reformed Confessions of the Sixteenth Century*
RCH	*Reformed Confessions: Harmonized*
RCIA	*Rite of Christian Initiation of Adults [Ordo Initiationis Christianae Adultorum]*
TDNT	*Theological Dictionary of the New Testament*

1

—

MAPPING DIVERSE PATTERNS OF INITIATION

Since the very first public proclamation of the gospel on the day of Pentecost, the church has been adding to its number. At the conclusion of the Pentecost narrative, Luke writes, "Those who accepted his message were baptized, and about three thousand were *added to their number that day*" (Acts 2:41 NIV). The phrase "added to their number" is important, for it signals the existence of a visible body of persons, a fellowship of the faithful ("their number"). It is this existing church that is initiating new members into its midst. Here, we see one of the clearest examples of Christian initiation. Unfortunately, readers will not have to think long about the theology and practice of Christian initiation or some of its most prominent elements, such as baptism, teaching (i.e., catechesis), and Communion, to be reminded of the deep divisions that exist among Christian denominations on these matters.[1]

The book you are reading is an attempt to think through the many and varied ways in which local fellowships have conducted such initiation or entrance. It also considers the way in which broad traditions of the Christian church (from Eastern Orthodoxy to Quakerism) have construed this relationship. This book will, therefore, bring many different

---

1. This chapter will offer an argument for why we are focusing on these three elements. Preliminarily, one should note the presence of all three in this passage. Baptism is most obvious (Acts 2:41). However, we also see that this body of disciples "were continually devoting themselves to the apostles' teaching and to fellowship, to the breaking of bread and to prayer" (2:42). Thus, those being added were also being instructed (i.e., catechized) in the faith and participating in worship together. The reference to the breaking of bread is a probable reference to the celebration of Communion. Welcomed into the fellowship via baptism, new members now devoted themselves to the apostles' teaching and to the fellowship of the Lord's Supper.

conversations into dialogue with one another, and as such it is a work in comparative or ecumenical theology. In one sense, this book will not say much that is new. The goal is not to say something that has never been said before, but rather to look at old paths in a new way. Here we will seek to identify and map patterns of liturgical logic and explore what these patterns teach us about the nature of Christian initiation and even the Christian life that follows it.

INITIATORY STRUCTURE: THEOLOGICAL
REFLECTIONS AND PROJECTIONS

The way we add to our number reflects and projects a set of theological commitments. The process itself exerts formative pressure and force that shapes and reshapes the church in a particular way. The connection between physical architecture and theology offers us a helpful analogy that illustrates this foundational point.

From third grade through my high school years, my family attended a small, rural Southern Baptist church in central Arkansas. The yellow-bricked meetinghouse had a large steeple and was situated on a broad clearing just off of a state highway. The sanctuary contained a large, built-in baptistery that overlooked a pew-filled room capable of seating roughly three hundred. The baptistery was situated behind the main stage and elevated above the choir loft so everyone from the back to the front could see it. It was deep enough to immerse and large enough for the minister to baptize from inside the pool. Importantly, the architecture of this baptistery was reflecting and projecting certain theological commitments. First, the elevation of the baptistery above the congregation reflected the credobaptist convictions of the church: baptism was celebrated as a public profession of faith on the part of the one being baptized. Second, the visibility of the pool also signaled that everyone in the congregation was a witness to this public profession. Third, the permanency and fact that the baptistery was always visible, even when not being used, functioned as an icon that we as a local church were a baptized community. In these ways, the architecture reflected the church's theological convictions about the nature and recipients of baptism, but it also projected a certain view of the church as well.

In her book *A Place for Baptism*, the Catholic liturgical scholar Regina Kuehn catalogs a number of baptismal fonts (both ancient and modern) and explains how their various shapes and features reflect and project theology.[2] Keuhn highlights several different shapes:

- Womb-shaped font: A round laver font deep enough to immerse infants. It reflects the notion that baptism is new birth. This also projects a view of the church as mother.[3]

- Cruciform font: Being an empty cross, this font symbolizes both the death of Christ as well as his resurrection. These fonts often have stairs leading in one side (often from the west; the direction of sunset and death) and leading out the other (eastward; the direction of sunrise and new life). This not only allowed for access but demonstrated transition from death to life.[4] This font shape also projects the view that baptismal life is cross-shaped and costly.

- Tomb-shaped font: Some fonts are rectangular, in the shape of a coffin or sarcophagus. The meaning reflected here is similar to that of the cruciform font. The image of death and burial is also a reminder of the life that springs forth from the death of Christ and reminds viewers of his victory over the grave.[5]

---

2. See Martin Dudley, "Baptistry," in *The New SCM Dictionary of Liturgy and Worship*, ed. Paul F. Bradshaw (London: SCM, 2013), 55–56; J. G. Davies, *The Architectural Setting of Baptism* (London: Barrie & Rockliff, 1962); Peter Hammond, ed., *Towards a Church Architecture* (London: Architectural, 1962); Regina Keuhn, *A Place for Baptism* (Chicago: Liturgy Training, 1992); Everett Ferguson, *Baptism in the Early Church* (Grand Rapids: Eerdmans, 2009), 819–60.

3. Keuhn, *Place for Baptism*, 3. See Robin M. Jensen, *Baptismal Imagery in Early Christianity* (Grand Rapids: Baker Academic, 2012), 56–58, 162–65.

4. Cf. Keuhn, *Place for Baptism*, 75. In his analysis of early church baptisteries, Everett Ferguson observes that very often baptisteries with steps had three steps in and out, symbolizing the three days Jesus was in the tomb. At the same time, Ferguson offers caution about reading too much speculation into the symbolism behind the font shapes of the early church due to a lack of explicit symbolic explanation (see Ferguson, *Baptism in the Early Church*, 820). Citing Ristow, Ferguson provides the following approximate breakdown of the archaeological evidence about baptistery shapes in the early church: (1) round (30 percent), (2) cross-shaped (16 percent), (3) rectangular (14 percent), (4) octagonal (11 percent), (5) square (9 percent), and (6) hexagonal (5 percent). These numbers add up to only 85 percent, and the remaining shapes are presumedly mixed. See Sebastian Ristow, *Früchristliche Baptisterien*, Jahrbuch für Antike und Christentum, Egänzungsband 27 (Münster: Aschendorff, 1998), 77–81.

5. Keuhn, *Place for Baptism*, 25; Jensen, *Baptismal Imagery*, 161–62.

- Polygonal font: Some fonts are shaped in either an octagon or hexagon. The octagon represents the number eight, symbolizing the day after Holy Saturday, when Jesus rose from the dead. The hexagon represents the number six, symbolizing the sixth day of the week, when Jesus suffered and died on the cross (i.e., Good Friday).[6] Thus, each shape respectively places emphasis on either Christ's death or resurrection.

- Font as tub: Kuehn contends that this round font shape (often deep enough for adult or at least infant immersion) conveys cleansing from sin.[7] This shape projects the view of the church as a sanctified body and emphasizes the holiness of postbaptismal life.

Just as there is a connection between the physical architecture of baptisteries that reflects and projects certain theological meanings, this book contends that there is a theological-liturgical architecture or shape to Christian initiation and its key initiatory elements: baptism, catechesis, and Communion. As we will seek to show, the varieties of ordering and structure of these three elements within the Christian church reflect and project convictions about a host of theological issues. Pastorally speaking, the shape of these initiatory structures brings the church into visible form in the world, but this shape or pattern of initiation also continues to reform the church as it is applied over and again within a church's life. Therefore, careful attention to the way in which persons are added to the number of the faithful is not only an interesting intellectual pursuit but a pursuit of key theological and pastoral importance.

Broadly speaking, the three key aspects of the initiation process that merit special attention are baptism, catechesis (i.e., teaching), and Communion. The first two are especially prominent within the Great

---

6. Kuehn, *Place for Baptism*, 53; cf. 65. Jensen notes, "One hexagonal font, in Grado (Italy), is housed within an octagonal building. ... Perhaps the initiate was reminded of Christ's death on entering the font and of his resurrection on emerging from it" (*Baptismal Imagery*, 162).

7. Kuehn, *Place for Baptism*, 76. Ferguson notes that the two key symbolic meanings reflected in baptismal-font shapes of the early church are that of "the tomb of death and resurrection" and "the womb of new birth" (*Baptism in the Early Church*, 819).

Commission, while the third is presupposed by it.[8] In the Great Commission recorded in Matthew's Gospel, Jesus commands his apostles, and by inference all Christians ("of all the nations ... to the end of the age"), to make disciples (Matt 28:18-20). In his commission the risen Christ names two means for carrying out the task of making disciples: baptizing and teaching.[9] As the church has continued to read Christ's command and sought to fulfill it across the centuries, distinctive ways of relating these means to each other in the process of making disciples have surfaced.[10] Subtraditions have arisen within the great tradition of the church as a result of competing answers to a host of questions, such as: What is the proper ordering of these means? Which should receive priority? How do they work together toward discipleship? How do they relate to each other in the process of bringing persons into the visible fellowship of the church? Additionally, the variety of ways in which this relationship has been viewed has been compounded by the emergence of competing baptismal theologies and the differing ways in which these theologies relate teaching to baptism.[11] The

8. Communion, the Lord's Supper, the Lord's Table, Eucharist, or mass (as it is variously called) is presupposed in the Great Commission's phrase "teaching them to follow all that I commanded you" (Matt 28:20) since it is directly commanded by Christ earlier in the Gospel ("Take, eat," "Drink from it, all of you," "Do this in remembrance of me"; Matt 26:26-27; cf. Luke 22:19; 1 Cor 11:24-25).

9. The main verb of the passage is μαθητεύσατε (aorist active imperative plural), "to make a disciple of, teach." According to Daniel Wallace, the participles βαπτίζοντες ("baptizing") and διδάσκοντες ("teaching") are best understood as participles of means, i.e., "the means by which the disciples were to make disciples was to baptize and then to teach." See Wallace, Greek Grammar beyond the Basics: An Exegetical Syntax of the New Testament (Grand Rapids: Zondervan, 1996), 645. Wallace understands πορευθέντες ("going") as a participle of attendant circumstance rather than means ("go and ... "; i.e., "a participle ... used to communicate an action that, in some sense, is coordinate with the finite verb"). In this case "make disciples" is the verbal idea on which "go" is placed in coordinate relation (Wallace, Greek Grammar, 640, 645). Cf. Donald A. Hagner, Matthew 14-28, Word Biblical Commentary 33B (Dallas: Word, 1995), 882, 886-87; Craig L. Blomberg, Matthew, New American Commentary 22 (Nashville: Broadman, 1992), 431.

10. Baptism alone has a host of issues that been variously answered, namely, the proper recipients, meaning, mode, administration, nature or necessity, and the connection to church membership.

11. These competing theologies at times come with competing histories. The historical questions related to infant baptism have been mined extensively in the debate between Joachim Jeremias and Kurt Aland. Joachim Jeremias makes a historical case for originality of infant baptism in Infant Baptism in the First Four Centuries (London: SCM, 1960); Jeremias, The Origins of Infant Baptism (London: SCM, 1963). Kurt Aland counters Jeremias's interpretation of the evidence in Did the Early Church Baptise Infants? (London: SCM, 1963); Aland, Die Stellung der Kinder in der frühen christlichen Gemeinden und ihre Taufe (Munich: Kaiser, 1967);

infant-baptism debate represents the chief example of this phenomenon; however, debates over other aspects of Christian initiation such as confirmation and first Communion contribute to it as well.

The process of initiation (or entrance) into the full visible fellowship of the local church or parish has historically been the key point at which the relationship between baptism and instruction (or catechesis) manifests itself. The question has been, How do the disciple-making means of baptism and catechesis function in the process of initiating a person into the full, visible fellowship of the local church or parish? In both theory and practice, this question has been answered in a variety of ways that will be considered in due course. Before examining the complexity of the various answers to this question, we will briefly highlight some of the pastoral implications of this study, define key terms, and establish a common axis of comparison by which to coordinate the differing answers.

PRELIMINARY PASTORAL IMPLICATIONS

The initial chapters of this book necessarily cover a number of terminological and methodological issues. This work will prove harder for some than others. Acknowledging this, it seems prudent to highlight some of the pastoral fruit that this labor will yield. Four key pastoral insights are worth mentioning up front. First, the framework constructed and explored in this book forces one to consider a network of issues that may otherwise be missed. Whereas the questions surrounding baptism, catechesis, and first Communion are often considered in isolation from one another, the framework proposed here forces one to consider the interrelationship of all three. While an examination of each constituent part has its place, the constituent parts do not exist or function in isolation. Rather, it is better to understand each part of initiation (catechesis, baptism, and entrance) as occupying unique orbits within the same galaxy. Like celestial bodies, baptism, catechesis, and the Lord's Supper exert gravitational force on one another. If one is interested in exploring the ways in which changing the order and sequence of these bodies and their orbits also changes the function of each in the process of entrance, then this book will offer aid.

Aland, *Taufe und Kindertaufe: 40 Sätze zur Aussage des Neuen Testaments und dem historichen Befund, zur modernen Debatte darüber* (Gütersloh: Gütersloher Verlagshaus Gerd Mohn, 1971).

Second, this study will occasion more careful thinking about the role of the church in administering the ordinances or sacraments of initiation. What is the local church saying through its administration of baptism and Communion? What is she saying through the catechesis connected to these rites? As we will see, the mere ordering of these elements says something. Just what is that something? Similarly, while most traditions would affirm the importance of administering the ordinances "discriminately," this study will highlight the negative implications of *indiscriminate* administration and how indiscriminate administration corrupts the theological-liturgical connections between baptism, catechesis, and Communion.

Third, the age-old discussion of divine initiative and human responsibility raises its head in our initiatory theology. Do these ordinances or sacraments of initiation primarily communicate the grace of God to the initiate, or are these rites of initiation functioning primarily as means of response to God's grace? How does the ordering of relationship support one approach over another?

Finally, while the ordinances or sacraments of initiation lie at the front of one's life in the visible church, they have an ongoing role in the life of the believer. The way in which a church deploys these rites will have a shaping effect on the understanding of all who observe them. Thus, carefully considering the theology communicated in a church's chosen initiatory structure has wide-ranging implications for how congregants and parishioners think about themselves and the nature of life together.

DEFINING THE KEY ELEMENTS: BAPTISM, CATECHESIS, AND ENTRANCE

As with any good sandbox, one must first frame the box and fill it with sand before it is ready for play. This sort of first work is our labor here. Because of the confessional breadth undertaken in this study, it is important to set forth the use of several key concepts and their related terms up front. However, beyond the mere use of terms, this section seeks to lay an important conceptual foundation for the comparative framework on which the study as a whole will build. So, my aim in this section goes well beyond vocabulary definition. We are here setting up the means by which we will compare the various models of liturgical logic explored in the chapters to follow.

The goal of this work is to construct a comparative theology of Christian initiation for "the common good" (1 Cor 12:7). The first element of consideration is baptism, an element of Christian worship that has occasioned as much debate within the church as any other element. Unless otherwise stated, "baptism" will designate water baptism, as opposed to Spirit-baptism or martyrdom (i.e., baptism of blood). Some traditions, such as Southern Baptists, will define baptism more narrowly, designating immersion as the only valid mode of baptism: "Christian baptism is the *immersion* of a believer in water in the name of the Father, the Son, and the Holy Spirit."[12] However, the book in hand is an attempt to construct an explanatory framework for baptism within the process of initiation as interpreted *across major Christian traditions*. That is to say, this book is neither an argument for one tradition nor a screed against other traditions. Therefore, the definition of "baptism" within this work will be understood relative to the particular confessional tradition in view at any given time. This approach relativizes important theological questions, especially of the proper nature, mode, and recipients of baptism.[13] While these questions are important, the descriptive task of this book will be pursued with polemical restraint and with charity toward those on the other side of the font, as it were.

A number of baptismal terms will be used over the course of this book and include the following:

- "Adult baptism" refers to the baptism of anyone who has attained discretion (child or older).

- "Baptizand" refers to the person baptized.

- "Credobaptism" is the baptism of a person on the basis of a personal profession of faith. Credobaptism is synonymous with "believer's (or believers') baptism."[14]

---

12. Article VII: Baptism and the Lord's Supper, Baptist Faith and Message (2000; *BCF*, 516), emphasis added.

13. For considerations of the merits of the various views on these matters, consider Sinclair B. Ferguson, Anthony N. S. Lane, and Bruce Ware, *Baptism: Three Views*, ed. David F. Wright (Downers Grove, IL: IVP Academic, 2009); Thomas J. Nettles, Richard L. Pratt Jr., Robert Kolb, and John D. Castelein, *Understanding Four Views on Baptism*, ed. John H. Armstrong (Grand Rapids: Zondervan, 2007).

14. Diversity exists within credobaptist literature in the spelling of this term. Sometimes the singular possessive form is used (believer's baptism), and at other times the plural

- "Credobaptist" refers to one who baptizes persons only on the basis of a personal profession of faith. "Baptist" will be capitalized when referring to those who apply the appellation to themselves; "baptist" (lowercase) will be used when referring to credobaptists in general.[15]

- "Paedobaptism" (i.e., "infant baptism") is the baptism of infants and young children prior to their attainment of discretion.

- "Paedobaptist" is one who practices paedobaptism or infant baptism.

- "Mode of baptism" refers to the way in which water is used in baptism. Three modes are well-known in church history: immersion (complete submersion in water), affusion (pouring water over the baptizand, typically the forehead), and aspersion (sprinkling).

- "No baptism" views are views of baptism in which Spirit baptism has replaced water baptism.

- "Triune formula" designates the threefold baptismal formula: "in the name of the Father and the Son and the Holy Spirit" (Matt 28:19).

CATECHESIS

"Catechesis" is a term that has fallen out of favor in some sectors of the church over the past century, but one with a long history in the church. The term has been used historically to refer to the process within the church of teaching or instructing someone in the fundamental doctrinal and ethical content of the Christian faith. The term derives from the Greek word κατηχεω, meaning "to teach or instruct." Κατηχεω appears eight times in the

---

possessive is used (believers' baptism). This diversity is illustrated in a 2006 monograph on credobaptism. The title of the work uses the singular possessive spelling, while the plural possessive spelling is used in the foreword. Cf. Thomas R. Schreiner and Shawn D. Wright, *Believer's Baptism: Sign of the New Covenant in Christ*, NAC Studies in Bible and Theology (Nashville: B&H Academic, 2006); Timothy George, "Foreword," in Schreiner and Wright, *Believer's Baptism*, 1–9.

15. This practice is borrowed from Anthony R. Cross, *Recovering the Evangelical Sacrament: Baptisma Semper Reformandum* (Eugene, OR: Pickwick, 2013), 2n9.

New Testament, exclusively within the writings of Luke and Paul. Luke states that his purpose in writing his gospel to Theophilus was that he "may know the exact truth about the things you have been taught [κατηχήθης]" (Luke 1:4). Of Apollos, Luke writes, he was "an eloquent man ... proficient in the Scriptures" who "had been instructed [κατηχημένος] in the way of the Lord" such that "he was accurately speaking and teaching things about Jesus" (Acts 18:24–25). James and the elders at the Jerusalem Council tell Paul that many of the believing Jews "have been told [κατηχήθησαν] about" Paul that he is teaching Jews outside Israel to forsake the law (Acts 21:21). They counsel him to show that this is not true by purifying himself. In so doing "everyone will know that there is nothing to what they have been told [κατήχηνται] about" him (Acts 21:24).

Hermann Beyer notes that Paul uses the verb κατηχεω "exclusively in the sense ... 'to give instruction concerning the content of faith.' "[16] This is true whether the instruction is in the true Christian faith (e.g., Gal 6:6) or a Judaized faith (Rom 2:18, "instructed from the Law"). Paul uses the word to contrast the use of tongues within the congregation with the beneficial use of intelligible speech. He writes, "Nevertheless, in the church I prefer to speak five words with my mind so that I may instruct [κατηχήσω] others also, rather than ten thousand words in a tongue" (1 Cor 14:19). The participial form of κατηχεω can refer either to the instructor or the instructed. Paul writes, "The one who is taught [κατηχούμενος] the word is to share all good things with the one who teaches [κατηχοῦντι] him" (Gal 6:6). Here "the word [τὸν λόγον]" refers generally to the Scriptures but most specifically to "the gospel [τὸ εὐαγγέλιον]" (cf. Gal 1:11; 2:2, 5, 7, 14; 3:8; 4:13).

A host of terms are associated with "catechesis." The catechumenate is formal initiatory catechesis associated with baptism or confirmation. Catechesis is conducted by a catechist and received by a catechumen (see Gal 6:6). The action of catechesis is signified by the verb "catechize," and a formal manual or handbook called a catechism (often in question-and-answer format) has been used at times in church history. The study of catechesis is called catechetics.[17]

---

16. Hermann Wolfgang Beyer, "κατηχεω," TDNT 3:638–40.

17. A helpful summary of terms can be found in J. I. Packer and Gary A. Parrett, *Grounded in the Gospel: Building Believers the Old-Fashioned Way* (Grand Rapids: Baker, 2010), 27–28.

Catechesis has enjoyed a special relationship with baptismal preparation, examination, and confession.[18] J. I. Packer and Gary Parrett identify three distinctions within the usage of the term "catechesis"; they are as follows:

- *procatechesis* (or *protocatechesis*): "catechizing those whom many contemporary church leaders would call 'seekers' and whom the ancients might have called 'inquirers' ";

- catechesis proper: "the formal catechetical work of preparing children or adult converts for baptism or confirmation—that is, for their full inclusion in the life of the church"; and

- ongoing catechesis: "the ministry of teaching and formation that really is neverending as believers are continually nurtured in the way of the Lord."[19]

The present work will touch all three levels, but it deals primarily with "catechesis proper."[20] In fact, the wording above ("preparing children or adult converts for *baptism or confirmation*—that is, for their full inclusion in the life of the church") manifests the key concern of this project, namely, to consider how catechesis has been variously related to baptism for the purpose of "full inclusion in the life of the church"—a status referred to within this work as "entrance." This leads to the consideration of the study's axis of comparison.

---

18. "Creedal statements," Leith writes, "were from the beginning associated with baptism. The importance of this rite for the development of creeds is very considerable. Hans Lietzmann went so far as to say that the root of all creeds is the formula of belief pronounced by the baptizand or pronounced in his hearing and assented to by him before baptism. This statement does not do justice to the great variety of situations that called for creedal affirmation in the life of the Church, but it does indicate the importance of baptism for the development of creeds." See John H. Leith, "Creeds and Their Role in the Church," in *Creeds of the Churches*, 3rd ed. (Louisville: John Knox, 1982), 6. Leith's observation is supported by the interrogatory nature of creedal confession in the Apostolic Tradition of Hippolytus (ca. 215); cf. Leith, *Creeds of the Churches*, 7, 23. The connection of creedal confession with baptism stands behind statements such as that of Thomas Oden, who writes, "Christian theology [is] best thought of largely as a commentary on baptism," and, "The history of Christian theology is best understood as an extended commentary on the baptismal formula." See Thomas C. Oden, *Systematic Theology* vol 1. (San Francisco: HarperSanFrancisco, 1987–1992), 181, 202.

19. Packer and Parrett, *Grounded in the Gospel*, 29.

20. All three senses will be touched on at some point or another. Where significant, distinctions in terms will be made.

FIRST COMMUNION: THE AXIS OF COMPARISON

Broadly speaking, this study is a comparative theology of Christian initiation. The focus of this work, however, is narrower than the term "initiation" may first imply. The term "initiation" is most frequently associated with baptism but may also refer to the three "sacraments of initiation," namely, (1) baptism, (2) chrismation or confirmation, and (3) Communion.[21] In some cases the idea of initiation or incorporation is even applied to enrollment as a learner or baptismal candidate (i.e., catechumen).[22]

When infant baptism is practiced as an initiatory option, especially in traditions that do not practice infant Communion (i.e., nonpaedocommunion traditions),[23] a liminal space is created in which the baptizand is already a member of the community but not yet a participant in the community's ongoing expression of fellowship: Communion or the Lord's Supper. In whatever way the respective tradition explains the initiate's exclusion from the Lord's Supper, something is incomplete with regard to his or her inclusion into the visible corporate life of the church.

Consequently, the term "initiation" sometimes suffers from an oscillation between the inauguration into a *process* of initiation and the inauguration or *completion* of initiation into full, visible communion with a local church or parish. The focus of this study is the latter. Therefore, the term "entrance" is used technically here to designate the completion or terminus

---

21. Michael Dujarier refers to the "sacraments of initiation" or "sacramental initiation." See Dujarier, *A History of the Catechumenate: The First Six Centuries*, trans. Edward J. Haasl (New York: Sadlier, 1979), cf. 43, 46. An association of baptism with the term "initiation" is found in diverse traditions. On the one hand, in Lumen Gentium: The Dogmatic Constitutions on the Church, the Roman Catholic Church affirms, "While [Christ] expressly insist[s] on the need for faith and baptism (see Mark 16:16; John 3:5), at the same time [he] confirmed the need for the church, *into which people enter through baptism as through a door*" (Lumen Gentium 2.14 [*CCFCT* 3:585], emphasis added). On the other hand, the Orthodox Creed (1678, Baptist) is representative of the broader credobaptist tradition when it describes water baptism as "a sign of our entrance into the covenant of grace, and ingrafting into Christ, and into the body of Christ, which is his church" (Orthodox Creed 28 [*BCF*, 326]).

22. Vatican II's Lumen Gentium describes incorporation through intention as follows: "Catechumens who, under the impulse of the Holy Spirit, expressly ask to be incorporated into the church are by that very desire joined to it, and Mother Church already embraces them with love and care as its own" (Lumen Gentium 2.14 [*CCFCT* 3:586]).

23. Paedocommunion is the administration of the Lord's Supper to infants upon baptism (strict paedocommunion) or children prior to confirmation (soft paedocommunion). The concepts of soft and strict Communion will be developed further in a later section.

of Christian initiation: the inauguration of full, visible fellowship with a local body of believers as it is expressed through admission to and participation in the Lord's Supper (i.e., "first Communion").[24]

Several considerations commend the Lord's Supper as an axis for comparing how baptism and catechesis are functionally related to entrance. First, there is near-universal agreement that the sacraments or ordinances (especially baptism and the Lord's Supper) are visible signs of fellowship.[25] Whether sacramental or nonsacramental, all traditions practicing these physical signs are agreed that they do function in this way.

For example, credobaptists following a nonsacramentarian approach to the ordinances emphasize that the ordinances are signs or marks of personal faith and corporate fellowship. The Anabaptist Schleitheim Confession (1527) limits baptism to believers only, specifically

all those who have learned repentance and amendment of life, and who believe truly that their sins are taken away by Christ, and to all those who walk in the resurrection of Jesus Christ, and wish to be buried with Him in death, so that they may be resurrected with him, and to all those who with this significance request it [baptism] of us and demand it for themselves.[26]

---

24. In one sense, the oft-used term "first Communion" is virtually synonymous with "entrance." The term "entrance," however, emphasizes the point that full initiation into the church—inclusion into its visible, liturgical life—finds its locus here. The Catechism of the Catholic Church affirms the larger point that the Lord's Supper marks full initiation: "*The holy Eucharist completes Christian initiation. Those who have been raised to the dignity of the royal priesthood by Baptism and configured more deeply to Christ by Confirmation participate with the whole community in the Lord's own sacrifice by means of the Eucharist*" (CCC, 1322 [368], emphasis added).

25. The distinction in terms between "sacrament" and "ordinance" refers primarily to the way in which the sign is understood to function *invisibly*. On the one hand, the term "sacrament" derives from the Greek term μυστήριον ("mystery"; cf. 1 Tim 3:16; Eph 5:32), which was often translated into Latin as *sacramentum* ("a thing set apart as sacred" as well as "a military oath of obedience"). The concept of sacrament has been variously defined, but Augustine's definition—"a visible sign of a sacred thing"—is common. McKim defines sacrament as "an outward sign instituted by God to convey an inward or spiritual grace." See Donald McKim, *Westminster Dictionary of Theological Terms* (Louisville: Westminster John Knox, 1996). On the other hand, the term "ordinance" (from the Latin *ordinans*, "arranging") has been preferred by traditions (typically nonsacramental) that affirm only a symbolic or sign nature of the rite. The term highlights that the rite was ordained by the Lord, and it refers only to baptism (cf. Matt 28:18-20) and the Lord's Supper (cf. Matt 26:26-29; Mark 14:22-25; Luke 22:14-23).

26. Schleitheim Confession (1527, Anabaptist; BCF, 25-26).

With other credobaptist traditions, baptism here functions as a visible sign of faith. Additionally, the Schleitheim Confession makes baptism the visible means of incorporation into the church and prerequisite for fellowship at the Lord's Supper.[27] "All those who wish to break one bread in remembrance of the broken body of Christ, and all who wish to drink of one drink as a remembrance of the shed blood of Christ, shall be united beforehand by baptism in one body of Christ which is the church of God and whose Head is Christ."[28] As a sign of visible fellowship with Christ and with each other, the sign of the Supper must be reserved for those who have visibly identified with Christ and his church. "Whoever has not been called by one God to one faith, to one baptism, to one Spirit, to one body, with all the children of God's church, cannot be made [into] one bread with them, as indeed must be done if one is truly to break bread according to the command of Christ."[29]

Those who would want to say more about the nature of the sacraments (especially with regard to Christ's presence within the Supper) do not want to say less about them. The Lutheran Augsburg Confession affirms, "[The] sacraments were instituted *not only* to be marks of profession among human beings but much more to be signs and testimonies of God's will toward us, intended to arouse and strengthen faith in those who use them."[30] Absent

---

27. Not all credobaptists understand baptism as a prerequisite to the Lord's Supper. For example, the Confession of Free-Will Baptists (1834, 1868) states, "It is the privilege and duty of all who have spiritual union with Christ thus to commemorate his death [via the Lord's Supper]; and no man has a right to forbid these tokens to the least of his disciples." As Philip Schaff notes, this statement "commits the Free-Will Baptists to the principle and practice of *open* communion." See Confession of Free-Will Baptists (1834, 1868), in *The Creeds of Christendom*, ed. Philip Schaff, 6th rev. ed. (New York: Harper & Brothers, 1877), 3:756. Nonetheless, both ordinances are still understood as visible signs, and the Lord's Supper retains its function as a visible sign of fellowship. Though contrary to the denomination's current confession of faith, a 2012 study of pastors in the Southern Baptist Convention found that more than half (52 percent) offer the Lord's Supper to "anyone who has put faith in Christ." An additional segment offer it to "anyone who wants" to participate (5 percent), and another segment has "no specifications" (4 percent). See Carol Pipes, "Lord's Supper: LifeWay Surveys Churches' Practices, Frequency," *Baptist Press*, 2012, http://www.bpnews.net/38730.

28. Schleitheim Confession (*BCF*, 26).

29. Schleitheim Confession (*BCF*, 26). Cf. Dordrecht Confession (1632, Mennonite) 7–8 (*BCF*, 67–68). These emphases are readily found in Baptist confessions. See English Declaration at Amsterdam (1611, Baptist) 10, 13 (*BCF*, 111); Second London Confession (1677 [1689], Baptist) 30.1 (*BCF*, 292); Baptist Faith and Message (2000) 7 (*BCF*, 516).

30. Augsburg Confession 13 (*BC*, 47), emphasis added. Remarkably similar to this is the statement of the Anglican Thirty-Nine Articles (1562): "Sacraments ordained of Christ be

from this statement is any denial that the sacraments are visible marks. In fact, the Eastern Orthodox Jeremias II quotes the Augsburg Confession affirmatively on this point.[31] Similarly, though the Roman Catholic Council of Trent anathematizes those who reduce the sacraments to mere external signs, it does not deny that the sacraments have this function.[32]

Positively, in the Vatican II Dogmatic Constitution of the Church, Lumen Gentium, the Church itself is said to be a kind of sacrament: "Since the Church is in Christ as a sacrament or instrumental sign of intimate union with God of the unity of all humanity, the council, continuing the teaching of previous councils, intends to declare with greater clarity to the faithful and the entire human race the nature of the church and its universal mission." It further affirms that the visible bonds of the church are the "profession of faith, *the sacraments*, and ecclesiastical government, and communion."[33] Thus, while the Roman Church, the epitome of a sacramental

not only badges or tokens of Christian men's profession, but rather they be certain sure witnesses, and effectual signs of grace, and God's good will towards us, by the which he doth work invisibly in us, and doth not only quicken, but also strengthen and confirm our Faith in him" (Thirty-Nine Articles 25 [Schaff, *Creeds of Christendom*, 3:502]).

31. "Your thirteenth article, which says that the use of the divine sacraments was instituted not only in order that they might be some type of symbols or marks, or tokens to distinguish Christians from the outsiders, but much more, that they be signs and witnesses of the kindness and grace of God toward us. We also confirm this and have the same opinion concerning them." See Jeremias II, *The Reply of Ecumenical Patriarch Jeremias II to the Augsburg Confession* 1.13 (CCFCT 1:428).

32. "If anyone says that the sacraments of the new law do not contain the grace which they signify; or do not confer that grace on those who place no obstacle in the way, as if they were *only* external signs of grace or justice received by faith, and some kind of mark of the Christian profession by which believers are distinguished from unbelievers in the eyes of people: let him be anathema." See Dogmatic Decrees of the Council of Trent [1545–1563] 7 can. 1.6 (CCFCT 2:840), emphasis added.

33. Lumen Gentium 1.1 (CCFCT 3:570); 2.14 (CCFCT 3:585), emphasis added. The document notes that the sacraments are the instrumental means whereby one is united with Christ. The following statement evinces this dynamic and provides descriptions of what happens in the sacraments of baptism and the Eucharist: "In this body the life of Christ is communicated to believers, who by means of the sacraments in a mysterious but real way are united to Christ who suffered and has been glorified. By baptism we are made into the likeness of Christ: 'For by one Spirit we were all baptized into one body' (1 Cor 12:13). *Through this sacred rite the union with the death and resurrection of Christ is both symbolized and effected*: 'We were buried with Him by baptism into death,' but if 'we have been united with him in a death like his, we shall certainly be united with him in a resurrection like his' (Rom 6:4–5). *When we really participate in the body of the Lord through the breaking of the eucharistic bread, we are raised up to communion with him and among ourselves*. 'Because there is one bread, we who are many are one body, for we all partake of the one bread' (1 Cor 10:17). *In this way all of us are made*

tradition, wishes to make the sacraments more than visible symbols of fellowship, it does not make them less than visible symbols of fellowship. Second, of the three "sacraments of initiation"—baptism, confirmation (chrismation in the East), and Lord's Supper—only the Lord's Supper and baptism are common to all major traditions.[34] While the Roman and Eastern churches affirm seven sacraments,[35] the traditions springing from the Reformation have only ascribed the title of sacrament or ordinance to baptism and the Lord's Supper. Luther argues that it is "proper to restrict the name of sacrament to those promises which have signs attached to them. ... Hence there are, strictly speaking, but two sacraments in the church of God—baptism and the bread."[36] Luther's opinion regarding the number of sacraments is ubiquitous for Protestants. Even the Thirty-Nine Articles (1562), a rather moderate Reformation confession, is representative of the broader Protestant tradition on this point:

There are two Sacraments ordained of Christ our Lord in the Gospel, that is to say, Baptism, and the Supper of the Lord. Those five commonly called Sacraments, that is to say, Confirmation, Penance, Orders, Matrimony, and Extreme Unction, are not to be counted

members of this body (see 1 Cor 12:27) 'individually members one of another' (Rom 12:5)" (Lumen Gentium 1.7 [CCFCT 3:576], emphases added).

34. Confirmation is a poor candidate for marking full, visible fellowship for several reasons. First, even where a form of confirmation was retained, confirmation is rarely if ever given the same stature as either baptism or the Lord's Supper. For example, confirmation has the status of a rite within the Anglican, Methodist, and Lutheran churches. Second, confirmation in the vast majority of cases is a corollary rite to baptism or the Lord's Supper or both. The only time it takes on a force roughly equivalent to either baptism or Communion is when soft paedocommunion (administering Communion in childhood prior to confirmation) is practiced. This practice will be considered later in this work. Finally, confirmation has an uneven history of both use and meaning within church history. In some cases, it is conjoined to baptism as a sign of the Holy Spirit. In other cases, it is a completion of infant baptism and connected to a profession of faith at or around puberty. While the meaning and placement of confirmation is a key variable for explaining the models of the proposed framework, by itself it is an unstable axis for comparing visible entrance into the fellowship of the church.

35. (1) Baptism, (2) chrismation (i.e., confirmation), (3) Communion, (4) penance, (5) holy orders, (6) matrimony, (7) extreme unction (i.e., unction with oil); cf. Longer Catechism of the Orthodox, Catholic, Eastern Church, q. 285, in Schaff, Creeds of Christendom 2:490; Dogmatic Decrees of the Council of Trent (1545-1563), 7 can. 1.1, CCFCT 2:840.

36. Luther, Babylonian Captivity of the Church, 113-260, in Three Treatises, trans. A. T. W. Steinhäuser, rev. Frederick C. Ahrens and Abdel Ross Wentz (Minneapolis: Fortress, 1970), 258. Luther wrestled with the status of penance (cf. Babylonian Captivity, 132), but concludes, "The sacrament of penance, which I added to these two, lacks the divinely instituted visible sign, and is, as I have said, nothing but a way and a return to baptism" (258).

for Sacraments of the Gospel, being such as have grown partly of the corrupt following of the Apostles, partly are states of life allowed in the Scriptures; but yet have not like nature of Sacraments with Baptism, and the Lord's Supper, for that they have not any visible sign or ceremony ordained of God.[37]

While theologies of the Lord Supper vary widely, the practice and function of the sacrament or ordinance as a sign of visible fellowship is as close to universal as one could ask.[38]

Finally, unlike baptism and chrismation or confirmation, the Lord's Supper is repeatable. Thus, the Lord's Supper functions as *the* ongoing liturgical sign of fellowship within local churches. Relatedly, the highest level of discipline to be taken on a member is excommunication, or "the ban," as it is sometimes called. While the degree to which excommunication affects social interaction outside corporate gatherings is variously interpreted, there is widespread agreement that it means exclusion from celebrations of the Lord's Supper.[39] One who has been disfellowshiped may not participate in the august liturgical sign of Table fellowship.

Though fellowship with other believers is ultimately rooted in love for one another (John 13:34–35), in terms of liturgical symbols of full visible fellowship, the Lord's Supper stands above all others. Since the Lord's Supper functions as *the* final step of initiation and the ongoing liturgical

---

37. Thirty-Nine Articles (1562), 25, in Schaff, *Creeds of Christendom* 3:502–3.

38. That the Eucharist functions as a sign of full fellowship is illustrated within the Catholic and Eastern Orthodox traditions, where catechumens are "dismissed" prior to the celebration of the Eucharist. As the *RCIA* explains, "They [i.e., the catechumens] must await their baptism, which will join them to God's priestly people and empower them to participate in Christ's new worship" (*RCIA*, 75 [37–38]). Lacking baptism, they are not yet eligible to participate in the eucharistic service with the faithful.

39. The *textus classicus* for this position is 1 Cor 5:11: "But actually, I wrote to you not to associate with any so-called brother if he is a sexually immoral person, or a greedy person, or an idolater, or is verbally abusive, or habitually drunk, or a swindler—not even to eat with such a person." For examples of this view see CCC 1463 [408] (Catholic); Smalcald Articles 9 (Lutheran; *BC*, 323); Westminster Confession 30.4 (Anglican; *CCFCT* 2:644); Hans de Ries, Short Confession of Faith (1610) 36 (Baptist/Mennonite; *CCFCT* 2:766 [cf. *BCF*, 103]). The English Declaration at Amsterdam (1611, Baptist) states that any who are unrepentant following the steps of admonition (see Matt 18) are "to be excluded from the communion of the Saints" but that this exclusion does not pertain to "civil society" (English Declaration at Amsterdam 17–18 [1611, Baptist; *BCF*, 112]; spelling and punctuation modernized). Compare with the Waterland Confession 36 (1580, Mennonite; *BCF*, 59), in which the banning of an unrepentant member results in a more comprehensive withdrawal from the individual.

sign of fellowship in the church, inaugural admission to the Supper will serve as the marker of "entrance" into the visible fellowship of the local church for our study.

Several terms associated with the Lord's Supper should be noted. "Eucharist" (Greek εὐχαριστῶ; lit. "thanksgiving"), "mass" (Latin *Missa*; lit. "to dismiss" or "to send"),[40] "Holy Communion," and "Sacrament of the Altar" are all terms used by various traditions for this celebration. The term "Table" is used as a reference to this meal, and "Table fellowship" refers to the fellowship, mutual participation of life, and reconciliation that celebrants express through the meal. "Fencing the Table" means to restrict the administration of the Lord's Supper in some way. The Lord's Supper is administered by some (typically the Eastern traditions) to infants (paedocommunion) but is most frequently administered within Western traditions to those who have attained faculties of discretion and made a credible profession of faith (credocommunion).

Additional terms will be defined as the study moves forward, and more nuance and specificity will be given to the terms that have already been introduced. With the axis of comparison in place, we are in position to begin examining the wide variety of ways in which baptism, catechesis, and entrance have been related to one another.

THE PROBLEM OF COMPLEXITY

The phrase "problem of complexity" refers to the diverse array of answers to the relationship between baptism, catechesis, and entrance to the church. The problem of complexity may at first appearance seem to be merely an ecumenical problem, namely, the denominational boundary lines and

---

40. Regarding the sense of "dismissal," the *Missa Fidelium* ("the mass of the faithful") "is so named because in early times the (unbaptized) catechumens were dismissed before the Offertory and only the baptized (the 'fideles') remained to join in the Eucharistic offering." See F. L. Cross and E. A. Livingstone, eds., "Faithful, Mass of the," in *Oxford Dictionary of the Christian Church*, 3rd rev. ed. (New York: Oxford University Press, 2005), s.v. Regarding the sense of "sent," the CCC states that the sacrament of the Eucharist, though it goes by many other appellations, is sometimes called "Holy Mass (*Missa*)." This title, it argues, is appropriate "because the liturgy in which the mystery of salvation is accomplished concludes with the sending forth (*missio*) of the faithful, so that they may fulfill God's will in their daily lives" (*CCC*, 1332 [370]).

the polemical struggles from which they emerged.[41] While the plurality of denominations certainly contributes to the complexity problem, the problem should not be reduced to this phenomenon. Instead, "problem" must be expanded to include the fact that a mere listing of denominational models is insufficient to account for the data. Thus, the problem of complexity manifests in at least three ways. First, there is expected diversity between traditions (interdenominational diversity). Second, there is surprising affinity between divergent traditions (interdenominational affinity). Finally, there is somewhat surprising internal complexity within particular traditions (intradenominational diversity).

INTERDENOMINATIONAL DIVERSITY

First, one is unsurprised to find a diversity of approaches between different Christian traditions. For example, the practice of infant Communion (i.e., paedocommunion) among the Eastern Orthodox is well known. John Karmiris, an Eastern Orthodox theologian, writes, "The importance of [the Eucharist] for our salvation is so great as to make it equally important with the sacrament of baptism."[42] In 1576 Jeremias II, an ecumenical patriarch in the Eastern Orthodox Church, gave an extended reply to the Augsburg Confession (1530). Jeremias provides an Orthodox response to

---

41. Careful studies in comparative symbolics (i.e., the study of confessional material) offer us help in seeing this complexity clearly. F. E. Mayer and Arthur Carl Piepkorn offer the following principle: "Christian fellowship demands a comparative study of the various creeds in the light of God's Word and, on the basis of such studies, the sifting of truth from error." See *The Religious Bodies of America*, 4th rev. ed. (St. Louis: Concordia, 1961), 4. An approach such as this acknowledges real differences rather than minimizing or obscuring them for the sake of "unity."

42. John Karmiris, "Concerning the Sacraments," in *Eastern Orthodox Theology: A Contemporary Reader*, ed. Daniel B. Clendenin (Grand Rapids: Baker Academic, 2003), 28. Earlier Karmiris reviews several key liturgical and patristic sources that manifest the close connection between salvation (esp. deification) and eucharistic communication. According to the liturgy associated with John Chrysostom, communicants in the Eucharist receive the body and blood of Christ "for the purification of the soul, for the remission of sins, for the fellowship of [the] Holy Spirit, for the fulfillment of the kingdom of heaven." See the Divine Liturgy of St. John Chrysostomos (*CCFCT* 1:287). Other cited examples of the great soteriological weight freighted on the Eucharist by the Orthodox include Maximus the Confessor, *Hermeneia to Prayer* (PG 90:877), and John of Damascus, *On the Divine Images* 3.26 (PG 94:1348). Karmiris summarizes this stream of thought, writing, "In the Holy Eucharist men are united with and incorporated into the God-man, receiving that divine quality necessary for their deification" (Karmiris, "Concerning the Sacraments," 27).

each section of the Lutheran standard. His response on the relationship between baptism and first Communion illustrates the diversity between these two traditions:

> The ninth article [of your Augsburg Confession] says that infants should be baptized and that baptism should not be postponed. We also, must act in this manner so that nothing may happen because of postponement. ... Moreover, as has been said, we give to them afterwards holy communion. According to Basil the Great, he who is born again needs spiritual food, also.[43] And the Lord says: "Unless you eat the flesh of the Son of man and drink his blood," you cannot enter into the kingdom of God. Consequently, both are necessary: baptism and communion.[44]

In addition to the omission of infant Communion in the Augsburg Confession, several statements about the proper reception of the Lord's Supper within the larger Book of Concord militate against the practice. Luther, speaking of worthy eating of the Lord's Supper in his *Small Catechism*, writes,

> Who, then, receives this sacrament [of the Altar] worthily? Answer: Fasting and bodily preparation are in fact a fine external discipline, but a person who has faith in these words, "given for you" and "shed for you for the forgiveness of sins," is really worthy and well prepared. However, a person who does not believe these words or doubts them is unworthy and unprepared, because the words "for you" require truly believing hearts.[45]

In his *Large Catechism* Luther states, "So everyone who wishes to be a Christian and to go to the sacrament [of the Altar] should know [the words Christ used to institute it]. For *we do not intend to admit to the sacrament*

---

43. Pelikan and Hotchkiss note that this is a possible reference to Basil of Caesarea, *On the Holy Spirit* 15.35–36 (*NPNF²* 8:22).

44. Jeremias II, *Reply of Ecumenical Patriarch* 1.9 (1576; *CCFCT* 1:419). Article IX of the Augsburg Confession states, "Concerning baptism it is taught that it is necessary, that grace is offered through it, and that one should also baptize children, who through such baptism are entrusted to God and become pleasing to him" (*BC*, 42). The article does not mention paedocommunion. Jeremias is thus addressing the omission.

45. Luther, *Small Catechism* (1529; *BC*, 363).

and administer it to those who do not know what they seek or why they come."
For Luther and his successors the essence of the sacrament is "the Word
... joined to the external element." The verbal nature of the treasure of the
sacrament means that preparation is a heart matter, not an external one.[46]
This elevates the need for discretion by communicants.[47]

The ability to "recognize the body" and examine oneself is affirmed elsewhere within the Book of Concord. For example, the Augsburg Confession
defends the devotion displayed in the celebration of the Lord's Supper by its
subscribing churches, stating, "People are admitted only if they first had an
opportunity to be examined and heard. The people are also reminded about
the dignity and use of the sacrament—how it offers great consolation to
anxious consciences—so that they may learn to believe in God and expect
and ask for all that is good from God."[48] This position stands against the
administration of the Supper to infants but has left room for some to allow
for preconfirmation Communion for children who have an acceptable level
of discretion.[49] In requiring the capacity for discretion, self-examination,

---

46. Luther, *Large Catechism* (1529; BC, 469.2; 468.10; 470.36), emphasis added.

47. Frank Senn notes that infant Communion in the West began fading around the ninth
and tenth centuries. "The Fourth Lateran Council," he writes, "linked the first reception of
communion with attainment of an age of discretion, without precisely defining what an age
of discretion might be. This decision was reaffirmed by the Council of Trent (session of July
16, 1552)." See Frank C. Senn, "Confirmation and First Communion: A Reappraisal," *Lutheran
Quarterly* 23.2 (1971): 178–91. Trent affirmed the permissibility of paedocommunion but said
it was not necessary; cf. Council of Trent and Henry Joseph Schroeder, *Canons and Decrees of
the Council of Trent* (Rockford, IL: Tan Books, 1978), 134.

48. On standard practice of confession as prerequisite to Communion see Augsburg
Confession (BC, 73.1); Apology of the Augsburg Confession (BC, 258.1).

49. A Lutheran argument for soft paedocommunion is offered in Berthold Von Schenk,
"First Communion and Confirmation," *Concordia Theological Monthly* 42.6 (1971): 353–60. A
Lutheran counterargument to soft paedocommunion is offered by Senn, "Confirmation and
First Communion," 178–91. The two articles are not in direct dialogue. In my view, the strong
emphasis on the objective validity of the sacrament apart from subjective disposition or
preparation leaves the theoretical possibility for infant Communion within the Lutheran
sacramental framework. For example, the Formula of Concord leaves more room for infant
Communion when it emphasizes the objective validity of the sacrament apart from subjective
preparation: "We believe, teach and confess that there is only one kind of unworthy guest,
those who do not believe." If combined with an infant-faith view, this statement leaves the
door open for infant Communion. Additionally, it states, "We believe, teach, and confess that
the entire worthiness of the guests at the table of his heavenly meal is and consists alone in
the most holy obedience and perfect merit of Christ. We make his obedience and merit our
own through true faith, concerning which we received assurance through the sacrament.
Worthiness consists in no way in our own virtues, or in internal or external preparations" (Formula
of Concord [BC, 506.18, 506.20], emphasis added).

and a level of understanding of what the elements represent, the Lutheran tradition makes catechesis prerequisite to first Communion. This practice starkly contrasts Orthodox paedocommunion.

INTERDENOMINATIONAL AFFINITY

Second, upon closer examination there are points of surprising affinity between traditions that are otherwise divergent. It is unsurprising that two traditions as divergent as the Lutheran and Orthodox would find disagreement over any number of issues, much less the sacraments. Indeed, it was sacraments that occasioned so much diversity among the Reformers themselves, marking divisions between the Reformed, Lutherans, and Anabaptists. The Marburg Colloquy stands as a permanent divide between the Reformed and Lutheran traditions on the issue of Christ's presence in the Lord's Supper. Despite their differences on this pivotal issue, at first blush the Reformed and Lutheran traditions would seem to stand together against the paedocommunion practice of the Eastern Church. The confessional standards of each tradition agree that the administration of the Supper should be postponed until a child has acquired discretion. In terms similar to the Lutheran standards above, the Westminster Larger Catechism (1647) states,

> Q. 177. Wherein do the sacraments of baptism and the Lord's Supper differ?

> A. The sacraments of baptism and the Lord's Supper differ, in that baptism is to be administered but once, with water, to be a sign and seal of our regeneration and ingrafting into Christ, and that even to infants; whereas the Lord's Supper is to be administered often, in the elements of bread and wine, to represent and exhibit Christ as spiritual nourishment to the soul, and to confirm our continuance and growth in him, and *that only to such as are of years and ability to examine themselves.*[50]

---

50. Westminster Larger Catechism (1647), q. 177 (*RCH*, 215), emphasis added. This distinction between the sacraments of baptism and the Lord's Supper is found in Calvin. John Calvin focuses on the necessity of examination prior to reception of the Supper and observes that infants are incapable of this (*Institutes* 4.16.30).

The Westminster Shorter Catechism (1646) describes the kind of examination in view:

Q. 97. What is required for the worthy receiving of the Lord's Supper?

A. It is required of them that would worthily partake of the Lord's Supper, *that they examine themselves of their knowledge to discern the Lord's body, of their faith to feed upon him, of their repentance, love, and new obedience*; lest, coming unworthily, they eat and drink judgment to themselves.[51]

In addition to self-examination, the Westminster Larger Catechism makes it clear that proper reception of Lord's Supper involves a complex of issues that require care and discernment, such as "thankful remembrance," and "renewing the exercises of [the] graces" of the Christian life (e.g., faith, repentance, etc.).[52] Similarly, the Heidelberg Catechism (1563) emphasizes that the Lord's Supper is for those who are sorrowful for sin and desire to grow in godliness, prerequisites that are beyond the capacities of infants.[53]

Notwithstanding the antipathies of the larger tradition toward paedocommunion,[54] some contemporary Reformed expressions have adopted paedocommunion. Cornelius Venema offers two categories of paedocommunion: soft and strict. "Soft paedocommunion" is the admitting of children to the Lord's Supper "at an earlier age than is customary." The Reformed Church in America has adopted this practice, allowing infant-baptized,

---

51. Westminster Shorter Catechism (1646), q. 97 (*RCH*, 223), emphasis added.

52. Cf. Westminster Larger Catechism (1647), qq. 169, 171–75 (*RCH*, 223, 225).

53. Heidelberg Catechism (1563), cf. q. 81 (*RCH*, 230). Similar affirmations are held by Lutherans and bear the same implications for postponement for them as well. Luther, in his *Small Catechism*, writes, "Who, then, receives this sacrament [of the Altar] worthily? Answer: Fasting and bodily preparation are in fact a fine external discipline, but a person who has faith in these words, 'given for you' and 'shed for you for the forgiveness of sins,' is really worthy and well prepared. However, a person who does not believe these words or doubts them is unworthy and unprepared, because the words 'for you' require truly believing hearts" (*BC*, 363). The preparations and dispositions described here are not applicable to infants (even where infant faith is asserted).

54. On those that blur the distinction between the prerequisite faculties for baptism and the Lord's Supper, Calvin concludes, "If these men had a particle of sound brain left, would they be blind to a thing so clear and obvious?" *Institutes* 4.16.30 (trans. Battles).

unconfirmed children to participate in the Supper.[55] While soft paedo-communion reorders a more traditional approach of baptism, catechesis, confirmation, and first Communion, it honors the spirit of the confessional statements above that require communicants to have certain faculties of discernment and spiritual dispositions in order to receive Table fellowship. "Strict paedocommunion" is "the admission of any baptized child of believing parents who is physically able to receive the Communion elements."[56] Some within the Reformed tradition have taken up this latter view, believing it to be a more consistent expression of their covenantal theology. Contemporary arguments in favor of strict paedocommunion among the Reformed have come from those within the "federal vision" movement, a movement advocating what it believes to be a more thoroughgoing covenant theology.[57] Though there are differences to be parsed in the particulars of their respective sacramental theologies, the Reformed federal-vision proponents and Eastern Orthodox have become strange bedfellows with

---

55. Cf. "Baptized Non-communicants and the Celebration of the Lord's Supper" (1977 and 1984, respectively); "Baptized Children and the Lord's Table," Reformed Church in America Theological Commission, 1990, https://www.rca.org/baptism.

56. Cornelius P. Venema, *Children at the Lord's Table: Assessing the Case of Paedocommunion* (Grand Rapids: Reformation Heritage Books, 2009), 2–4.

57. At the heart of the federal vision is the conviction that the covenant promises of God regarding the children of believers are taken in a more objective sense than has often been the case. Parents should believe that their children *are* God's children, whom he promises to save. As Douglas Wilson puts it, "Covenant children are placed in covenant homes by a sovereign God, and we are required as Christians to believe the promises of Scripture concerning these children." Unlike the children of unbelievers, "Our children are *saints* (1 Cor 7:14). ... So the promise is to us and to our children." See Wilson, "Union with Christ: An Overview of the Federal Vision," in *The Auburn Avenue Theology, Pros and Cons*, ed. E. Calvin Beisner (Fort Lauderdale, FL: Knox Theological Seminary, 2004), 3, emphasis original. Calvin Beisner's edited volume of essays is helpful for hearing both sides of the debate on a variety of salient topics both soteriological and sacramental. Other key exemplars of the federal vision (i.e., Auburn Avenue theology) include Steve Wilkins and Duane Garner, eds., *The Federal Vision* (Monroe, LA: Athanasius, 2004); Andrew Sandlin, ed., *Backbone of the Bible: Covenant in Contemporary Perspective* (Nacogdoches, TX: Covenant Media, 2004). A cumulative case for paedocommunion or covenant Communion is made by the contributors to Gregg Strawbridge, ed., *The Case for Covenant Communion* (Monroe, LA: Athanasius, 2006). Critiques of the federal vision include Venema, *Children at the Lord's Table*; Guy Prentiss Waters, *The Federal Vision and Covenant Theology: A Comparative Analysis* (Phillipsburg, NJ: P&R, 2006); Orthodox Presbyterian Church, *Justification: Report of the Committee to Study the Doctrine of Justification* (Willow Grove, PA: Committee on Christian Education of the Orthodox Presbyterian Church, 2007).

regard to their practice of strict paedocommunion.[58] It is at this point that a tradition-based model of interpreting the data becomes problematic. How is one to account for an affinity across a divide as deep as the one between the Reformed and the Orthodox?

INTRADENOMINATIONAL DIVERSITY

Finally, there may be surprising instances of *internal* complexity within a tradition and its construal of the relationship between baptism, catechesis, and entrance. The variety of paedocommunion and postponed Communion among the Reformed illustrates this observation. Similar complexity is observed among Baptists on the issue of open and closed Communion as well as open and closed membership.[59] For example, John Bunyan allows

---

58. After a book-length examination of federal-vision proponents' respective views on covenant and a wide variety of other theological loci, Guy Waters concludes, "The FV is most properly seen not as a series of refinements of or deviations from classical Reformed theological formulations. It is, properly, a different system altogether." He observes, however, "For any number of reasons ... most FV proponents have *not* institutionally broken from the Reformed faith. A number vehemently believe their views to be the most consistent expression of the Reformed faith formulated in the church's history" (*Federal Vision and Covenant Theology*, 300, emphasis added). Waters's assessment signals that there may be internal theological affinities leading to the shared practice of paedocommunion between the federal-vision proponents and the Eastern Orthodox. Nonetheless, that federal-vision proponents remain institutionally allegiant to the Reformed tradition supports larger point here, namely, that a merely denominational approach to the problem of complexity is insufficient.

59. Helpful summaries of these issues as they appeared among English Baptists and American or Southern Baptists respectively are provided by Michael Walker, *Baptists at the Table: The Theology of the Lord's Supper amongst English Baptists in the Nineteenth Century* (Didcot: Baptist Historical Society, 1992), esp. 32–83; and Gregory A. Wills, "Sounds from Baptist History," in *The Lord's Supper: Remembering and Proclaiming Christ until He Comes*, ed. Thomas R. Schreiner and Matthew R. Crawford, NAC Studies in Bible and Theology 10 (Nashville: B&H Academic, 2010), 285–312. While the larger English and American debates over these issues are instructive, both issues (i.e., open Communion *and* open membership) are present in the dispute between John Bunyan and William Kiffin. Thus, this particular debate is of interest; cf. Harry L. Poe, "John Bunyan's Controversy with the Baptists," *Baptist History and Heritage* 23.2 (1988): 25–35; John Bunyan, *Differences in Judgment about Water-Baptism, No Bar to Communion*, MWJB 4:189–264; William Kiffin, *A Sober Discourse of Right to Church-Communion*, Baptist Distinctives Series 31 (repr., Paris, AR: Baptist Standard Bearer, 2006). Concerning open membership, James Leo Garrett writes, "Currently, a movement has been launched to convince Baptist churches to adopt open membership. That means that Baptist churches should no longer insist that all persons received into membership (barring some physical disability) have been baptized upon and after profession of faith in Jesus Christ by the mode of immersion. Instead, persons who have had only infant baptism, who have had baptism by pouring or sprinkling, and possibly those who have had no baptism may be received into Baptist churches without immersion so long as they profess faith in Jesus. (This movement

for both Communion and membership apart from what he is willing to call a biblically valid baptism.[60] Harry Poe notes that in *A Confession of My Faith, and a Reason of My Practice* (1672) Bunyan distinguished "the practice of baptism and the doctrine of baptism."[61] The latter referred to belief in the foundational elements of the gospel, namely, "the saving death and resurrection of Christ, and the believer's death and resurrection with Christ." The former referred to the external sign of faith. While this sign, Poe writes, "symbolizes the salvation experience of the believer with Christ, its absence does not invalidate the experience."[62] On Bunyan's view, churches were to listen for an authentic, internal experience of faith more than to look for the external symbol. Bunyan held "that by the word of faith, and of good works, moral duties gospelized, we ought to judge of the fitness of members by, by which we ought also to receive them to fellowship."[63] Poe concludes, "Rather than as a basis for church membership, Bunyan believed that baptism provided a 'sign to the person baptized, and a help to his own faith.' "[64]

John Bunyan articulated his distinctive views on open Communion in several major works, most notably *Differences in Judgment about Water-Baptism, No Bar to Communion*. One of the most important of Bunyan's interlocutors was William Kiffin (e.g., *A Sober Discourse of Right to Church-Communion*). Poe aptly notes, "This understanding of the basis for fellowship in the church and the conspicuous absence of baptism as a rite of

---

toward open membership is to be clearly differentiated from open communion, even though open communion has sometimes led to open membership.)" See Garrett, "Should Baptist Churches Adopt Open Membership," The Center for Theological Research, Southwestern Baptist Theological Seminary (2010), http://www.baptisttheology.org/baptisttheology/assets/File/ShouldBaptistChurchesadoptOpenMembership-Garrett.pdf. For trends toward open membership among Baptists see Curtis W. Freeman, *Contesting Catholicity: Theology for Other Baptists* (Waco: Baylor University Press, 2014), 379n180; Paul S. Fiddes and Bruce Matthews, *Conversations around the World 2000-2005: The Report of the International Conversations between the Anglican Communion and the Baptist World Alliance* (London: Anglican Communion Office, 2005), 4.49-50.

60. Harry L. Poe, "John Bunyan," in *Baptist Theologians*, ed. Timothy George and David S. Dockery (Nashville: Broadman, 1990), 38.

61. John Bunyan, *A Confession of My Faith, and a Reason of My Practice* (1672), in *Works of John Bunyan*, ed. George Offor (London: Blackie and Son, 1861), 2:609.

62. Poe, "John Bunyan," 39.

63. Bunyan, *Confession of My Faith*, 610.

64. Poe, "John Bunyan," 39.

entry in his theology set Bunyan at odds with many Baptists who held strict communion views."[65] Open Communion views such as Bunyan's make catechesis (especially in the form of gospel preaching) and examination prerequisite for first Communion. Baptism, on his view, is not a prerequisite for first Communion. Open Communion stands in contrast to strict(er) Communion views[66] that understand both catechesis and baptism to be prerequisites to the Lord's Supper. The complexity within a tradition on the relationship between baptism, catechesis, and entrance is not restricted to external polemical debates; complexity within a tradition on this issue can also be found at the atomic level of *internal* competing norms and polities.

The Roman Catholic liturgist Aidan Kavanagh has drawn attention to the competition of norms and polities between infant and adult or conversion baptism within his tradition. Important liturgical reforms emanating from Vatican II include revisions to infant or children's baptism (1969), confirmation (1971), and adult initiation (1972). In the last reform document—Rite of Christian Initiation of Adults—the council lays forth a return to a robust catechumenate that culminates in baptism, confirmation, and first Communion.

Kavanagh argues that the Rite of Christian Initiation of Adults recenters adult baptism as the norm for all baptisms. He writes,

The notion that infant baptism must be regarded as something less than normal cannot set easily with many Catholics, lay as well as clerical, who have never known anything else. But its abnormality does not require one to conclude that it is illegitimate: tradition clearly seems to know the baptism of infants from the beginning. But tradition with equal clarity does *not* know one thing often implied by the conventional frequency of infant baptism, namely,

---

65. Poe, "John Bunyan," 38.

66. There are varying degrees of strictness on the issue of eligibility. The distinction between close and closed Communion is sometimes made, especially among Baptists. "Close Communion" designates those of "like faith and practice" who affirm that baptism is reserved for those baptized as believers. See, e.g., Andrew Fuller, *Baptism and the Terms of Communion: An Argument*, 3rd ed. (repr., Paris, AR: Baptist Standard Bearer, 2006). "Closed Communion" designates the limiting of participants to the membership of a particular local church (most notably within the Landmark movement). This distinction is irrelevant to the point made here, because both positions—in opposition to open Communion—understand baptism to be prerequisite to admission to the Lord's Supper.

that baptism in infancy is the normal manner in which one becomes
a Catholic Christian.[67]

On his view, infant baptism is adult baptism in miniature: all the elements are there; they simply are not as developed or pronounced. Thus, on
Kavanagh's view, while both are valid, to understand fully the miniature,
one must look to the mature.[68] Despite the absence of a direct statement to
this effect in the Rite of Christian Initiation of Adults, Kavanagh defends
his observation that the document makes the catechesis–baptism–first
Communion sequence the pastoral norm of the church.

If this is not the case ... then the document not only makes no sense
but is vain and fatuous. Its extensive and sensitive dispositions for
gradually incorporating adult converts into communities of faith
nowhere suggest that this process should be regarded as the rare
exception. On the contrary, from deep within the Roman tradition
it speaks of the process presumptively as normative.[69]

---

67. Aidan Kavanagh, *The Shape of Baptism: The Rite of Christian Initiation* (New York: Pueblo,
1978), 106, emphasis original. Interestingly, from within the Lutheran tradition, Frank Senn
approaches conclusions and proposals very close to those of Kavanagh (though not motivated
by the *RCIA*). His examination of patristic catechesis and confirmation combined with his
observations of the current post-Christian or pagan cultural context lead Senn to conclude
that it would be healthy for the practice of infant baptism to diminish. He makes this com-
ment longingly, but he acknowledges that at the time of his writing a "moratorium on infant
baptism" would not be well received. See Frank C. Senn, "Confirmation and First Communion:
A Reappraisal," *Lutheran Quarterly* 23.2 (1971): 190. Cf. *RCIA*.

68. William Harmless, agreeing with this assessment, provides the following metaphor:
"Set against such a norm [of adult baptism], infant baptism will seem a mere 'piano reduction' compared to the *RCIA*'s 'symphonic orchestration': the key melodies may all be there,
but scarcely with their proper richness and full-voiced tonality. In other words, the *RCIA*
should, over time, quietly but profoundly challenge the standards and presuppositions that
undergird our long-standing habit of infant baptism." See William Harmless, *Augustine and
the Catechumenate* (Collegeville, MN: Liturgical, 1995), 14.

69. Kavanagh, *Shape of Baptism*, 106. Illustrating the validity of Kavanagh's assessment,
the *RCIA* states, "The time spent in the catechumenate should be long enough—several years
if necessary—for the conversion and faith of the catechumens to become strong. By their
formation in the entire Christian life and a sufficiently prolonged probation the catechumens
are properly initiated into the mysteries of salvation and the practice of an evangelical way of
life. By means of sacred rites celebrated at successive times they are led into the life of faith,
worship, and charity belonging to the people of God" (76 [38]). The "successive" nature of the
RCIA is seen in its three steps for initiating adults (i.e., persons with discretion): (1) acceptance
into the order of catechumens, (2) election or enrollment for baptism, (3) reception of the
sacraments of initiation (baptism, confirmation, and Eucharist) (6 [3]).

Based on this perceived shift of baptismal norms, Kavanagh believes that the Rite of Christian Initiation of Adults, if it has its full effect, will lead to a reconsideration of how catechesis and confirmation are currently performed. A key point of interest for him in this regard is the separation of confirmation from infant baptism, a practice he finds unwise. He writes,

The alternative will be to sustain two different sets of meanings, catecheses, and ritual forms for the "sealing" of confirmation. The first will be that for adults and children of catechetical age who are baptized, confirmed, and communicated within the same liturgical event even if the bishop is absent. The second will be that for children and others who are baptized years previously. The sacramental ethos of the first is directly baptismal, paschal, and Trinitarian: that of the second has more to do with marking an educational or life-crisis point in the personal development of the recipients, and it is enhanced by the presence of the bishop at the event.[70]

Kavanagh continues, adding detail to this bifurcated catechetical structure.

The Roman Rite thus finds itself affirming in practice *two* initiatory theories and polities that have successively held sway in its history: the first is antique and paschal, meant to consecrate and initiate a Christian wholly; the second is medieval and socio-personal in emphasis, stressing "growth" on all fronts (*ad robur*). The first presupposes the presence of catechumens in local churches together with the evangelical and catechetical structures necessary to prepare them for baptism. The second presupposes a sustained Catholic birthrate and functioning forms of religious education such as the parochial school. The two project rather different models of the Church as well, the second being a "Christendom model" currently wracked with enervating problems that arise not from the hostility of the modern state so much as from its massive indifference. The first projected model, on the contrary, does not presuppose the state at all: it was, in fact, developed historically not

---

70. Kavanagh, *Shape of Baptism*, 196.

only without recourse to state benevolence but often in opposition to its pretensions.[71]

If Kavanagh's observations of his own tradition are accurate, it is plausible (even likely) that other paedobaptist traditions have analogous complexity within their own initiatory structures as well. Kavanagh's logic suggests that competing answers to the baptismal norm question will lead to bifurcation within any paedobaptist tradition.

The internal diversity that has been highlighted above, both within credobaptist and paedobaptist traditions, demonstrates the need for an explanatory framework that goes beyond a merely denominational or traditional approach. In response, this book provides a different kind of framework for explaining the diverse ways in which baptism and catechesis have been related to one another to bring persons fully into the visible fellowship of the local church or parish.

RESEARCH QUESTIONS

Two basic questions are pursued in this book. First, how might the various ways of relating baptism, catechesis, and entrance as highlighted in the previous section be explained in coordination to one another? In response, the book will provide an explanatory framework that accounts for the major historical varieties of relationship between baptism and catechesis as entrance to the church. Defined as inaugural participation in the Lord's Supper, "entrance" is used as a prism through which a spectrum of logical-liturgical relationships between baptism and catechesis will be refracted into several primary colors (or models). The intention is not to squeeze historical exemplars into narrow categories, but rather to create conceptual models flexible enough to account for distinctive affinities of function and liturgical logic. The models proposed here are distinguished from each other by the attendant functions and meanings they assign to baptism or catechesis or both in relation to entrance.

The categories for framing the varieties of relationship between baptism and catechesis as entrance are independent and interdependent. Each of these categories has two related models associated with it. Put briefly,

---

71. Kavanagh, *Shape of Baptism*, 196–97.

baptism and catechesis function either *independently* or *interdependently* for entrance. On the one hand, independent models make either baptism or catechesis the *sole* means of entrance. Thus, the related models are the baptism model and the catechesis model. We will develop these in the following chapter. For now, however, we can represent the independent models as follows:

Category	Independent	
Model	Baptism	Catechesis
Sequence	Baptism ↓ **Entrance** ↓ Catechesis	Catechesis ↓ **Entrance** ↓ (Baptism)

On the other hand, interdependent models make baptism and catechesis a *tandem* means for entrance. Interdependent models demonstrate variety in their ordering—sequence and priority—of baptism or catechesis. For example, when baptism functions as the foundation for catechesis, the model is described as *retrospective* since catechesis as a means of entrance looks back to baptism. When catechesis functions as the foundation for baptism, the model is described as *prospective* since catechesis as a means of entrance looks forward to baptism. Each of these models will be treated in separate chapters (chs. 3-4). For now, however, we can represent the interdependent models as follows:

Category	Interdependent	
Model	Retrospective	Prospective
Sequence	Baptism ↓ Catechesis ↓ **Entrance**	Catechesis ↓ Baptism ↓ **Entrance**

Once the proposed explanatory structure has been built, consideration will turn to a second question: causality. Namely, is there a discernible catalyst that gives rise to the existence of one model over another? If so, what is it? By necessity, I will narrow the question of causality to the varieties of *interdependent* relationship developed in its framework (see ch. 2).

THESIS

In a broad sense this book functions as an extended argument for the cogency of its proposed explanatory framework of models (chs. 2–4). The broad argument, however, I will narrow to a more specific one related to the question of causality (ch. 5). In this latter regard, I will argue that the theological catalyst that gives rise to one interdependent model over the other is the way in which a local church or parish connects baptism to the confirmation of personal faith that is decisive for entrance.

METHODOLOGY

The methodology deployed in this study is essentially that of a typology. In a broad sense, typologies are useful for summarizing themes or families of thought. They stand to contribute both to our understanding and our appreciation of divergent approaches to the same question.

The history of theological typologies extends at least to the work of Ernst Troeltsch, *The Social Teachings of the Christian Churches.*[72] Three works in particular have shaped the use of typologies as found in this book and are therefore useful for describing and qualifying the methodology as deployed here: Avery Dulles's *Models of the Church* and *Models of Revelation* as well as H. Richard Niebuhr's *Christ and Culture.*[73] First, Niebuhr's *Christ and Culture* offers an example of a framework of types. Further, Niebuhr's work examines the relationship between two entities (Christ and culture), which corresponds well to the way baptism and catechesis are being considered in relation to Communion in the current work. Niebuhr's method of laying out the polar options and then discussing intermediate ones is followed here as well. That is, we will consider the polar models (independent

---

72. Earnst Troeltsch, *The Social Teachings of the Christian Churches*, 2 vols. (New York: Macmillan, 1931); cf. Avery Dulles, *Models of Revelation* (Maryknoll, NY: Orbis Books, 1992), 25.

73. Avery Dulles, *Models of the Church* (New York: Doubleday, 1978); Dulles, *Models of Revelation*; H. Richard Niebuhr, *Christ and Culture* (New York: HarperCollins, 1951, 2001).

models) in chapter 2 and then devote attention to the models in the middle (interdependent models) in chapters 3 and 4 respectively.

Second, typologies can help us both to *explain* patterns of thought or logic and *explore* the implications of these patterns. Dulles's work highlights this feature. Dulles employs the term "models" rather than "types," but his approach is similar to Niebuhr's. He identifies two levels of models: explanatory and exploratory. First, models serve an explanatory function when they "synthesize what we already know or at least are inclined to believe. A model is accepted if it accounts for a large number of biblical and traditional data and according with what history and experience tell us about the Christian life." Second, models serve an exploratory or "heuristic" function through "their capacity to lead to new theological insights."[74] In short, such an approach stands to help one see what may otherwise be missed.

Though Dulles's models of the church are much broader than the present study (i.e., Dulles considers the church as a whole, and this study considers only the process of entrance to the local church or parish), the same basic levels are at work in it. The emphasis of the present work will be on the taxonomic-explanatory level. The liturgical markers utilized to distinguish one model from another are concrete enough to categorize the historical and confessional evidence without much dispute. Nonetheless, the explanatory framework produced within this study (chs. 2–4) has the potential to function in an exploratory or typological-heuristic sense as well (chs. 5–6).[75]

Finally, while there are many values to typologies, both Niebuhr and Dulles offer guidance regarding the limitations of a typology. For example,

---

74. Dulles, *Models of the Church*, 24–25. By "heuristic" Dulles does not mean a new norm, for "theology has an abiding objective norm in the past—that is, in the revelation that was given once and for all in Jesus Christ" (25).

75. For example, credobaptists are not unified in their employed models of entrance. Some have favored an interdependent model (e.g., Balthasar Hubmaier) and others an independent model (e.g., John Bunyan's open-Communion or open-membership view). It could be argued persuasively that credobaptists who administer baptism indiscriminately (i.e., without examination of the candidate) are functionally employing an independent model. The proposed framework and catalyst offer a means by which to see and explore the dynamics at work in these differences. Cf. Balthasar Hubmaier, *A Christian Catechism*, in *Balthasar Hubmaier: Theologian of Anabaptism*, ed. H. Wayne Pipkin and John H. Yoder, Classics of the Reformation 5 (Scottdale, PA: Herald, 1989), 339–65; Harry L. Poe, "John Bunyan," in *Baptist Theologians*, ed. Timothy George and David S. Dockery (Nashville: Broadman, 1990), 38–39.

Niebuhr cautions, "a type is a mental construct to which no individual wholly conforms." Additionally, because of this approximate quality, "[the type] must be used ... only as a means toward understanding the individual and not as a statement of necessary connections, so that the rational is given precedence over the empirical."[76] Similarly, Dulles, in his work *Models of Revelation*, describes typological models as having two key limiting qualities. First, "The type is simplified: it omits many qualifications and amplifications which the theologians make." Second, "The type is schematic: it represents a pure position or ideal case from which any given theologian will presumably diverge at certain points, especially if one considers the full output of the individual over a span of years." To illustrate the tension of similarity and dissimilarity, Dulles likens models to a tailor's mannequin. The mannequin is not a real person, but it approximates a real person and in so doing serves the tailor's purpose of producing clothes. While further adjustments will have to be made to fit a particular person's idiosyncrasies, the clothes are constructed so that only minor adjustments are required.[77] While there are limitations to the use of typologies or models, they hold promise for exploring the ideal relationships between baptism, catechesis, and entrance.

The proposed models are intended to illuminate patterns or dynamics of relationship between baptism, catechesis, and entrance. The models are not intended to account for all practices or theological eccentricities of a particular person or tradition. As Kavanagh has noted of the contemporary Roman Catholic Church, a tradition may actually have two separate "polities" of catechesis or baptism or both at work within it. Thus, for the purposes of this study, historical exemplars are used in an illustrative sense, *not* as thoroughgoing representatives.

With these methodological considerations in place, there are three key values that this study offers. First, the explanatory framework developed in this book offers an instrument for comparing and contrasting foundational initiatory patterns of liturgical logic regardless of the denominational context in which they occur. As noted earlier, the complex mosaic of initiatory practices that manifests across and within denominations

---

76. Niebuhr, "Introduction: Types of Christian Ethics," in *Christ and Culture*, xxxviii.
77. Dulles, *Models of Revelation*, 30.

(interdenominational diversity, interdenominational affinity, and intra-denominational diversity) benefits from an approach that is *not* rooted in denominational distinctives. While denominational distinctives must be acknowledged, the logical-liturgical relationships that the models of this study will map have promise for seeing the initiatory mosaic more clearly. Not only does this clarify how other traditions differ from one another or are similar to one another, but it also clarifies where distinctions of logic have developed or (interestingly) are developing within a particular tradition.

Second, whereas studies of Christian initiation typically approach historical evidence diachronically looking at issues of development, this study approaches the evidence synchronically looking at issues of liturgical logic. In other words, rather than working through how initiatory patterns developed over time, this study seeks to create models that map distinctive families of initiatory logic. The synchronic approach *must not* replace the diachronic approach, but it does offer a way to explore the historical data in a fresh way. Thus, the synchronic approach deployed here provides a supplemental consideration of the basic patterns and moves of initiation (or entrance, as we are calling it). Studies that consider the historical and theological development surrounding baptism, catechesis, and entrance are important and must continue. The produce of such diachronic studies, however, should only lead to further refinement of the specific models or of the larger framework that will be constructed synchronically in this project.

Finally, theology should always operate in service to the church. In a pastoral sense, I believe the explanatory framework of this study will allow readers to better understand the initiatory logic of their own traditions in relation to other traditions, and (hopefully) better appreciate the rationale and coherence of other approaches (presuppositional differences notwithstanding). The exploratory chapters of this book (chs. 5–6) will seek to draw out some of the pastoral implications on a host of issues more clearly. While the explanatory and exploratory goals of the work are related, they are not inseparably conjoined. In other words, regardless of the relative success that the later exploratory chapters enjoy in convincing you, the explanatory framework holds value in and of itself.

USE OF SOURCES

The scope of inquiry in this book is expansive. The traditions that will be examined span from Eastern Orthodoxy to Quakerism. In order to filter the evidence to a manageable corpus the study takes creeds, confessions, and catechisms as its primary sources. This decision also functions to stabilize the evidence. The corporate nature of these documents and their continued use over time mitigate the liability that the evaluations and conclusions drawn from them are simply isolated outliers of the tradition in view. Even if the document proves to be a minority report within a tradition, the corporate nature of the selected genres offers more stability than the writings of a specific individual. Liturgies, church manuals, and church constitutions will be used sparingly to supplement the discussion.

Some traditions, such as Quakerism and the Stone-Campbell Restoration Movement, are anticreedal. In such cases, a key luminary's writings have been used to approximate the confessional nature of the materials used for other traditions.[78] Importantly, readers should remember that the intended goal is not to make ultimate claims about the tradition as a whole or an author in particular (i.e., "this was the author's or tradition's lone or early or late or final position on X, Y, or Z"). The confessional documents surveyed in this study are therefore intended only to *illustrate* the liturgical-logical pattern(s) in view.

Care has been given to select confessional material that is recognized, relatively well-known, and accessible. The editorial instincts of Philip Schaff, John Leith, Jaroslav Pelikan, and Valerie Hotchkiss in their respective ecumenical, confessional collections have aided in the selection process throughout.[79] Cues for this selection process for particular traditions (where possible) have been taken from other published collections of confessional material as well.[80]

---

78. For example, Robert Barclay is used in this way in the discussion of Quaker initiation in ch. 2. Similarly, Alexander Campbell is used in ch. 4 as a key exemplar of Stone-Campbell doctrine.

79. Schaff, *Creeds of Christendom*; John H. Leith, ed., *Creeds of the Churches: A Reader in Christian Doctrine from the Bible to the Present*, 3rd ed. (Louisville: Westminster John Knox, 1982); CCFCT.

80. E.g., BC; RCH; BCF.

PROGRAM

Chapter 2 has two main objectives: (1) introducing and orienting the reader to the proposed framework and (2) narrowing the focus of the study. With regard to the former, the chapter contains a visual illustration of the framework and explains its structure and categories (i.e., independent or interdependent and prospective or retrospective). Though not the focus of the study, the two independent models will be sketched there in order to introduce the dynamics of the framework as well as demonstrate each model's contours and viability. The chapter functions programmatically to narrow the focus of subsequent chapters to the seam separating the retrospective and prospective interdependent models. Some of the most important material in the book comes in chapters 3–4, but this material cannot be appreciated without chapter 2.

Chapters 3–4 will examine the retrospective and prospective models in turn. Each chapter provides a definition and profile of its model, looking at core attributes and implications. Key issues include the following:

1. The relation between baptism and entrance

2. The grounds, validity, subjective, objective, and functional aspects of baptism

3. The orientation of catechesis to baptism

4. The nature and relation of faith to baptism

5. The nature and timing of confirmation

6. The objective-subjective flexibility of the model

7. The view of the church projected by the model

The profiles created in these chapters synthesize biblical and confessional-theological evidence to illustrate the liturgical logic of entrance summarized by each model.

Having erected the explanatory framework (ch. 2) and developed the interdependent models in greater detail (chs. 3–4), chapter 5 will take up a heuristic and exploratory analysis of the central seam separating the two interdependent models. Specifically, this chapter will seek to identify the theological catalyst that (logically and liturgically speaking) gives rise to one model of interdependent relationship over the other. Key catalyst candidates include (1) the *ex opere operato/sola fide* sacramental divide, (2) the affirmation or denial of baptismal regeneration, (3) the distinction between infant baptism and adult baptism, and (4) the grounds of baptismal validity. Insights from the discussion of chapters 2–4 will be used to narrow the search for a catalyst. I will then make a case for the key catalytic element in an interdependent model's pattern of entrance. I will highlight the implications for this conclusion as well as the usefulness of the framework as a whole in chapter 6.

2

—

CONSTRUCTING THE
EXPLANATORY FRAMEWORK

Recently my wife and I purchased a trampoline for our four children. Of course, the kids wanted to jump on as soon as I unloaded the box in the backyard, but before the canvas could hold their weight and rebound them blissfully into the air, we had to spend several hours assembling the frame, attaching the springs, and securing the safety netting. The assembly process was somewhat tedious, but the tedium was tempered by the fact that blissful bouncing was just around the corner. This chapter is a bit like the assembly process for that trampoline. In order to enjoy the unique perspective, understanding, and appreciation that this study seeks to provide, we must set up the framework that will make such insights possible. Some of the bouncing will begin in chapter 3. So, stay with me through the assembly process.

This chapter constructs the proposed framework of models of relationship between baptism, catechesis, and entrance. The chapter contains a visual illustration of the framework and explains its structure and categories. Though not the focus of the study, the two independent models will be sketched here in order to introduce the dynamics of the framework as well as demonstrate each model's contours and viability. Programmatically, by the end of the chapter the focus of the study will be narrowed to consider the two interdependent models, which will be developed in greater detail in the subsequent chapters.

FRAMEWORK

Chapter 1 introduced the categories of independent and interdependent. That is, catechesis and baptism either function alone or together to bring one into the visible fellowship of a local church or parish. The framework below arranges these categories and their related models to one another across a spectrum, with the models prioritizing baptism on the left and the models prioritizing catechesis on the right. This section will orient the basic structural features of this framework.

Category	Independent	Prerequisite(s) of entrance? / Baptism or catechesis or both?	Interdependent			Prerequisite(s) of entrance? / Baptism or catechesis or both?	Independent
Model	Baptism		Retrospective		Prospective		Catechesis
Sequence	Baptism ↓ **Entrance** ↓ Catechesis		Baptism ↓ Catechesis ↓ **Entrance**	Orientation of catechesis to baptism	Catechesis ↓ Baptism ↓ **Entrance**		Catechesis ↓ **Entrance** ↓ (Baptism)

◄──────── OBJECTIVE			SUBJECTIVE ────────►

The above framework consists of four models classified in two categories. The broader categories are Independent and Interdependent: baptism and catechesis function either *independently* or *interdependently* for entrance. On the one hand, independent models make either baptism or catechesis the *sole* means of entrance. Thus, baptism alone or catechesis alone renders a candidate eligible to participate in the visible fellowship of the local church as displayed in the Lord's Supper ("entrance"). So, while the baptism model allows for catechesis after entrance, catechesis is not an integral means of entrance. The alternative is also true; while the catechesis model allows for baptism after entrance, baptism is not an integral means of entrance.

On the other hand, interdependent models make baptism and catechesis a *tandem* means of entrance. Here, baptism and catechesis function together to render a candidate eligible for visible fellowship with the local church around the Table of the Lord. Interdependent models demonstrate variety in their ordering—sequence and priority—of baptism and catechesis. When baptism functions as the foundation for catechesis, the *retrospective model* is operative, because catechesis as a means of entrance looks back to baptism. Alternatively, when catechesis functions as the foundation for baptism, the *prospective model* is operative, because catechesis as a means of entrance looks forward to baptism.

It may be helpful to draw out the questions to which these models offer their respective answers. The diagnostic questions for distinguishing the various models of relationship are as follows:

- Independent or interdependent: What are the prerequisites of entrance: baptism or catechesis or both? Do baptism and catechesis function together or independently in the process of entrance?

- Independent model: If baptism or catechesis are functioning independently, which one is operative in the entrance process?

- Interdependent model: If baptism and catechesis are functioning together, how is catechesis oriented to baptism in the entrance process? Is it looking back to baptism (retrospective) or anticipating baptism (prospective)? Put differently, is baptism the *basis for* catechesis (catechesis is retrospectively oriented to baptism), or is baptism *grounded on* catechesis (catechesis is prospectively oriented to baptism)?

MODEL DESCRIPTIONS (BRIEF)

As shown in the preceding graphic, four major models are proposed for understanding the relationship between baptism, catechesis, and entrance. Each will be developed in turn, but provisional definitions are offered here:

1. The baptism model is an independent model in which baptism is the sole prerequisite for entrance. Catechesis is subsequent to entrance and grounded on baptism and Lord's Supper.

2. The retrospective model is an interdependent model in which baptism and catechesis are both prerequisites for entrance. Catechesis is grounded on and looks back to baptism. The catechetical process is typically concluded with a rite of confirmation that is prerequisite for entrance.[1]

---

1. This, however, is not always the case. The practice of soft paedocommunion allows unconfirmed, baptized children to participate in the Lord's Supper. More will be said about

3. The prospective model is an interdependent model in which
    baptism and catechesis are both prerequisites for entrance.
    Here, however, catechesis is prerequisite to baptism and pro-
    vides the basis for baptism. The catechetical process culmi-
    nates in baptism and leads to entrance.

4. The catechesis model is an independent model in which cat-
    echesis is the sole prerequisite for entrance. Baptism, if it is
    given at all, is subsequent to entrance and viewed as a means
    of personal growth.

The independent model names are straightforward. The titles "retrospective" and "prospective" frame the interdependent models in terms of *how
catechesis relates to baptism* in the process of entrance. Thomas Finn writes,
"Baptism, whether ancient or modern, is the hinge upon which Christian
identity turns."[2] Understood in terms of the visibility of faith and the reality to which baptism points (i.e., union with Christ in his death, burial, and
resurrection), Finn's description is certainly correct. Unlike catechesis,
baptism is a *visible* sign and, therefore, receives the emphasis in the framing of these models of entrance into *visible* fellowship.

ATTRIBUTES

The sequence of baptism, catechesis, and entrance is the key attribute
defining each model. There are, however, subsidiary attributes to consider,
including but not limited to the model's projection of the nature of confirmation, the nature the church, and faith's relation to baptism (assuming
baptism is practiced).[3]

Regarding confirmation, does the model project a view of confirmation
that makes it the capstone of catechesis, or is it an objective seal connected
to baptism, or some combination of these? Idiosyncrasies on the issue of
confirmation abound. For example, what is its status: Is it a valid sacrament

---

this in subsequent discussion of this model.

2. Thomas M. Finn, *Early Christian Baptism and the Catechumenate: West and East Syria*, ed.
Thomas Halton, Message of the Fathers of the Church 5 (Collegeville, MN: Liturgical, 1992), 1.

3. Since the focus of this chapter is laying out the structure of the framework. These
and other subsidiary attributes will be noted in the sketches of the two independent models
below, but they will not be fully developed.

or merely a rite? What is its function: Is it an immediate, objective sign or seal of the Holy Spirit, or a later, subjective completion of baptism? What is its nature: Is it an objective gift to the recipient, or is it a subjective affirmation of the faith once delivered to the saints, or some combination of these? The variety of answers to these questions is wide. In fact, Paul Turner, a Roman Catholic theologian, identifies three forms of confirmation within the Catholic tradition alone: as a rite of (1) initiation, given in infancy at baptism; (2) maturity, given at a (varying) age of discretion; or (3) reception, given to a proselyte from another Christian denomination.[4] In subsequent discussion, attention will be given to these issues as necessary for explaining the relationship between baptism, catechesis, and entrance within a particular model. For now, however, I simply want to note that the various sequences of the proposed models tend to cast or project a particular view of confirmation.

Regarding the church, does the model project a view that the church is a mixed body (corpus permixteum) or regenerate body? That is, does the model of entrance leave the church expecting that there are those within her visible fellowship who have not yet expressed personal faith in Christ and his gospel? A model of initiation or entrance that projects such a view will have downstream effects on a host of issues such as discipleship, church polity, church discipline, and many more.

Regarding faith's relation to baptism, does the model project a view that faith is an objective gift flowing from the baptismal sign or that the baptismal sign is an emblem of prior faith or even an instrument through which the subjective faith of the baptizand is actualized? This also has a multitude of practical reverberations. For example, it affects how persons are led to the baptismal waters, what they are taught is happening in baptism, and how they are to think about their baptism after the fact.

The development of models within this study will also consider the elasticity of each, examining the ideal extremes of its logic. These extremes will be considered along an objective-subjective continuum. This continuum is not essential to the framework we are developing, but it holds explanatory strength that I will demonstrate along the way. Of the two means of entrance named—baptism and catechesis—baptism, being an elemental

---

4. See Paul Turner, "Confusion over Confirmation," *Worship* 71.6 (1997): 539–40.

symbol or sign, adds weight to a model's so-called objectivity. Likewise, catechesis, in its instruction of the baptismal subject, is the more subjective of the two means. Thus, models that prioritize baptism to a higher degree than catechesis are here categorized as more *objective*, and models that prioritize catechesis to a higher degree than baptism are understood to be more *subjective*.[5] While there is explanatory power on the larger level of how the models stand in relation to one another, this power extends to the lower, more granular level of diversity that we find within each model. Traditions that construe the relationship between baptism, catechesis, and entrance as interdependent will vary in their understandings of the nature of baptism, confirmation, and the Lord's Supper. For example, while two separate traditions, such as Lutheranism and Presbyterianism, have historically divergent views on both baptism and Communion, they share similar patterns of liturgical logic in how they connect baptism, catechesis, and entrance. If the models we are constructing are not flexible enough to accommodate such differences, then we are forced to take a merely denominational approach.

The models that follow seek to account for a breadth of specific practices while adequately summarizing the family of liturgical logic to which they belong. Thus, it will be helpful for readers to consider each model as defining internal space that allows for more objective views on the left and more subjective ones on the right. This internal (horizontal) space within each model allows for varieties of specific doctrinal eccentricities. At the same time, each model accounts for similarities of liturgical logic, which is marked by the outer boundaries of each model. It is at the level of liturgical logic that each model in particular and the framework as a whole are intended to have explanatory power.

LAYOUT

The models above have been laid out in a way that shows a logical progression from model to model. The independent models have been separated and situated at either end. These models (baptism model and catechesis

---

5. There is admittedly overlap in these designations. Baptism has subjective aspects to it (e.g., the faith of participants, administrators, witnesses, etc.), and catechesis has objective aspects to it (e.g., the faith once for all delivered to the saints). However, the physicality of the sign of baptism as well as the connection of grace to it (by many traditions though in various ways) give it a stronger objectivity. Similarly, the instructional aspect of catechesis gives it a stronger subjectivity.

model) represent the polar ends of an objective-subjective continuum. The baptism model is the most objective of the four models, as it does not require catechesis of the baptizand as a prerequisite for entrance; the catechesis model is the most subjective of the four models, as it bases entrance on the subjective elements of personal faith and experience of the candidate apart from the sign of water baptism. The models in the middle follow this pattern as well, placing the retrospective model to the left of the prospective model because of its grounding of catechesis on the objective sign of baptism.[6] The prospective model is deemed more subjective than the retrospective model because it administers baptism on the basis of the catechization of the baptizand.[7]

DISCRIMINATE ADMINISTRATION

Though examples may exist that mix some of the dynamics of the proposed models, the discriminate administration of both baptism and the Lord's Supper are presupposed in the presentation of this framework. This methodological decision aids presentation by (1) protecting the liturgical logic of each model and (2) narrowing the scope of inquiry.

First, the development of each model will presuppose that *baptism* is administered discriminately. This means that the respective model in view involves the examination either of the candidate or of the parents and sponsors. The problem of indiscriminate baptism is a real one, affecting paedobaptist and credobaptist traditions alike. For example, credobaptism according to its own logic is indiscriminate when it is administered apart from proper examination of the baptizand. Paedobaptism according to its own logic is indiscriminate when it is administered to the children of unbelieving parents of whom the church has no legitimate basis for expecting that they will raise the child toward personal confession at a later point (often marked by confirmation).

The World Council of Churches *Lima Report* on baptism, Eucharist, and ministry notes,

> In many large European and North American majority churches infant baptism is often practiced in an apparently indiscriminate

---

6. More will be said about this in ch. 3.

7. The relative objectivity-subjectivity of each model will be discussed in the development of each model.

way. This contributes to the reluctance of churches which practice
believers' baptism to acknowledge the validity of infant baptism;
this fact should lead to more critical reflection on the meaning of
baptism within those majority churches themselves.[8]

The concern that baptism be administered on the grounds of personal
faith of the recipient or of sponsors is echoed within paedobaptist traditions. For example, the baptismal liturgies assume the presence of parents or sponsors or both. Luther, speaking of the role of those present at
baptism (especially sponsors), writes,

> See to it that you are present there in true faith, that you listen
> to God's Word, and that you pray along earnestly. For wherever
> the priest says, "Let us pray," he is exhorting you to pray with him.
> Moreover, all sponsors and the others present ought to speak along
> with him the words of his prayer in their hearts to God. For this
> reason, the priest should speak these prayers very clearly and slowly,
> so that the sponsors can hear and understand them and can also
> pray with the priest with one mind in their hearts, carrying before
> God the need of the little child with all earnestness, on the child's
> behalf setting themselves against the devil with all their strength,
> and demonstrating that they take seriously what is no joke to the
> devil.[9]

The presence and role of sponsors is assumed throughout the liturgy. The
climax of the ceremony that culminates in baptism is the interrogation of
the infant whose answers are given through his or her sponsors.[10]

Similarly, the Westminster Larger Catechism asks, "Unto whom is
Baptism to be administered?" It responds, "Baptism is not to be administered to any that are out of the visible church, and so strangers from
the covenant of promise, till they profess their faith in Christ, and obedience to him, but *infants descending from parents, either both, or but one of*

---

8. *Baptism, Eucharist and Ministry: The Lima Report*, Faith and Order Paper 111 (Geneva: World Council of Churches, 1982), V.21.Commentary (b).

9. Luther, *Baptismal Booklet* (appended to *Small Catechism*, 1529; BC, 372–73).

10. Luther, *Baptismal Booklet* (appended to *Small Catechism*, 1529; BC, 374–75).

*them, professing faith in Christ, and obedience to him, are in that respect within
the covenant, and to be baptized."*[11] Likewise, Dositheus and the Synod at
Jerusalem in 1672 articulate a similar position in the Orthodox Confession
of the Eastern Church:

> Justin in his fifty-sixth Question, who says expressly, "And they
> [i.e., infants] are vouchsafed the benefits of Baptism by the faith of
> those that bring them to Baptism." And Augustine says that it is an
> Apostolic tradition, that children are saved through Baptism; and
> in another place, "The Church gives to babes the feet of others, that
> they may come; and the hearts of others, that they may believe; and
> the tongues of others, that they may promise"; and in another place,
> "Our mother, the Church, furnishes them with a particular heart."[12]

Discriminate baptism is also at the heart of credobaptist ecclesiology.
Baptism is reserved only for those giving a credible profession of faith.
The Mennonite Waterland Confession (1580) declares that baptism in the
triune formula is reserved for "those who hear, believe and freely receive
in a penitent heart the doctrine of the holy gospel; for such Christ commanded to be baptized, but by no means infants."[13] The Baptist London
Confession (1644) states that baptism is "to be dispensed onely upon persons professing faith or that are Disciples, or taught, who upon profession
of faith, ought to be baptized."[14] Discriminant baptism is here tied to the
catechizing of the baptizand, for proper subjects are "Disciples" or, as it
clarifies, "taught." The Second London Confession (1677) affirms, "Those
who do actually profess repentance towards God, faith in, and obedience, to our Lord Jesus, are the only proper subjects of this ordinance [i.e.,

---

11. Westminster Larger Catechism (1647), q. 166 (*RC*, 217), emphasis added. See also Belgic
Confession 34 (1561; *RCH*, 216, 218, 220); Heidelberg Catechism (1563), q. 74 (*RCH*, 220); Second
Helvetic Confession 20.6 (1566; *RCH*, 218); Westminster Confession 28.4 (1647; *RCH*, 217);
Westminster Shorter Catechism (1647), q. 95 (*RCH*, 217).

12. Dositheus and the Synod of Jerusalem, Confession 16 (1672; *CCFCT* 1:626–27). Patristic
references as noted by Pelikan are Justin Martyr, *Legation to the Orthodox* 56 (PG 6:1297);
Augustine, *On the Merits and Forgiveness of Sins, and on the Baptism of Infants* 1.26.39 (*NPNF*[1]
5:30); Augustine, *On Marriage and Concupiscence* 1.20.22 (*NPNF*[1] 5:273); Augustine, *On the Merits
and Forgiveness of Sins, and on the Baptism of Infants* 1.25.38 (*NPNF*[1] 5:30).

13. Waterland Confession 31 (1580; *BCF*, 57).

14. London Confession 39 (1644; *BCF*, 155).

baptism]."[15] Similar statements are characteristic of credobaptist confessions and catechisms from the sixteenth century to present.[16]

Despite the great confessional emphasis on discriminant baptism of believers only, indiscriminate baptism is still a live danger within the broader credobaptist tradition. The problem of "serial baptism" (i.e., multiple administrations of believers' baptisms to the same individual) has been noted at times among Southern Baptists.[17] Timothy George describes the phenomena of serial baptism (or "re-baptism," as he calls it here) among Southern Baptists as follows:

> In the process of an evangelistic service, or perhaps through introspective soul-searching, many church members come to believe that they have never had a genuine conversion experience at all. They have been baptized, perhaps been in the church for many years, perhaps have even served as deacons, Sunday School teachers, but they discover they have never really been converted. Whereupon, they

---

15. Second London Confession 29.2 (1677, Particular Baptist; *BCF*, 291). Similarly, the Orthodox Creed limits baptism to "those which do really profess repentance towards God, and faith in, and obedience to our Lord Jesus Christ" (Orthodox Creed 28 [1678, General Baptist; *BCF*, 317–18]).

16. New Hampshire Confession (1833, American Baptist): "Christian Baptism is the immersion in water of a believer, into the name of the Father [and] Son, and Spirit" (*BCF*, 382). All three versions of the Baptist Faith and Message (1925, 1963, and 2000; articles 13, 7, and 7 respectively; Southern Baptist) use this sentence as found in the New Hampshire Confession. The 1963 and 2000 editions, which are identical on their statements of baptism and the Lord's Supper, add further emphasis on the baptizand's faith with the following statements: "It is an act of obedience symbolizing *the believer's faith* in a crucified, buried, and risen Saviour, the believer's death to sin, the burial of the old life, and the resurrection to walk in newness of life in Christ Jesus. *It is a testimony to his faith* in the final resurrection of the dead" (Baptist Faith and Message 7 [1963; *BCF*, 413–14]; Baptist Faith and Message 7 [2000; *BCF*, 516], emphasis added).

17. See Hendricks, "Baptism: A Baptist Perspective," 30; Bill Stancil, "Rebaptisms in the Southern Baptist Convention: A Theological and Pastoral Dilemma," *Perspectives in Religious Studies* 21.2 (1994): 127–41. I was baptized twice as a Southern Baptist: once at twelve and then again at fifteen. The question of rebaptism and baptismal validity is much bigger than serial credobaptism, and its scope exceeds our purpose here. Rebaptism has been a point of debate since at least the second century as churches wrestled with how to receive those from heretical movements. Augustine's controversy with the Donatists over the validity of baptisms administered by priests who surrendered the Scriptures, and the Anabaptist controversy with the Magisterial Reformers over the validity of infant baptism, are also part of this discussion. See E. F. Harrison, "Rebaptism," in *Evangelical Dictionary of Theology*, 3rd ed., ed. Daniel J. Treier and Walter A. Elwell (Grand Rapids: Baker Academic, 2017), s.v. The term "serial baptism" is used by William L. Hendricks in "Baptism: A Baptist Perspective," *Southwestern Journal of Theology* 31 (1989): 30.

make another profession of faith and are then re-baptized upon this now allegedly genuine, authentic confession and conversion. … There are a number of churches that have re-re-baptized people, again and again and again. This is a practice which undercuts our traditional and theological understanding of baptism.[18]

Reasons adduced for such rebaptisms span from baptizing too early ("toddler baptisms") to inadequate prebaptismal preparation and examination.[19] Bill Stancil writes,

The Baptist tradition of receiving baptismal candidates on a profession of faith is in itself a repudiation of isolated individualism and points to the role of the community of faith as the guardian of baptism. When the congregation votes on a candidate for baptism, church members are called on to discern the signs of regeneration in the candidate. Unfortunately, in most Baptist churches this voting procedure is rarely practiced anymore, and only occasionally are baptismal candidates allowed or required to testify to the congregation of their Christian experience. What you are more likely to hear today in SBC churches is something like this: "Everyone who's glad Mr. Jones came forward for baptism, say amen!" When the church fails to exercise its function as discerner of signs of regeneration in the baptismal candidate, it repudiates its role as the guardian of baptism and casts the candidate for baptism afloat in a sea of subjectivity.[20]

---

18. Timothy George, "The Southern Baptists," in *Baptism and Church*, ed. Merle D. Strege (Grand Rapids: Sagamore Books, 1986), 48.

19. Jeffrey Bingham, "The Relationship between Baptism and Doctrine in the Second Century," Day-Higginbotham Lectures (Southwestern Baptist Theological Seminary, 2012), http://media.swbts.edu/item/390/the-relationship-between-baptism-and-doctrine-in-the-second-century. Timothy George terms the baptism of children five and under as "toddler baptism." See George, *Theology of the Reformers* (Nashville: Broadman & Holman, 1988), 318. James Emery White notes, "In 1985, SBC churches baptized more than nine hundred children ages five and under. That number, in 1986, had grown to more than three thousand." See White, "Rebaptism in the Life of the Church," *Search* 19.2 (1989): 26; cf. George, "Southern Baptists," 47.

20. Stancil, "Rebaptisms in the Southern Baptist Convention," 137. In addition to congregations taking their responsibility to examine baptismal candidates more carefully, Stancil argues for a stronger view of baptismal validity (esp. 133–38).

Regardless of why it is sometimes practiced, the judgment of the *Lima Report* against indiscriminate baptism is surely right. The overwhelming majority of denominations formally share this judgment—even those that are struggling to rid their ranks of the practice. As a result, the models in this study will be developed and illustrated on the assumption that when baptism is administered, it is done on a basis consistent with the respective tradition's confessional theology (i.e., the faith of the baptizand, parent, or sponsor). This methodological presupposition is important because the formal introduction of indiscriminate baptism into any one of the proposed models corrupts the basic nature of the model.

Indiscriminate baptism has a corrupting effect on both baptism and catechesis. First, indiscriminate baptism corrupts the nature of baptism within both credobaptist and paedobaptist frameworks. It corrupts paedobaptism by administering the covenant sign to children of parents who themselves are not believers and thus not members of the covenant community. It corrupts credobaptism, because it administers the sign of faith to one without faith or whose faith has not been credibly established via examination.

Second, indiscriminate baptism corrupts the integrity of catechesis. On the one hand, it undermines prebaptismal catechesis (prospective model) either by failing to give instruction or by failing to examine the candidate following instruction to ensure the candidate's personal faith.[21] On the other hand, it undermines postbaptismal catechesis (retrospective model) or postentrance catechesis (baptism model) because there is no reason to believe that the baptizand will submit to or be schooled in the faith by faithful parents and sponsors. Thus, *discriminate* baptism will be assumed throughout the development of these models.

Similarly, this study assumes the discriminate administration of the Lord's Supper. The development and illustration of all models will assume that when the Lord's Supper is offered to a communicant, such an offer is made on either covenantal or confessional grounds.

---

21. One should note the absence of the catechesis model here. "Indiscriminate entrance" would be the synonymous concept for the catechesis model, since baptism is not a means of entrance in that model. Indiscriminate entrance is the admission to the visible fellowship of the church without examination.

An example of the indiscriminate administration of the Lord's Supper is found in some contemporary Episcopalian churches that practice "radical inclusion." This practice has been described as "Communion without baptism." This designation is used technically by Michael Tuck. The phrase protects the view from conflation with "open Communion"—a term often used in Baptist debates over the communicant eligibility of persons who have received baptism as an infant, via a mode other than immersion, or (in some cases) no baptism. However, the issue of nonprofessing communicants is rarely if ever the issue in the Baptist debates. Contrastingly, "Communion without baptism" seeks to use the Lord's Supper as an evangelistic tool or "converting ordinance."[22]

By inviting nonprofessing visitors to communicate with the local church in the Lord's Supper, "Communion without baptism" advocates believe that the radically inclusive love of Jesus—especially as he expressed it through his meal ministry—is manifested. Writing in favor of Communion without baptism, Kathryn Tanner argues,

When ... accounts of the Lord's Supper are read in light of Jesus' willingness to eat with sinners, what stands out about the Lord's Supper is that Jesus is eating with sinners here too—with his betrayers on the night in which he will be betrayed, with Judas who hands him over, with "all of you who will become deserters" (Mark 14:27), with Peter who will deny three times that he is Jesus' associate, with disciples who immediately begin to wrangle over which one is greatest (Luke 22:24), and who lack even the strength to stay awake with Jesus in his hour of testing and agonized anticipation of the brutal death to come. It is hard to argue then that the disciples'

---

22. Michael Tuck, "Who Is Invited to the Feast? A Critique of the Practice of Communion without Baptism," *Worship* 86.6 (2012): 505-27. For more on recent debate over Communion without baptism, see James Farwell, "Baptism, Eucharist, and the Hospitality of Jesus: On the Practice of Open Communion," *Anglican Theological Review* 86 (2007): 215-38; Farwell, "A Brief Reflection on Kathryn Tanner's Response to 'Baptism, Eucharist, and the Hospitality of Jesus,'" *Anglican Theological Review* 87 (2007): 303-9; Kathryn Tanner, "In Praise of Open Communion: A Rejoinder to James Farwell," *Anglican Theological Review* 86 (2009) 473-85; Stephen Edmondson, "Opening the Table," *Anglican Theological Review* 91 (2009): 213-34; Benjamin Durheim and David Farina Turnbloom, "Having Patience with the Practice: A Response to Michael Tuck Regarding Communion without Baptism," *Worship* 87.3 (2013): 212-25.

commitment is what makes them proper participants; they are neither worthy in virtue of that commitment nor well informed.[23]

In addition to its direct contradiction of the confessional standards of the Episcopal Church,[24] Communion without baptism undermines a coherent signification of covenant fellowship because it intentionally serves the elements to those who are known either as not having believed in or even to have rejected Christ and his bride, the church. Communion without baptism is, therefore, not included in the catechesis model, discussed below, because the practice is not grounded on any discernable response to the gospel or identification with Christ. As such, the practice undermines a coherent understanding of visible fellowship, because the persons communing together visibly are not (even in pretense) manifesting union with Christ or with one another in Christ.

INDEPENDENT MODELS

The remainder of this chapter will develop the two independent models of our framework. The development of these models will be briefer than the interdependent models because I want to explore more deeply the relationship between baptism, catechesis, and entrance. Because the independent models cut off either baptism or catechesis from the process of entrance, they will not be developed in detail in pursuit of the stated research question. Nonetheless, some development is necessary to show the viability of the proposed framework—particularly the distinctions between the independent and interdependent models. Once these distinctions have been clarified, attention will narrow in the following chapters to a fuller development and analysis of the interdependent models and the seam that separates them.

---

23. Tanner, "In Praise of Open Communion," 476.

24. "No unbaptized person shall be eligible to receive Holy Communion in this Church." See Episcopal Church, *Constitution and Canons of the Episcopal Church* (New York: Church Publishing, 2012), 1.17.7 (59), http://www.episcopalarchives.org/CandC_2012.pdf.

BAPTISM MODEL

Category	Independent		Interdependent					Independent
Model	Baptism	Prerequisite(s) of entrance? / Baptism or catechesis or both?	Retrospective		Prospective	Prerequisite(s) of entrance? / Baptism or catechesis or both?		Catechesis
Sequence	Baptism ↓ Entrance ↓ Catechesis		Baptism ↓ Catechesis ↓ Entrance	Orientation of catechesis to baptism	Catechesis ↓ Baptism ↓ Entrance			Catechesis ↓ Entrance ↓ (Baptism)

As noted above, the baptism model is an independent model in which baptism is the sole prerequisite for entrance. Catechesis is subsequent to entrance and grounded on baptism and Communion. The baptism model invests in baptism all that is necessary for entrance into the church. From one's baptism forward, one is fully eligible to participate in the visible corporate life of the congregation.

Key Mark

Historically, this model finds expression primarily (if not exclusively) in the form of infant or child Communion or "paedocommunion."[25] As noted in the introduction, strict paedocommunion has a long history within the Eastern Orthodox tradition.[26] The following offers a clear statement of the Orthodox practice:

---

25. It is theoretically possible that an adult could be baptized without any substantive knowledge of the faith and communicated the Supper on either a strongly *ex opere operato* understanding of sacramental efficacy or on a strongly symbolic understanding of the ordinances as instruments of proclamation. In either of these theoretical scenarios the unwitting baptizand or communicant could be subsequently catechized. This author is unaware of any confessional statement approximating such an understanding. Further, such a practice would aptly be categorized as indiscriminate and, therefore, would be beyond our range of consideration.

26. For a concise, annotated historical overview of paedocommunion from the early church to the Reformation see Christian L. Keidel, "Is the Lord's Supper for Children," *Westminster Theological Journal* 37.3 (1975): 301–41 (esp. 301–5). See also Nick Needham, "Children at the Lord's Table in the Patristic Era," in *Children and the Lord's Supper*, ed. Guy Waters and Ligon Duncan (Ross-shire, UK: Christian Focus, 2011), 145–62.

One should immediately anoint with the divine myrrh the one who has been baptized. For this chrism is the seal and the mark of Christ. We receive grace from it. By virtue of the chrismation, we are called Christians and are the anointed ones of the Lord. For the Lord does not deem us unworthy to be named after him because by grace he calls us sons of God and gods. And when the priest anoints the one baptized, he says: "The seal of the gift of the Holy Spirit, Amen." Therefore, it is reasonable that chrismation follows baptism and is not postponed for a time. It also follows, therefore, that the one baptized should be given the communion. For that is the end purpose of the entire sacrament, that having been freed of error and the filth of sin, and having been cleansed anew and sealed by the holy myrrh, we may have communion with his body and his blood, and be united completely with him. Then Christ will dwell in us, walk among us, and be with us forever.[27]

On the Eastern Orthodox understanding, the complex of administration is whole: baptism, chrismation, and Eucharist are administered in one event.[28] A delay in administration is not accounted for or envisioned, and this unified complex of administration is true for all ages of initiates from infants to adults.

---

27. Jeremias II, *Reply of Ecumenical Patriarch* 1.3 (1576; CCFCT 1:400). The authority of confessions within Eastern Orthodoxy is more subsidiary than it is within the Reformed, Lutheran, or Roman Catholic traditions. The key place of confessional authority is given to the first seven ecumenical church councils, which Pelikan calls "the formal deposit of normative dogma for Eastern Orthodox teaching." See Jaroslav Pelikan, *Credo* (New Haven: Yale University Press, 2003), 413. "No later actions of any church," he writes, "neither those actions that lay claim to the title 'ecumenical' in Western dogmatics and canon law nor even the actions of the East itself since 787 at 'provincial synods' nor the Eastern Orthodox 'confessions' may be ranked on a level with the seven councils" (413–14). Pelikan, however, notes that comparative theology may glean helpful insights from subsequent confessions and catechisms, as they "make possible an inter-confessional comparison of doctrine that would be difficult without them, and they do help to clarify various doctrinal emphases in the liturgy, and even in the decrees of the councils, that could otherwise remain quite obscure" (426). Cf. George Mastrantonis, *Augsburg and Constantinople: The Correspondence between the Tübingen Theologians and Patriarch Jeremiah II of Constantinople on the Augsburg Confession* (Brookline, MA: Holy Cross Orthodox, 1982), xvii–xviii. Mastrantonis's work includes translations of all three rounds of exchange between the Tübingen theologians and Jeremias.

28. While Jeremias's *Confession of Faith* is noted for its moderate, ecumenical tone and Westernizing tendencies (cf. CCFCT 1:475), his statement here is not idiosyncratic (e.g., Ware, *Orthodox Way*, 145).

The extended quotation above may give the impression that chrismation should be treated as a new member to the study's triad, broadening the focus to the relationship between baptism, chrismation or confirmation, catechesis, and Communion. Certainly, the Roman and Eastern churches recognize chrismation or confirmation as a distinct sacrament from baptism, and more will need to be said later regarding the role and nature of confirmation in each model. Rather than adding chrismation or confirmation as a fourth member to the group, it is more appropriate to recognize the way in which the rite or function of confirmation is conjoined to baptism or catechesis. In this regard, the baptism model conjoins chrismation to baptism. This is true in regard to timing (immediately following baptism) and to function (as an "amen" to baptism).[29]

Subjective-Objective Continuum

The models of the proposed framework have been sequenced along an objective-subjective continuum. The criterion used to determine the relative sequence of each model along this continuum was the priority and nature of the key means of entrance. As already noted in this chapter, the priority and function of baptism as an objective, visible sign of initiation serves to make a model more or less objective than its counterparts. After all, baptism is a visible, corporate, liturgical act that can be observed directly, whereas catechesis is often carried out in smaller settings and is in a sense less observable. Thus, the priority and role of catechesis as a subjective means of initiation into visible fellowship serves to make a model more or less subjective than its counterparts.

The baptism model is the most objective of the four proposed models. This objectivity is seen in several ways. First, in the baptism model the baptizand is not catechized prior to baptism or entrance. Indeed, such instruction is impossible given the undeveloped or underdeveloped capacities of infants and small children to speak, reason, and verbally respond. As is the case with all paedobaptist liturgies, responses to baptismal interrogation, namely, the verbal profession of faith (e.g., "Jesus is Lord"), must be given by the parents and sponsors on behalf of the infant or young child. While

---

29. Cf. Critopoulos, *Confession of Faith* 8.1 (*CCFCT* 1:515).

all other proposed models require catechesis of some sort to precede first Communion, the baptism model does not.

Second, the baptism model projects an objective understanding of confirmation, tethering the rite (or least its function) inseparably to baptism and limiting its meaning to that of an objective seal or gift.[30] In his *Confession of Faith,* Metrophanes Critopoulos, patriarch of Alexandria, explains, "The church commands that those who have been granted holy baptism should immediately be anointed with the holy chrism, which has previously been prepared by the bishops and distributed by them to all the churches within their jurisdiction." Regarding the function and "power" of chrismation, he writes, "[Chrismation] is the King's seal, which, as it were, confirms and ratifies holy baptism, just as the word 'Amen' confirms and ratified the creed."[31] In the case of infants, chrismation, like baptism, is given apart from a personal confession of the faith and is thereby made wholly objective.[32] Thus, in the baptism model entrance to the Table is based solely on the objective validity of baptism and often an accompanying rite or sacrament of chrismation. Subjective elements on the part of the baptizand are not connected to entrance into the visible fellowship of the church.

Paedocommunion Expressions

The rationale supporting Eastern Orthodox paedocommunion is explained by Critopoulos as follows: "All partake at the Lord's table in both kinds, I mean both of the bread and of the cup, clergy and laity, men and women.

---

30. Chrismation has a strong connection to the reception of the Spirit across the history of the church (cf. Jensen, *Baptismal Imagery,* 91–135). The earliest practices connected it and the laying on of hands to baptism, creating a complex event. Jensen summarizes three forms: (1) two-stage, prebaptismal anointing (Eastern, Syrian; first the forehead, then the body); (2) postbaptismal anointing plus laying on of hands (North African [e.g., Tertullian and Augustine]); and (3) pre- and postbaptismal anointing (Rome, Milan, and Jerusalem [e.g., apostolic tradition, Ambrose, and Cyril]; Jensen, *Baptismal Imagery,* 106–10).

31. Critopoulos, *Confession of Faith* 8.2 (*CCFCT* 1:515). Baptism also has a strong objective quality as "those who undergo it are washed and cleansed from original sin, which is the irrational inclination and tendency towards all that is evil."

32. It is conceded that several major traditions will affirm the objective validity of the sacraments apart from personal faith. The point being made here is not about the validity of administration of the rite or sacrament, but rather the *condition* of administration as it relates to the recipient. As will become clear later, in other models of entrance the administration of the rite or sacrament is only granted on the condition of personal faith as shaped by instruction.

Yes, and even infants, first of all immediately after their holy baptism, and afterwards as well, whenever their parents wish them to." He continues, "The reason for everyone partaking of the Lord's supper in both kinds is that all need that life which they cannot receive except through partaking of the Lord's body and blood." It is through this eucharistic feeding on Christ that communicants are "healed from the ancestral curse of death, and gain immortality."[33]

Paedocommunion, however, is a practice not limited to the Eastern Orthodox Church.[34] There are those within Reformed circles who practice or are advocating the practice within their respective tradition.

The predominant practice regarding children at the Table among the Reformed traditions is to require a credible, public profession of faith (sometimes via a rite of confirmation). Communion administered in this way is called credocommunion.[35] However, a vocal minority within the Reformed tradition is arguing for paedocommunion.

Cornelius Venema notes that paedocommunion comes in two varieties: soft and strict.[36] Soft paedocommunion is the admitting of children to

---

33. Critopoulos, *Confession of Faith* 9.9–10 (*CCFCT* 1:520). The feeding of infants at the Supper is typically done through intinction, the dipping of the bread—which is leavened within the Eastern tradition—in the consecrated wine. Roman Catholic theology differs with the way in which salvation of infants is connected to eucharistic feeding here. For example, the Canons and Decrees of the Council of Trent states, "Children under the age of discernment *are not bound by any obligation to sacramental holy communion,* seeing that after rebirth by the water of baptism and incorporation in Christ they are not at that age able to lose the grace they have received of being children of God. Nor are times past to be condemned if they sometimes observed that custom in some places. For those holy fathers had good reason for their practice in the situation of their time, and *we must certainly believe without dispute that they did not do this for any necessity of salvation"* (Dogmatic Decrees of the Council of Trent 21.4 [1545–1563; *CCFCT* 2:860], emphasis added).

34. Paedocommunion receives commendation by the ecumenical *Lima Report*: "If baptism, as incorporation into the body of Christ, points by its very nature to the eucharistic sharing of Christ's body and blood, the question arises as to how a further and separate rite can be interposed between baptism and admission to communion. *Those churches which baptize children but refuse them a share in the eucharist before such a rite may wish to ponder whether they have fully appreciated and accepted the consequences of baptism"* (*Baptism, Eucharist and Ministry,* IV.B.14.Commentary [b], emphasis added).

35. This term and the following terms are taking from Venema, *Children at the Lord's Table,* 2–4. John Calvin's credocommunion (antipaedocommunion) position has been the majority view within the Reformed tradition; this view will be discussed in the ch. 3. Relevant passages within the *Institutes* include 4.16.30 and 4.19.13.

36. Venema laments that these views are not always distinguished in the literature (*Children at the Lord's Table,* 3).

the Lord's Supper "at an earlier age than is customary ... (middle to late adolescence)." This position requires "a simple but credible profession of the Christian faith" prior to admission; as such, Venema calls it a "modification" of the majority credocommunion view.[37]

For example, paedocommunion became the official position of the Reformed Church of America in 1990. Two principles ground the Reformed Church of America position: (1) children are "members of the church" by virtue of their baptism, and (2) the nourishing and strengthening nature of the Lord's Supper as a "means of grace." Alone, the same principles could be used to justify strict paedocommunion; however, the Reformed Church of America position lists additional prerequisites for participation such as personal desire, "faith and love for the Savior, ability to experience the grace of Christ expressed in the bread and the cup, and the sense of belonging to the covenant community." Thus, it is not merely baptism, but baptism plus several qualities (including "faith and love for the Savior") that make a child eligible to participate in the Supper. For this reason, the position illustrates soft paedocommunion.[38]

Strict paedocommunion is "the admission of any baptized child of believing parents who is physically able to receive the Communion elements."[39] Theoretically, infants are qualified to communicate in the Supper via intinction, but Reformed versions of strict paedocommunion often delay until the child can take and eat. Douglas Wilson's personal account evinces the Reformed strict paedocommunion impulse to offer the Supper later than infancy but prior to a profession of faith and mature catechesis. He writes,

> Just a short time ago, another grandchild came to his first observance of the Lord's Supper. ... He is a year and a half old, and doesn't

37. Venema, *Children at the Lord's Table*, 2–4.

38. Reformed Church in America Theological Commission, "Baptized Children and the Lord's Table," (1990), http://images.rca.org/docs/synod/BaptizedChildrenAtTable1990.pdf. This position was the culmination of multiple reports given by the theological commission spanning a period of thirteen years by the Reformed Church in America Theological Commission: (1) "Baptized Non-communicants and the Celebration of the Lord's Supper," (1977), http://images.rca.org/docs/synod/BaptizedNonComm1977.pdf; (2) "Baptized Non-communicants and the Celebration of the Lord's Supper" (1984), http://images.rca.org/docs/synod/BaptizedNonComm1984.pdf; (3) "Children at the Table" (1988), http://images.rca.org/docs/synod/BaptizedChildrenAtTable1988.pdf.

39. Venema, *Children at the Lord's Table*, 3.

really talk yet. But he worships with his family throughout our worship service, and he has a basic sign language catechism down. "Where is Jesus?" He pats his heart. "Where is God?" He points to heaven. "Are you baptized?" He pats his head. At the conclusion of our worship service, we all sing the *Gloria Patri* with hands upraised, which he used to do also. But as he began to notice the communion tray going by and he didn't get any, it began to distress him. About a month before he came to the Table, he stopped raising his hands in the *Gloria Patri*, and just watched. He was starting to learn how to observe as a detached outsider. When it was decided he should come to the Table, he was carefully instructed in the meaning of the Supper as he held the bread. When he partook, together with his family, one of the first things he did was pat the heads of everyone around him—mother, father, grandmother. We are all baptized, he said, discerning the body. At the *Gloria Patri*, his hands shot up in the air. Glory to God indeed.[40]

The term "covenant Communion" is picked up by strict paedocommunionists as a way to emphasize that the only "basis for admission to the Table of the Lord" is "membership in the covenant community," not a profession of faith.[41]

Though it appeals to the historic practice and precedent of the early church and Eastern Church, the rationale for Reformed paedocommunion differs in respect to the highly sacramental view of the East. Recognition of the covenant is the key issue among Reformed advocates. Venema identifies four arguments commonly advanced by Reformed paedocommunionists[42]:

1. The historical argument draws on the paedocommunion practice of the Eastern Orthodox from the mid-third century to present day and the practice of Western church until the

---

40. Douglas Wilson, "Union with Christ: An Overview of the Federal Vision," in Beisner, *Auburn Avenue Theology*, 4.

41. Venema argues that the traditional Reformed "credocommunion" practice has equal right to the term "covenant communion," since the view is based on a particular understanding of the *new covenant* dynamic of full inclusion in the community by faith (*Children at the Lord's Table*, 4).

42. Venema, *Children at the Lord's Table*, 4–8.

Fourth Lateran Council (1215). It reasons that the practice is well attested within the early church and thereby has stronger historical grounds than the antipaedocommunion position.[43]

2. The covenant argument equates the denial of the Lord's Supper with a denial of a child's status of covenant membership. It critiques advocates of credocommunion as having fallen prey to "baptistic" and "dispensational" pitfalls regarding the nature of the sacraments and distinction between the covenants respectively.[44]

3. The "analogy with the Passover" argument says that the Passover meal and Lord's Supper are parallel in their meaning and administration. Thus, on the basis that children were included in the former, they should be included in the latter.[45]

4. The 1 Corinthians 11 argument states that the sin Paul addresses here (11:27, 29) is focused on acting with partiality and failing to include one another appropriately. In so doing, paedocommunionists seek to reclaim this passage from their detractors, charging their detractors with committing the sin that Paul is addressing: excluding those they should be including.[46]

Many of the contemporary advocates for paedocommunion are lobbying for the practice from within a confessional tradition that officially opposes

---

43. At the same time, Reformed paedocommunionists want to maintain distance from some of the rationales that were often provided by the early fathers. Cf. Robert Rayburn, "A Presbyterian Defense of Paedocommunion," in Strawbridge, *Case for Covenant Communion*, 13.

44. Cf. Gregg Strawbridge, "The Polemics of Infant Communion," in Strawbridge, *Case for Covenant Communion*, 147–65, esp. 157–63.

45. James B. Jordan, "Children and the Religious Meals of the Old Creation," in Strawbridge, *Case for Covenant Communion*, 49–68. Cf. Rayburn, "Presbyterian Defense of Paedocommunion," 5n3.

46. For example, Jeffrey Meyers contends that not only does 1 Cor 11 not mean what credocommunists assert, but "those who fail to commune the youngest, weakest members of the body of Christ (1 Cor 12:14–26) are themselves not 'judging the body' (that is, *the church* as the communal body of Christ) and are therefore eating the Lord's Supper in an unworthy manner." See Meyers, "Presbyterian, Examine Thyself," in Strawbridge, *Case for Covenant Communion*, 20, emphasis original. Cf. Tim Gallant, *Feed My Lambs* (Grande Prairie, AB: Pactum Reformanda, 2002), 72–105.

it.[47] Some, however, have embraced it fully as a confessional distinctive. For example, the Federation of Reformed Churches' Book of Order highlights paedocommunion as a denominational distinctive. It grounds the practice in a theological understanding of the Lord's Supper as "the covenantal meal of the visible Church of Jesus Christ, in which the people of God are ever more incorporated into Christ's body, participating together in the power of endless life."[48] It also points to the full-scale participation of the Old Testament covenant community in feasts[49] and of the corporate reception of the water from the rock in the wilderness as warrant for the practice. The Book of Order concludes, "The Lord's Supper should not be withheld from any New Covenant member in good standing. Baptized children, feeble-minded, and senile persons are to be joyfully welcomed into the Eucharistic celebration."[50]

Summary

In sum, the baptism model views baptism as the sole basis for entrance into the visible fellowship of the local church. God has spoken the only word that needs to be heard regarding a child's inclusion in the covenant community by virtue of the family to which the child has been born.[51] There is no disjunction or delay between baptism and entrance involving catechesis and confirmation via personal profession (formal or informal).

---

47. Gregg Strawbridge admits, "Paedocommunion is not the received tradition of the West, generally, nor of Reformed and Presbyterian traditions specifically." He notes several study committees that have argued for the practice within the Orthodox Presbyterian Church (G. I. Williamson, chair) and the Presbyterian Church of America (Robert Rayburn, chair) as well as other theologians who favor the practice, most notably N. T. Wright. See Strawbridge, "Polemics of Infant Communion," 147.

48. "Our Distinctives," in *Book of Order of the Federation of Reformed Churches (FRC)*, 11th rev. ed. (Williamsville, NY: Federation of Reformed Churches, 2013), I.B.5, http://www.federationorc.org/. The following prooftexts are cited: "John 6:47–58; Acts 2:38–39; 1 Corinthians 10:14–22; HC 75, 76; WCF XXIX:1; WLC 168."

49. "Our Distinctives," I.B.5.b, with the following prooftexts: Exod 12:43–48; Deut 16:1–17; Matt 26:26–27; Acts 2:38–42.

50. "Our Distinctives," I.B.5.d, with the following prooftexts: 1 Cor 10:1–4, 16–17; HC 75, 79; WLC 170. The Orthodox Creed (Baptist) acknowledges that Augustine and contemporary Eastern churches practice paedocommunion but explicitly rejects the practice on several grounds. It finds paedocommunion lacking in that infants can neither "examine themselves, nor give account of their faith, nor understand what is signified by the outward signs of bread and wine" (Orthodox Creed 33 [*BCF*, 322]).

51. Acts 2:39 is a favorite prooftext adduced on this point: "The promise is for you and your children."

If confirmation is practiced in an initiatory sense, it is given at the time of baptism via chrismation or by the laying on of hands. In such cases, it functions as an objective sealing of the individual and is closely connected to the reception of the Holy Spirit. Protestant versions of this model will view the baptism itself as a sign and seal of the covenant. The reception of the Spirit is related either to the baptismal event or to the laying on of hands or both. Entrance into the visible fellowship of the church is accomplished in one complex ceremony that concludes with infant Communion in the Eastern Church (via intinction) or, for Reformed paedocommunionists, Communion at the earliest point at which a child can take and eat.

The baptism model projects a mixed body (*corpus permixteum*) view of the church, since a later profession of faith is in no way guaranteed or assumed. While instruction will undoubtedly be given for many years to come, for the baptism model the only role that catechesis plays *in the process of entrance* is a vicarious one. Here, the instruction of the baptizand is mediated through the instruction and examination of sponsors.

CATECHESIS MODEL

Category	Independent	Prerequisite(s) of entrance? Baptism or catechesis or both?	Interdependent			Prerequisite(s) of entrance? Baptism or catechesis or both?	Independent
Model	Baptism		Retrospective		Prospective		Catechesis
Sequence	Baptism ↓ Entrance ↓ Catechesis		Baptism ↓ Catechesis ↓ Entrance	Orientation of catechesis to baptism	Catechesis ↓ Baptism ↓ Entrance		Catechesis ↓ Entrance ↓ (Baptism)

Key Mark

Just as the baptism model excludes catechesis from the process of entrance, the catechesis model excludes baptism. The catechesis model is an independent model in which catechesis is the sole prerequisite for entrance. Baptism, if it is administered at all, is subsequent to entrance and viewed as a means of personal growth. Thus, open membership (with its concomitant practice of open Communion) is the key mark of this model.[52]

Open membership is the practice of admitting persons to the membership of a local church regardless of what that church confesses to be a valid water baptism.[53] In contrast, closed membership refers to the requirement that a person have a valid water baptism in order to join the fellowship of a local church.

Debate over open membership has been of particular interest within the Baptist tradition[54] as churches have wrestled with how to receive new members from other denominations (esp. when the baptism was in infancy). Closed membership constitutes the majority tradition among Baptists. In its broadest (Baptist) sense, closed membership requires believers' baptism as a prerequisite of church membership. Other qualifiers may be added, such as proper mode (immersion) or context (credobaptist church, church with "Baptist" in the name, or even the particular local Baptist church the person is joining).[55]

---

52. As discussed above, open Communion, as used in this study, assumes discriminate administration to those with a credible profession of faith. Additionally, the term "membership" will be used within this section in a sense that is equivalent with "entrance." Entrance, as noted earlier, focuses on the inauguration of full, visible membership through the sign of the Lord's Supper. Bobby Jamieson summarizes this connection well: "[The term] membership names the relation the ordinances imply and normally create." See Jamieson, *Going Public: Why Baptism Is Required for Church Membership* (Nashville: B&H Academic, 2015), 148.

53. The term "valid" has a range of meanings depending on the context. The term may range from a broader designation of baptism in the triune formula—without respect to the kind (credo- or paedobaptism), denominational context, or mode of baptism—to a much narrower specification of believers' baptism administered by immersion by the specific congregation to which the person seeks to join.

54. Cf. Thorwald Lorenzen, "Baptism and Church Membership: Some Baptist Positions and Their Ecumenical Implications," *Journal of Ecumenical Studies*, 18.4 (1981): 561-74; George H. Shriver, "Southern Baptists Ponder Open Membership: An End of Re-baptism," *Journal of Ecumenical Studies* 6.3 (1969): 423-29; Garrett, "Should Baptist Churches Adopt Open Membership." Garrett distinguishes open Communion from open membership. Though the latter presupposes the former, the former does not necessarily lead to the latter. This is given historical weight by Curtis Freeman, who notes that trends toward open Communion are not synonymous with trends toward open membership, especially among British Baptists. See Freeman, *Contesting Catholicity: Theology for Other Baptists* (Waco: Baylor University Press, 2014), 353; cf. Peter Naylor, *Calvinism, Communion and the Baptists: A Study of English Calvinistic Baptists from the Late 1600s to the Early 1800s* (Milton Keynes: Paternoster, 2004).

55. Timothy George delineates six views of baptismal validity among cooperating churches of the Southern Baptist Convention. They are as follows: (1) radical landmark: requiring rebaptism by immersion upon the changing of local church membership;

The English Declaration at Amsterdam (1611) illustrates the broader position, when it requires believers' baptism but does not designate immersion as the proper mode:

> That every Church is to receive in all their members *by Baptism upon the Confession of their faith and sins* wrought by the preaching of the Gospel, according to the primitive institution (Matt 28:19) and practice (Acts 2:41). And therefore Churches constituted after any other manner, or of any other persons are not according to CHRIST'S Testament.[56]

The majority tradition among Baptists is to designate immersion as the proper mode of believers' baptism. The London Confession (1644) serves as a classic example:

> [39.] Baptisme is an Ordinance of the new Testament, given by Christ, to be dispensed onely upon persons professing faith or that are Disciples, or taught, who upon profession of faith, ought to be baptized.

> [40.] The way and manner of the dispensing of this Ordinance[57] the Scripture holds out to be dipping or plunging the whole body under water.[58]

---

(2) denominational landmark: receiving only those baptized as believers by immersion in an SBC church; (3) denominational credobaptist: receiving all who have been baptized as believers by immersion from any denomination with "Baptist" in the name; (4) applied credobaptist: receiving all who have been baptized as believers by immersion from any Christian denomination (credo- or paedobaptist); (5) open mode: receiving all who have been baptized as believers by any mode from any Christian denomination (credo- or paedobaptist); (6) open membership: receiving all who have been baptized as believers or as infants by any mode from any Christian denomination (George, "Southern Baptists," 47). One should note that open membership (view 6) is narrower within the Southern Baptist tradition, as described by George, than it is among Baptists outside this denomination *and the definition that is used in this study* since his definition still requires baptism of some sort (cf. Lorenzen, "Baptism and Church Membership," 561–74).

56. English Declaration at Amsterdam 13 (1611, Baptist; *BCF*, 111); spelling and punctuation modernized, emphasis added.

57. Lumpkin notes, "Later editions added, 'and after to partake of the Lord's Supper' " (*BCF*, 155n34.[b]).

58. London Confession 39–40 (1644; *BCF*, 155). Other prominent examples include Second London Confession 29.4 (1677; *BCF*, 292); Orthodox Creed 28 (1678; *BCF*, 326); the New Hampshire Confession 14 (1833; *BCF*, 382); A Treatise on the Faith of the Free Will Baptists 18.1 (1948; *BCF*, 392).

As a confessional distinctive, Thorwald Lorenzen observes, open member-ship is "seldom or never the official position of a national Baptist union," but "the open membership tradition is quite strong in regions like Great Britain, the U.S.A. ('American Baptist Churches'), South Australia, and parts of Canada." For open-membership Baptists, "Baptism is seen ... not as an essential, but as a desirable, mark of the church."[59]

While open membership is difficult to find explicitly in national or cooperative confessions,[60] it is more readily found in *local* church confes-sions and constitutions. For example, the Flinders Street Baptist Church (Adelaide, South Australia) expresses this view:

> *MEMBERSHIP*—The members of the Church shall be people who declare that they have come into personal fellowship with Jesus Christ, intend to follow Him in the strength of His spirit, pledge themselves to a life of Christian service and witness, and desire to become sharers in the fellowship of this Church.

> *BELIEVERS' BAPTISM*—The Church shall advocate the teaching and practice of believers' baptism by immersion. Its membership, how-ever, shall be open also to those who, after the matter of baptism has been discussed with them by a Pastor or other responsible Church officer, in conscience do not see it as their duty to be so baptized.[61]

A similar position is expressed in a German church constitution:

> Entry into our church takes place *usually* by baptism ... in the mode of immersion. ... It follows the confession of repentance and faith and the witness to the experienced divine grace before the

---

59. Lorenzen, "Baptism and Church Membership," 563, 567.

60. The possibility of open membership is implicit in the Doctrinal Basis of the Baptist Union of Victoria, Australia (1888). This statement defines the nature of the church as a "spiritual society" that is made up "of persons who have personally and intelligently accepted [Jesus Christ] as Saviour and Lord, and pledged themselves to discipleship and service in the kingdom of God" (art. 3). Additionally, it affirms "liberty of thought and of conscience, and the right of the believer and the Church, freed from any ecclesiastical or other external author-ity, to interpret His mind" (art. 4). Furthermore, it does not name baptism a prerequisite of church membership or the Lord's Supper (arts. 7–8); cf. *BCM*, 436–37. Though not prescribed, open membership is within the bounds of this confessional standard.

61. Flinders Street Baptist Church, Constitution and Regulations 1 (Adelaide, South Australia), as cited by Lorenzen, "Baptism and Church Membership," 567.

congregation. *Full membership, however, is open to all who in word and deed witness to God's action in their life and who, in the fellowship of the church, are prepared to serve each other and be witnesses in the world.*[62]

James Leo Garrett identifies three possible forms of open membership within Baptist churches, namely, granting membership to persons on the basis of:

1. infant baptism;

2. a mode other than immersion (aspersion or affusion);

3. a verbal confession apart from water baptism of any mode.[63]

Garrett's options are helpful in showing the possible range of meaning for open membership. A clear distinction exists, however, between the first two options and the last: the first two base membership on baptism (of some sort), but the third does not.

Lorenzen offers additional insight by distinguishing open membership from *modified* open membership. He defines open membership as the practice of admitting persons to the membership of a local church on the basis of a profession of faith apart from what the local church confesses to be a valid water baptism. Importantly, within open membership "baptism is seen … not as an essential, but as a desirable, mark of the church." Therefore, if "a member of the Salvation Army or a Quaker or a Darbyite" presents himself or herself for membership, their lack of baptism will not hinder them from being received. "If one's faith in Jesus Christ and one's commitment to discipleship is clear, one should be admitted into church membership."[64]

Modified open membership understands baptism to be "an *essential* mark of the church." Baptist churches practicing modified open

62. "Arbeitskreis 'Taufe und Aufnahmepraxis,' Bonn, Thesen zum neutestamentlichen Taufverständnis (II)," *Semester Zeitschrift* 23 (1971): 15. Quotation as cited and translated by Lorenzen, "Baptism and Church Membership," 567, emphasis added.

63. Garrett, "Should Baptist Churches Adopt Open Membership," 1. Shriver represents an argument in favor of open Communion ("Southern Baptists Ponder Open Membership," 423–29).

64. Lorenzen, "Baptism and Church Membership," 563, 573.

membership administer believers' baptism by immersion to new converts, but they accept persons from other denominational backgrounds *on the basis of a baptism* that the *person* believes to be valid.[65] In this view, the basis of membership is baptism along with a personal confession of faith. Here, the basis of baptismal validity is the *individual's* conviction, not the local church's confession. Baptism is integral to modified open membership; thus, someone who has not received baptism (of any kind) is not eligible for membership. Because membership is here based on baptism, a Baptist church employing modified open membership tacitly affirms the validity of infant baptism.

Lorenzen's distinction between open membership and modified open membership underscores an important issue for the catechesis model, specifically, the role that baptism plays in the entrance process. Within the catechesis model of entrance, baptismal validity is irrelevant; rather, the crucial question is whether or not water baptism is a prerequisite for entrance into the visible fellowship of the church.[66] Defined in this way, open membership—not *modified* open membership—is the sine qua non of the catechesis model.

Spiritualizing Tendencies

The catechesis model has strong spiritualizing tendencies. First, the catechesis model places a greater emphasis on the theology of baptism than the visible rite itself. John Bunyan's view of open membership illustrates this dynamic.[67]

---

65. Lorenzen, "Baptism and Church Membership," 569–71. Freeman expresses a modified open-membership understanding (*Contesting Catholicity*, esp. 365–83). Anthony N. S. Lane takes a similar view in his "Dual-Practice Baptism View," in Wright, *Baptism: Three Views*, 139–71.

66. Though he proposes the open-membership model as the best option for Baptist churches, Lorenzen still affirms the traditional theological impasse over baptism. "Baptists," he writes, "cannot recognize infant baptism as valid." Instead, he proposes that baptism be removed as a requirement for membership and, consequently, for Table fellowship (Lorenzen, "Baptism and Church Membership," 568).

67. Bunyan's open membership drew the ire of many of his Baptist contemporaries, and the practice has provided foundation for some to classify him as a Congregationalist rather than a Baptist. He wrote three significant polemical tracts on the matter: *A Confession of My Faith, and a Reason of My Practice* (1672), *Differences in Judgment about Water-Baptism, No Bar to Communion* (1673), and *Peaceable Principles and True* (1674). Cf. T. L. Underwood, "Introduction," *MWJB* 4:xxv–xxxvi.

Bunyan distinguishes between the "doctrine" of water baptism and "the practice of water baptism."[68] He writes,

I distinguish between the doctrin and practise of Water-baptism; The Doctrin being that which by the outward sign is presented to us, or which by the outward circumstance of the act is preached to the believer: *viz.*, *The death of Christ; My death with Christ; also his resurrection from the Dead, and mine with him to newness of life.* This is the doctrin which Baptism preacheth, or that which by the outward action is signifyed to the believing receiver. Now I say, he that believeth in Jesus Christ; that richer and better than that [of baptism in water], *viz.* is dead to sin, and that lives to God by him, he hath the heart, power and doctrine of Baptism: all then that he wanteth, is but the sign, the shadow, or the outward circumstance thereof; Nor yet is that despised, but forborne for want of light. The best of Baptisms he hath; he is Baptized by that one spirit; he hath the heart of water-baptism, he wanteth only the outward shew, which if he had would not prove him a truly visible Saint; it would not tell me he had grace in his heart.[69]

On Bunyan's view, the richness of baptism is what baptism signifies, not the baptism itself. The doctrine of baptism is none other than the gospel truths of Jesus' death, burial, and resurrection and the prospective member's identification with Jesus in his saving activity (buried with and raised with Christ *by faith*).

Though the outward sign of water baptism may be lacking, Bunyan argues that one's faith is visible in other ways. Bunyan holds, "By the word of faith, and of good works; moral duties Gospellized, we ought to judge the fitness of members by, by which we ought also to receive them into fellowship."[70] In other words, a personal profession of faith in the gospel and a pattern of godly living that is consistent with it are the marks of a

---

68. John Bunyan, *Confession of My Faith* (1672; *MWJB* 4:172); cf. Bunyan, *Confession of My Faith*, in Offor, *Works of John Bunyan*, 2:609.

69. Bunyan, *Confession of My Faith* (*MWJB* 4:172; Offor 2:609), emphasis original.

70. Bunyan, *Confession of My Faith* (*MWJB* 4:165; Offor 2:607). "Gospellized" is a unique term. A similar statement is found two paragraphs below this line (Bunyan, *Confession of My Faith* [*MWJB* 4:166; Offor 2:607]). There he describes the moral law as received through Christ, "the perfect law, which is the moral precept Evangelized or delivered to us by the hand of Christ."

true Christian.[71] If a person bears these marks of fellowship with God (i.e., if God has received that person), then fellowship in the local church must be extended. But what of the "practice" of water baptism?

The key mark of the catechesis model is that it removes water baptism from the membership equation altogether; such is the outcome of Bunyan's position. Bunyan argues that the possession of the external sign of water baptism apart from the marks of faith and holiness do not make one eligible for membership: "If he appear not a Brother before [water baptism], he appeareth not a Brother by that." Rather than seeing water baptism as a matter of admission into the local church, Bunyan saw it as "a sign to the person baptized, and a help to his own faith." Removed from the process of entrance and described in this way, baptism is privatized as an act of *mere* personal profession or spiritual growth.[72]

Second, the catechesis model marginalizes water baptism in favor of Spirit baptism. The baptism that matters for entering the membership of the local church and sharing in its Table fellowship is not water baptism but Spirit baptism. Speaking to the change wrought by the Spirit, Bunyan cites Romans 2:28–29, "For he is not a Jew, which is one outwardly; neither is that circumcision, which is outward in the flesh: But he is a Jew, which is one inwardly; and circumcision is that of the heart, in the spirit, ... whose praise is not of men, but of God" (Rom 2:28–29 KJV).[73] This inner circumcision, brought about by the Spirit is the "antitype" of circumcision, which was the "entering ordinance" of the Old Testament. He continues, "Now a confession of this by word and life, makes this inward circumcision visible; when you know him therefore to be thus circumcised, you ought to admit him to the Lord's Passover: he, if any, hath a share not only in church-communion, but a visible right to the kingdom of heaven."[74]

The phrases "moral duties Gospellized" and "moral precept Evangelized" are parallel. Thus, "Gospellized" seems best understood as "delivered to us by the hand of Christ."

71. Bunyan, *Confession of My Faith* (MWJB 4:167; Offor 2:607). Bunyan is fond of the phrase "the word of faith, and the moral precept." He uses "holiness" and "moral precept" interchangeably; he also calls this the "ten commandments."

72. Bunyan, *Confession of My Faith* (MWJB 4:172; Offor 2:610). "Mere" profession should here be understood to mean that corporate aspects have been filtered out (i.e., corporate witness, mutual covenant, etc.).

73. Bunyan, *Confession of My Faith* (MWJB 4:165.27–30; Offor 2:607); he excises the phrase "and not in the letter."

74. Bunyan, *Confession of My Faith* (MWJB 4:165.27–30; Offor 2:607).

According to Bunyan, the marks of faith and holiness show the reality of this greater circumcision, which is equated with baptism. Therefore, submission to believers' baptism in water is not viewed as a (necessary) mark of the Spirit's work in an individual.

Flexibility

As noted in the earlier sketch of the baptism model, each model of this study is flexible enough to accommodate a spectrum of views that share its fundamental liturgical logic. The catechesis model is flexible enough to include certain expressions of credobaptism as well as no-baptism views. Bunyan's version of open membership offers an example of a credobaptist version of this model, and, by virtue of the continued practice of the ordinances of baptism and the Lord's Supper, he represents the more objective side of the model. The Quakers (Society of Friends) offer an interesting example of the no-baptism version of this model, and, by virtue of their rejection of the physical ordinances, they represent the more subjective or spiritual end of the model's spectrum.[75]

The grouping of Bunyan and the Quakers within the same model is striking, for Bunyan engaged the Quakers polemically (e.g., *Some Gospel-Truth Opened* [1656] and *A Vindication of Gospel Truths Opened* [1657]). Chief among his concerns were what he perceived to be a spiritualized Christology, which he viewed as undermining the "atonement, ascension, bodily resurrection, second coming, and intercession of Christ."[76] With this acknowledgment in place, two reminders about the nature of our models are in order. First, remember that the proposed framework seeks to account for *unexpected affinities*. Assuming that the similarity of liturgical logic can be demonstrated, the grouping of Bunyan with the Quakers supports the value of the framework and its models. Second, the grouping of otherwise divergent examples is *not* an assertion of affinity at any level other than the distinctive liturgical logic of the respective model. Bunyan's critiques and disagreements with the Society of Friends (and vice versa) remain and will be further acknowledged in what follows.

---

75. For a helpful brief history and overview of Quaker worship theology and practice, see Paul N. Anderson, "Quaker Worship," in Bradshaw, *New SCM Dictionary*, 394–97.

76. Poe, "John Bunyan," 31; cf. 30.

Several theological differences between Bunyan and the Quakers regarding the *nature* of baptism, catechesis, and entrance will be noted below. There is, however, a unity in their approaches that manifest the essence of the catechesis model. Within their respective theological frames of reference, both Bunyan and the Quakers remove water baptism from the process of entrance.

Quaker beliefs are in no way monolithic. In what follows, the goal is simply to offer a prominent example of how a spiritualized Quaker approach to the relational trio of baptism, catechesis, and entrance manifests the key mark of the catechesis model. Robert Barclay's (1648–1690) widely distributed and influential *Theses Theologicae* (1675) and his *Apology* (1678) to that work offer helpful material for illustrating a more subjective version of the catechesis model.[77]

Barclay, like Bunyan, denies water baptism as a "visible sign or badge to distinguish Christians from infidels, even as circumcision did the Jews." He states, "There is no such command for baptism, so there is not any word in all the New Testament, calling it a badge of Christianity, or seal of the new covenant."[78]

---

77. Cf. Robert Barclay, *Theses Theologicae*, in Schaff, *Creeds of Christendom* 3:789–98, esp. 797; Barclay, *An Apology for the True Christian Divinity: Being an Explanation and Vindication of the Principles and Doctrines of the People Called Quakers* (New York: S. Wood and Sons for the Trustees of Obadiah Brown's Benevolent Fund, 1827); Barclay, *Barclay's Apology in Modern English* [*Apology-Friday*], ed. Dean Freiday (Newberg, OR: Barclay, 1991). Philip Schaff calls Barclay's *Apology* "the ablest and most authoritative exposition of the belief of the Quakers" (Schaff, *Creeds of Christendom* 1:864). Schaff notes that Barclay translated the English versions of the *Apology*. Use of Barclay as a key exemplar of Quaker theology is modeled by Jerry William Frost, who uses Barclay's works to compare Quaker theology with Puritan theology in his article "Dry Bones of Quaker Theology," *Church History* 39.4 (1970): 503–23.

78. Barclay, *Apology*, proposition XII.10.442. A key text undergirding Barclay's rejection of water baptism is Matt 3:11: "I indeed baptize you with water unto repentance: but he that cometh after me is mightier than I, whose shoes I am not worthy to bear: he shall baptize you with the Holy Ghost, and with fire" (KJV). The baptism of the Spirit supersedes and negates the practice of water baptism. Barclay addresses a number of texts that are raised as objections to the thesis that the only prescribed baptism in the NT is Spirit baptism; chief among these is Matt 28:19. Barclay interprets Matt 28:19 as Spirit baptism and defends his interpretation with the following hermeneutical principle: "We ought not to go from the literal signification of the text, except some urgent necessity force us thereunto. But no urgent necessity in this place forceth us thereunto: Therefore we ought not to go from it." That is, since water baptism is not specified in the verse, there is no need to interpret it as water baptism. He concludes, "That baptism which Christ commanded his apostles was such, that as many as were therewith baptized did put on Christ [see Gal 3:27]: But this is not true of water-baptism" (Barclay, *Apology for the True Christian Divinity*, proposition XII.8.431–32).

Barclay also shares Bunyan's view that the best visible sign of one's Christianity is faith and holiness. Unlike circumcision in the Old Testament, baptism does not leave a visible mark. Thus, "The professing of faith in Christ, and a holy life answering thereunto, is a far better badge of Christianity than any outward washing."[79] With this affirmation, Barclay manifests the essence of the catechesis model: entrance into visible fellowship is grounded not on water baptism, but on verbal and practical evidence of the inner regenerating work of the Holy Spirit (i.e., Spirit baptism or circumcision of the heart). While the essence of the catechesis model is shared, several distinctions from Bunyan's view must be made.

The key difference between Barclay's and Bunyan's approaches is the extent to which baptism, catechesis, and entrance are spiritualized. First, Barclay goes beyond Bunyan's relegation of water baptism as a matter of personal growth and denies its continuing status as an ordinance. Making water baptism a requirement of the new dispensation is "to derogate from the new covenant dispensation, and set up the legal rites and ceremonies, of which ... baptism, or washing with water, was one." If the gospel dispensation, "which puts an end to the shadows, be come, then such baptisms and carnal ordinances are no more to be imposed." For Barclay and the Quakers, clinging to water baptism is tantamount to Judaizing the faith: making outward that which is inward.[80]

Second, Barclay spiritualizes the catechesis connected with entrance.[81] As noted above, Bunyan sees the theology of baptism as having definite propositional content (e.g., Christ's death, burial, and resurrection). Further, he holds that one's entrance into the church as ultimately

---

79. Barclay, *Apology*, proposition XII.10.442.

80. Barclay, *Apology*, proposition XII.6.424-25, 427. Proposition XII: "As there is one Lord and one faith, so there is one baptism; which is not the putting away of the filth of the flesh, but the answer of a good conscience before God, by the resurrection of Jesus Christ. And this baptism is a pure and spiritual thing, to wit, the baptism of the spirit and fire, by which we are buried with him, that being washed and purged from our sins, we may walk in newness of life; of which the baptism of John was a figure, which was commanded for a time, and not to continue forever" (Barclay, *Apology*, proposition XII.6.409). Cf. Barclay, *Theses Theologicae* 3:797.

81. It is important to note that the Friends preach sermons, have formulated confessions of faith (e.g., A Confession of Faith Containing XXIII Articles [1673; *CCFCT* 3:137-48]), and have written catechisms (e.g., Barclay, *A Catechism and Confession of Faith* [Philadelphia: Friends' Book Store, 1673]). The point made here is that entrance into the community (although an admittedly vague concept due to the intensely spiritualized understanding) is not grounded in the communication of propositional content to the mind of the individual through preaching.

grounded on one's reception of that content *as discerned through examina-tion.*[82] Barclay, however, affirms a notion of inward teaching or "convince-ment" that stands in contrast with propositional views.

Convincement is the inner illumination of the Holy Spirit within the spirit of an individual. Freiday writes, " 'Convincement' preceded repen-tance (or 'self-conviction') in the early Friends' consideration of the way in which one became a follower of Christ. In a sense, it was a matter of being convinced, not only intellectually but also in the heart and by the power of the Spirit, of the truth of Christianity. 'Conversion,' which involved a con-scious turning toward God, sometimes followed, but for others it did not."[83] Convincement often occurs through one's attendance at a meeting of those worshiping the Lord inwardly. Barclay's own testimony demonstrates this:

For not a few have come to be convinced of the truth after this manner, of which I myself, in part, am a true witness, who not by strength of arguments, or by a particular disquisition of each doctrine, and convincement of my understanding thereby, came to receive and bear witness of the truth, but by being secretly reached by this life; for when I came into the silent assemblies of God's people, I felt a secret power among them, which touched my heart, and as I gave way unto it, I found the evil weakening in me, and the good raised up, and so I became thus knit and united unto them, hungering more and more after the increase of this power and life, whereby I might feel myself perfectly redeemed.[84]

He concludes,

And indeed this is the surest way to become a Christian, to whom *afterwards the knowledge and understanding of principles will not be wanting,* but will grow up so much as is needful, as the natural fruit of this good root, and such a knowledge will not be barren nor unfruitful. After this manner we desire therefore all that come

---

82. Bunyan: "By the word of God therefore, by which their faith, experience and conver-sation, *being examined,* is found good; by that the church should receive them into fellowship" (*A Confession of My Faith* [*MWJB* 4:165; Offor 2:606], emphasis added).

83. Barclay, *Apology-Freiday,* 254n19; cf. George Fox, *The Journal of George Fox,* 8th ed. (London: Friend's Bookstop, 1902), 2:282.

84. Barclay, *Apology,* proposition XI.7.357, emphasis added.

among us to be proselyted, knowing that *though thousands should be convinced in their understanding of all the truths we maintain, yet if they were not sensible of this inward life, and their souls not changed from unrighteousness to righteousness, they could add nothing to us.* For this is that cement whereby we are *joined as to the Lord, so to one another* (1 Cor 6:17) and without this none can worship with us.[85]

Barclay's statements evince a spiritualized notion of catechesis in connection to entrance. Further, he interiorizes the catechetical process to such an extent that very little (if any) of the catechesis that leads to entrance can be properly called public. Barclay's convincement was "not by strength of arguments, or by a particular disquisition of each doctrine, and convincement of my understanding thereby." He finds this pattern to be normative, even to be "the surest way to become a Christian." Nonetheless, he leaves an important role for the community in the inner catechesis he describes.

The assembled congregation of the faithful is the context in which the "secret power" of the Holy Spirit operates to weaken the evil and lift up the good in a person. He affirms that "knowledge and understanding of principles will not be wanting [later]," but intellectual instruction and its concomitant knowledge does not figure into the "convincement" of an individual or to their initiation or entrance into the community.

This power [i.e., internal power of the Holy Spirit] that hath oftentimes laid hold of our adversaries, and made them yield unto us, and join with us, and confess to the truth, *before they had any distinct or discursive knowledge of our doctrines,* so that sometimes many at one meeting have been thus convinced: and this power would sometimes also reach to and wonderfully work even in little children, to the admiration and astonishment of many.[86]

Thus, Barclay's understanding of the catechesis connected with entrance is much more private, internal, and spiritual than Bunyan's.

---

85. Barclay, *Apology*, proposition XI.7.357, emphasis added.
86. Barclay, *Apology*, proposition XI.8.359–60, emphasis added.

Finally, Barclay spiritualizes the notion of entrance into the community by spiritualizing the Lord's Supper and the communion of the saints. The Lord's Supper is spiritualized and relegated to a previous dispensation on grounds similar to those applied to water baptism.[87] Speaking of the spiritual and inward fellowship of believers meeting together, Barclay writes, "We are often greatly strengthened and renewed in the spirits of our minds without a word, and we enjoy and possess the holy fellowship and communion of the body and blood of Christ, by which our inward man is nourished and fed; which makes us not to dote upon outward water, and bread and wine, in our spiritual things."[88]

Despite his spiritualized understanding of the Supper, Barclay affirms the necessity of visible fellowship. Corporate gatherings are "necessary for the people of God; because, so long as we are clothed with this outward tabernacle, there is a necessity to the entertaining of a joint and visible fellowship, and bearing of an outward testimony for God, and seeing of the faces of one another." This visible, corporate fellowship "doth greatly tend to encourage and refresh the saints."[89] Thus, Barclay reports that Quakers neither view worship as merely a private endeavor, nor do they deny the necessity or value of visible fellowship.

Though the Quaker concept of entrance, as exhibited in Barclay, is spiritualized in such a way that its signification is different (i.e., spiritualized communion instead of a physical meal),[90] the fact that the Quakers receive persons into their visible fellowship on the basis of faith and holiness, not water baptism, manifests the essence of the catechesis model. In so doing, the Quakers represent a subjective or spiritualist extreme of the catechesis model's liturgical logic.

---

87. Barclay writes, "The communion of the body and blood of Christ is inward and spiritual, which is the participation of his flesh and blood, by which the inward man is daily nourished in the hearts of those in whom Christ dwells; of which things the breaking of bread by Christ with his disciples was a figure, which they even used in the Church for a time, who had received the substance, for the cause of the weak" (Barclay, *Theses Theologicae*, proposition XIII).

88. Barclay, *Apology*, proposition XI.7.355.

89. Barclay, *Apology*, proposition XI.3.348.

90. As defined in the introduction, the term "entrance" is used technically in this study to designate the terminus of Christian initiation: the inauguration of full, visible fellowship with a local body of believers as it is expressed through admission to and participation in the Lord's Supper (i.e., "first Communion").

Subjectivity

The catechesis model is the most subjective of the four proposed models. This subjectivity is seen in three ways. First, the objective sign of water baptism is irrelevant to the process of entrance (as discussed above). Water baptism is a personal matter of growth and may or may not be received, depending on the conscience and understanding of the individual.

Second, the sole basis of church Communion is the candidate's understanding of the gospel and manifestation of it in godly living. Consequently, catechesis through preaching and teaching (formal, informal, and in some instances spiritual) is the only means useful for bringing one into the fellowship of the church. Additionally, the function of confirmation is subjective, accomplished through the interrogation of the initiate's grasp of the gospel truth or simply on the grounds of one's personal testimony or experience of the truth as communicated by the Spirit (e.g., convincement).

Finally, the spiritualizing of baptism also weakens the objectivity of this model. The baptism that matters for entrance is the baptism of the Holy Spirit. While examples of all three other models will affirm the importance of Spirit baptism, only the catechesis model limits entrance into the fellowship of the visible church to the (invisible and inner) baptism of the Holy Spirit.

Corresponding with its focus on Spirit baptism, the catechesis model projects an individualized version of regenerate church membership (believer's church). In other words, in this model the church is a voluntary society composed of those who have experienced the inward and spiritual baptism of the Holy Spirit and who join the local church by virtue of their testimony alone, apart from any sign given to them by the church.[91]

---

91. Appendix 1 picks up on the individualized version of regenerate church membership of the catechesis model by describing its projected view of the church as "believer's church" (note the singular possessive). This stands in contrast to the more corporate projection of the prospective model (ch. 4); therefore, appendix 1 designates the prospective model's projected view of the church as "believers' church" (note the plural possessive). With respect to the discussion above the reader should simply note that the catechesis model bases entrance on an inward, invisible baptism that the church does *not* administer, while the prospective model bases entrance on an external, visible baptism that the church *does* administer.

NARROWING THE FOCUS

As noted in the first chapter, two basic questions are pursued in this book. First, how might the various ways of relating baptism, catechesis, and entrance be explained in coordination to one another? The explanatory framework and its four models are a direct response to this question. A second question that is related to the first but distinct from it is the question of causality. Namely, is there a discernible catalyst that gives rise to the existence of one model over another? If so, what is it? I will pursue this exploratory question only after the four models have been constructed. One may rightly think of the second question as a kind of heuristic experiment using the explanatory framework of models constructed in this book.

The proposed framework has three seams separating its four models. The two outer seams that separate the independent models from the interdependent models are defined by the question, What is prerequisite to entrance: baptism or catechesis or both? Independent models require either baptism or catechesis; however, interdependent models require both.

Within the interdependent category, the retrospective and prospective models are distinguished by the sequence and priority of baptism and catechesis. Such a phenomenological or external description is helpful, but we want to further explore these models, considering whether a theological catalyst can be discerned that gives rise to the manifestation of one *interdependent model* over the other. The following two chapters (chs. 3–4) will offer fuller developments of the retrospective and prospective models than what we have pursued with regard to the independent models outlined in the current chapter. The fuller development of the interdependent models in what follows will fund the heuristic discussion and testing of catalyst candidates in chapter 5.

3

—

RETROSPECTIVE MODEL

The previous chapter sketched the proposed framework of models. There, profiles of the independent models were provided to showcase their viability as well as the dynamics of the framework. While the independent models rely on either baptism or catechesis as the sole means of entrance into the visible fellowship of the local church, the interdependent models incorporate both baptism and catechesis in the process of entrance. The next two chapters will examine the interdependent models in turn: the retrospective model and the prospective model. Each chapter provides a profile of its model, looking at core attributes and implications.

DEFINITION

Category	Independent			Interdependent				Independent
Model	Baptism	Prerequisite(s) of entrance? Baptism or catechesis or both?	Retrospective		Prospective	Prerequisite(s) of entrance? Baptism or catechesis or both?	Catechesis
	Baptism		Baptism	Orientation of catechesis to baptism	Catechesis		Catechesis
	↓		↓		↓		↓
Sequence	**Entrance**		Catechesis		Baptism		**Entrance**
	↓		↓		↓		↓
	Catechesis		**Entrance**		**Entrance**		(Baptism)

◄———— OBJECTIVE   SUBJECTIVE ————►

The retrospective model is an interdependent model in which baptism and catechesis are both prerequisites for entrance. Catechetical preparation, whether formal or informal, prior to entrance is a key mark of this model. Here, however, catechesis is grounded on and looks back to baptism. The catechetical process is concluded with examination of some sort (e.g., a rite of confirmation), which is prerequisite to Communion.[1] Catechesis' orientation to baptism is what gives this category its name. The entire catechetical process for the baptizand is retrospective of baptism. As we will see, in this pattern baptism becomes part of the catechesis that leads one to first Communion.

Historically, this model finds expression primarily in the form of infant baptism that is separated in time from confirmation and first Communion (in this order).[2] In contrast to the baptism model (see ch. 2), both confirmation (when practiced) and Communion are reserved for those who have reached "the age of discernment."[3]

BAPTISM AND ENTRANCE

In order to develop the retrospective model's connection between baptism and entrance in greater detail, it is helpful to consider how this model relates to the others within our framework. Specifically, how does the retrospective model stand in relation to the other models with regard to baptism and entrance? First, the retrospective model is linked with those models requiring water baptism for entrance. Moving left to right, the first three models of the framework—baptism, retrospective, and prospective models—make water baptism prerequisite to entrance. In other words, without water baptism an individual remains ineligible to participate in the Lord's Supper. Because the retrospective model accepts infant baptism while rejecting infant Communion, the model creates a liminal space for children in which they are already members of the community but not yet a participant in the community's ongoing expression of fellowship: the Lord's Supper. While the church fully expects them to be confirmed into this fellowship at a later point on the basis of their personal confession of the faith, they are not yet fully members in a visible sense. To draw on eschatological language, they are proleptic or "already-not yet" members.

Second, the retrospective model is linked with those models that fence the Table from those who have yet to profess their faith credibly. Again,

---

1. The status of the rite as a sacrament or nonsacrament is incidental to this model. The key aspects are examination and personal confession of the Christian faith.

2. The inversion of confirmation and first Communion (baptism–first Communion–confirmation) will be discussed below.

3. Cf. Dogmatic Decrees of the Council of Trent 21.4 (1545–1563; CCFCT 2:860).

moving left to right, the last three models—retrospective, prospective, and catechesis models—presuppose a credible profession of faith along with certain capacities and dispositions for participation in the Lord's Supper. This position is known as "credocommunion." Credocommunion is the majority position in the Christian traditions of the West. The importance of and capacity for self-examination, personal confession, desire to partake of the elements, and ability to remember Christ's death (among other things) are cornerstones of the credocommunion position.

The key biblical foundation for the credocommunion position is 1 Corinthians 11. While the Eastern Church (with some followers in the West) has understood 1 Corinthians 11 as directed to adults without reference to children, the majority interpretation within the Western traditions—Catholic and Protestant alike—is to apply the passage both to adults and to children.[4] In other words, the Pauline exhortation to "do this in remembrance [ἀνάμνησιν] of Me" (1 Cor 11:24, 25) and strictures to "examine [δοκιμαζέτω]" oneself (v. 28), to "recognize [διακρίνων; or 'discern' or 'judge' or 'distinguish'] the body" (v. 29), and to "wait [ἐκδέχεσθε]" for one another (v. 33) are prerequisite activities for participation in the Supper. By extension, the *capacities* for these activities are also prerequisite.

Credocommunion is the official practice of the Catholic Church. For example, the Council of Trent advocates delayed Communion eligibility, leaving the timing of first Communion to the discretion of "the parents and confessor ... whether they [i.e., the children] have some knowledge of this admirable Sacrament [i.e., the Eucharist] and whether they desire to receive it."[5] The Catechism of the Council of Trent (1566; i.e., the Roman Catechism) offers three rationales why those under the age of discretion should be excluded from the Eucharist: they are unable (1) "to distinguish

---

4. As noted in ch. 2, there is intramural debate here among paedobaptists. Paedocommunionists such as Gregg Strawbridge charge that fellow paedobaptists are hermeneutically inconsistent. For while they often decry the application of "adult" texts to infants regarding baptism, when it comes to infant Communion, they fail to extend their hermeneutic to the Lord's Supper, applying "adult" texts such as 1 Cor 11 to infants. Cf. Strawbridge, "Polemics of Infant Communion," 158. Strawbridge makes his case via an examination of John Calvin's *Institutes* (4.16.28–30).

5. CCT, 267–68.

the Holy Eucharist from common and ordinary bread," (2) to prepare and bring the proper spiritual dispositions of "piety and devotion," and (3) to respond to the command "take and eat."[6]

The Westminster Larger Catechism is representative of the majority view among Protestants in its stricture that the Lord's Supper is to be administered "only to such as are of years and ability to examine themselves."[7] The Westminster Shorter Catechism (1646) describes the kind of examination in view:

Q. 97. What is required for the worthy receiving of the Lord's Supper?

A. It is required of them that would worthily partake of the Lord's Supper, that they examine themselves of their knowledge to discern the Lord's body, of their faith to feed upon him, of their repentance, love, and new obedience; lest, coming unworthily, they eat and drink judgment to themselves.[8]

Communicants must, therefore, be able to discern their own knowledge, faith, repentance, love, and obedience in order to partake.

In addition to self-examination, the Westminster Larger Catechism makes it clear that the proper reception of the Lord's Supper involves a complex of issues that require care and discernment, such as "thankful remembrance" and "renewing the exercises of [the] graces" of the Christian life (e.g., faith, repentance, etc.).[9] The Westminster standards echo the sentiments of the Heidelberg Catechism (1563), which emphasizes that the Lord's Supper is for those who are sorrowful for sin and desire to grow in godliness, prerequisites that are beyond the capacities of infants.[10] The larger Reformed tradition is not alone in this understand-

---

6. *CCT*, 267. The age of discretion is typically understood to be attained at age seven, assuming normal development. Cf. *The Code of Canon Law: In English Translation*, trans. Canon Law Society of Great Britain and Ireland (Grand Rapids: Eerdmans, 1983), can. 97 §2 [14].

7. Westminster Larger Catechism, q. 177 (1647; *RC*, 215). Cf. Calvin, *Institutes* 4.16.30; Second London Confession 30 (1677; *BCF*, 293); Luther, *Larger Catechism* (*BC*, 470.33–37).

8. Westminster Shorter Catechism, q. 97 (1646; *RC*, 223), emphasis added.

9. Cf. Westminster Larger Catechism, qq. 169, 171–75 (1647; *RC*, 223, 225).

10. Heidelberg Catechism, q. 81 (1563; *RC*, 230).

ing that eligibility for the Supper is to be delayed until certain capacities are manifested.[11]

THE NATURE AND TIMING OF CONFIRMATION

The retrospective model projects a subjective view of confirmation that differs from that of the baptism model, both in its nature and timing. To review, the baptism model (e.g., Eastern Orthodox infant initiation) projects a wholly objective understanding of confirmation. Here, confirmation is the sign and seal of the Holy Spirit given by the church alongside or through infant baptism. *Thus, with regard to timing, confirmation is conjoined with baptism either as an accompanying rite or as a function of baptism itself.*[12]

Concerning the nature of confirmation, the Eastern Orthodox express the notion of objective sealing in their postbaptismal anointing of the baptizand with chrism—a mixture of oil, balsam, and other spices that has been blessed by a bishop.[13] Timothy Ware writes, "What happened to the first Christians on the day of Pentecost happens also to each of us when, immediately following our Baptism, we are in the Orthodox practice anointed with Chrism or *Myron*. (This, the second sacrament of Christian

---

11. In addition to the examples above, similar affirmations are held by Lutherans. For example, Luther, in his *Small Catechism*, writes, "Who, then, receives this sacrament [of the Altar] worthily? Answer: Fasting and bodily preparation are in fact a fine external discipline, but a person who has faith in these words, 'given for you' and 'shed for you for the forgiveness of sins,' is really worthy and well prepared. However, a person who does not believe these words or doubts them is unworthy and unprepared, because the words 'for you' require truly believing hearts" (BC, 363). The preparations and dispositions described here are not applicable to infants (even where infant faith is asserted). Cf. Methodists (Articles of Religion 18 [CCFCT 3:205]). See also the Scots Confession (1560), which affirms that baptism "applies as much to the children of the faithful as to those who are of age and discretion." It maintains, however, "The supper of the Lord is only for those who are of the household of faith and can try and examine themselves both in their faith and their duty to their neighbors. Those who eat and drink at that holy table without faith, or without peace and goodwill to their brethren, eat unworthily" (Scots Confession 23 [1560; CCFCT 2:403]). Thus, even though infants and small children are considered members of "the household of faith," their participation in the Supper is deferred until such time as their capacities and dispositions meet these criteria.

12. With regard to the timing of confirmation, the prospective model also connects confirmation with baptism. The prospective model as a whole, however, is much more subjective than the baptism model. This will be discussed further in the next chapter.

13. The chrism is "made from oil and balsam blessed by a bishop, the oil symbolizing the gleaming brightness of conscience and balsam symbolizing the odor of a good reputation" (*Bull of Union with the Armenians* 15 [1439; CCFCT 1:759]). Cf. Philip Schaff, "§ 72. Catechetical Instruction and Confirmation," in *Ante-Nicene Christianity, A.D. 100-325*, History of the Christian Church 2 (Grand Rapids: Eerdmans, 1910), 257.

initiation, corresponds to Confirmation in the Western tradition.)" Ware goes on to describe this anointing as a "personal Pentecost."[14] The close association of confirmation with the bestowal of the Holy Spirit is evident in the words of institution, "The seal of the gift of the Holy Ghost, Amen."[15] Within the baptism model, confirmation or chrismation is conferred either immediately following an infant's baptism (via the laying on of hands or anointing with chrism or both) or through infant baptism itself (apart from hand-laying or anointing). In either case it is given apart from a personal profession of faith.

The retrospective model, in contrast to the baptism model reviewed above, projects a more subjective understanding of confirmation. When practiced as a rite of maturity (i.e., as a marker of spiritual discernment and understanding,[16] confirmation exemplifies this subjective turn. When confirmation as a rite continued within Reformation churches, it typically continued as a rite of maturity.[17] In this form, confirmation is the capstone of the catechetical process, an examination of a noncommunicant member's faith that leads to full-communicant status (i.e., entrance).

CONFIRMATION IN THE REFORMATION

John Calvin is a prominent example of confirmation as a maturity rite and the subjective emphasis given confirmation within the retrospective model. Having just outlined his distaste for the Roman practice of confirmation as a sacrament conferring the Holy Spirit, Calvin outlines what he believes to be the correct and most beneficial practice:

> How I wish that we might have kept the custom which ... existed among the ancient Christians before this misborn wraith of a sacrament [of confirmation] came to birth! Not that it would be a confirmation such as they fancy, which cannot be named without doing injustice to baptism; but a catechizing, in which children or those

---

14. Ware, *Orthodox Way*, 133.

15. Peter Moglia, *The Orthodox Confession of the Catholic and Apostolic Eastern Church* 105 (1638/42; CCFCT 1:603).

16. This statement assumes there are multiple forms of confirmation. These various forms will be discussed in greater detail below when the Roman Catholic tradition is examined.

17. G. W. H. Lampe, *Seal of the Spirit*, 2nd ed. (London: SPCK, 1967), 310.

near adolescence would give an account of their faith before the church.[18]

Calvin earlier describes in greater detail his understanding of the ancient practice of confirmation:

> In early times it was the custom for the children of Christians after they had grown up to be brought before the bishop to fulfill that duty which was required of those who as adults offered themselves for baptism. For the latter sat among the catechumens until, duly instructed in the mysteries of the faith, they were able to make confession of their faith before the bishop and people. Therefore, those who had been baptized as infants, because they had not then made confession of faith before the church, were at the end of their childhood or at the beginning of adolescence again presented by their parents, and were examined by the bishop according to the form of the catechism, which was then in definite form and in common use. But in order that this act, which ought by itself to have been weighty and holy, might have more reverence and dignity, the ceremony of the laying on of hands was also added. Thus the youth, once his faith was approved, was dismissed with a solemn blessing.[19]

In light of his understanding of church history and the Scriptures, Calvin believes the best practice for catechizing baptized children is to use a catechism, "containing and summarizing in simple manner most of the articles of our religion."[20] At the age of ten, a child would be examined in front of the entire congregation. Calvin reasoned that using this method of instruction and employing public examination at the end of the catechetical process would ensure the instruction of children in the faith. Not only would it measure whether the child had in fact been instructed, but it would motivate parents to fulfill their duty (if for no other reason than fear of public embarrassment).[21]

---

18. Calvin, *Institutes* 4.19.13 (trans. Battles, 2:1460–61). Cf. Geneva Catechism prologue (1541/42; CCFCT 2:320).

19. Calvin, *Institutes* 4.19.4 (trans. Battles, 2:1451–52).

20. Calvin, *Institutes* 4.19.13 (trans. Battles, 2:1461).

21. Calvin, *Institutes* 4.19.13 (trans. Battles, 2:1461).

Calvin's understanding of confirmation as a maturity rite is not idio-syncratic. Other Reformers evince the same understanding. For exam-ple, Zacharias Ursinus articulates the same view in his *Commentary on the Heidelberg Catechism*:

These children [i.e., those born to Christian parents], very soon after their birth were baptized, being regarded as members of the church, and after they had grown a little older they were instructed in the catechism, which having learned, they were confirmed by the laying on of hands and were dismissed from the class of Catechumens, and were then permitted, with those of riper years, to celebrate the Lord's Supper.[22]

Philip Melanchthon also affirms a maturity-rite definition of confirmation in his *Loci Communes*: "In days gone by they used to have an examination of the teaching in which individuals recited a summary of the doctrine and showed that they dissented from the heathen and the heretics; and there was also the very useful practice of instructing people in how to distinguish between the profane and the godly."[23] G. W. H. Lampe finds the practice of confirmation in the Reformation lacking in historical and biblical precedent. He maintains, however, that it is theologically correct. "Their [i.e., the Reformers'] development of Confirmation made it possible to retain infant Baptism along with the doctrine of justification *sola fide*. The Christian who was baptized in infancy was now able to make his nec-essary profession of faith after due instruction."[24]

CONFIRMATION IN THE ROMAN CATHOLIC TRADITION

The Council of Trent anathematizes the understanding expressed by Calvin, Ursinus, Melanchthon, and others. It avers, "If anyone says that confir-mation of the baptized is an empty ceremony, and not rather a true and proper sacrament; or that at one time it was nothing but a form of religious

---

22. Zacharias Ursinus, *The Commentary of Dr. Zacharias Ursinus on the Heidelberg Catechism*, 3rd American ed., trans. G. W. Williard (Cincinnati: Bucher, 1851), 10; cf. 12.

23. Philip Melanchthon, *Loci Communes* (1543), trans. J. A. O. Preus (St. Louis: Concordia, 1992), 141–42. See also Martin Bucer, *De Regno Christi* 5, in *Melanchthon and Bucer*, ed. and trans. Wilhem Pauck (Louisville: Westminster John Knox, 1969), 228–29.

24. Lampe, *Seal of the Spirit*, 314. Cf. Berthold von Schenk, "First Communion and Confirmation," *Concordia Theological Monthly* 42.6 (1971): 356.

instruction in which those approaching adolescence presented an account of their faith publicly to the church: let him be anathema."[25] Against the popular Reformation understanding, Trent maintains that confirmation is an objective sealing of an individual and is not merely a witnessing of an individual's confession of faith.

Yet, the Catholic tradition, along with Calvin and others of the Reformation, exemplifies the retrospective model's subjective turn away from the more objective confirmation view of the baptism model. Paul Turner summarizes a complex and confusing malaise of practices associated with the Roman Catholic sacrament of confirmation. He identifies five pastoral needs that have precipitated three forms of practice.[26]

Pastoral Needs

Turner cites the following pastoral needs as formative for the "history of confirmation" within the Roman Catholic tradition:

1. The need to develop "an expressive baptismal liturgy" that unified the variety of practices expressed in the early church (e.g., pre- and postbaptismal anointings, laying on of hands by bishop, invocation of the Holy Spirit, etc.)

2. The bishop's desire to retain "ritual contact between themselves and every baptized member of the diocese" over

---

25. Dogmatic Decrees of the Council of Trent 7, can. 3.1 (1545–1563; *CCFCT* 2:842).

26. Paul Turner, "Confusion over Confirmation," *Worship* 71.6 (1997): 537–45. This section will focus on the phenomenology of confirmation as a rite, not its chronological development. For key discussions of development, see Gregory Dix, *Confirmation, or Laying on of Hands* (London: Society for Promoting Christian Knowledge, 1936); Michel Dujarier, *A History of the Catechumenate: The First Six Centuries* (New York: Sadlier, 1979); John D. C. Fisher, *Christian Initiation: Baptism in the Medieval West; A Study in the Disintegration of the Primitive Rite of Initiation* (London: SPCK, 1965); Maxwell E. Johnson, *The Rites of Christian Initiation: Their Evolution and Interpretation*, 2nd ed. (Collegeville, MN: Liturgical, 2007); Aidan Kavanagh, *Confirmation: Origins and Reform* (New York: Pueblo, 1988); Hans Küng, "Confirmation as the Completion of Baptism (I): To Edward Schillebeeckx on His 60th Birthday," *Colloquium* 8 (1975): 33–40; G. W. H. Lampe, *The Seal of the Spirit: A Study in the Doctrine of Baptism and Confirmation in the New Testament and the Fathers*, 2nd ed. (London: SPCK, 1967); Arthur J. Mason, *The Relation of Confirmation to Baptism: As Taught in Holy Scripture and the Fathers* (London: Longmans, Green, 1891); Paul Turner, *Sources of Confirmation: From the Fathers through the Reformers* (Collegeville, MN: Liturgical, 1993); Paul Turner, "The Origins of Confirmation: An Analysis of Aidan Kavanagh's Hypothesis (with Response by Aidan Kavanagh)," in *Living Water, Sealing Spirit: Readings on Christian Initiation*, ed. Maxwell E. Johnson, 238–58 (Collegeville, MN: Liturgical, 1995).

against the increasing impracticality of doing this at baptismal services

3. The question of how to receive those baptized (in the triune
   formula) by "heretical" groups while maintaining the unrepeatability of baptism

4. The administration of last rites

5. The need to mark "the Christian maturity of adolescents"[27]

The only constants within the history of the practice of confirmation are
the "anointing with chrism, handlaying, and prayer for the Holy Spirit."
Beyond this, variety is the norm; the age, prerequisites, authorized administrators,[28] timing, and meaning may differ. As Turner concludes, "It has
been consistently inconsistent."[29]

Forms of Confirmation

According to Turner, the Catholic tradition has addressed the pastoral
needs above by three forms of confirmation:

1. Rite of initiation—administered with baptism[30]

2. Rite of maturity—administered at a varying age of discretion[31]

---

27. Turner, "Confusion over Confirmation," 538. Turner's *Sources of Confirmation* illustrates
the confusion he summarizes in his article.

28. In the East, baptism (infant or adult) is always accompanied by chrismation. Differing
polities of confirmation or chrismation exist between the Eastern and Western traditions.
The Orthodox tradition allows the priest to administer both baptism *and* chrismation (so long
as the oil has been consecrated by a bishop). The Roman tradition only permits the bishop
to administer confirmation. Thus, while both give emphasis to the authority of the bishop,
only the Roman tradition reserves administration for the bishop (cf. Critopoulos, *Confession
of Faith* 8.1 [*CCFCT* 1:515]; *CCC*, 1290 [360]).

29. Turner, "Confusion over Confirmation," 539. Similarly, Frank Quinn refers to what he
calls "the problem of confirmation," which includes the rite's origin, meaning, and relation
to baptism ("Confirmation Reconsidered," 225).

30. This can apply (1) to adults or children of catechetical age or (2) to infants (in the
Eastern Orthodox tradition).

31. Turner observes that while canon law makes the age of discretion seven, a conference
of bishops may designate a different age for receiving confirmation (anywhere from seven
to eighteen). Fluctuation in the age of eligibility bears on the meaning of the rite: "Later
ages emphasize the candidates' commitment," and "earlier ages stress the free gift of God's
grace." The common denominator in all situations, however, is that "confirmation belongs

3. Rite of reception—administered to a proselyte from another
Christian denomination[32]

Turner explains that in the Roman tradition the initiation form of confirmation (form 1) is expressed only in the rite of "adult" baptism.[33] Confirmation
as reception (form 3) is a remedial rite built on the assumption that the
authority to confer the Holy Spirit is grounded in the apostolic succession
of bishops, which denominations outside "the Church" (especially those
of the Reformation) have corrupted. Thus, the two primary forms of confirmation within the Roman Catholic tradition are that of initiation (form
1) and maturity (form 2).

As noted earlier, the Catholic sacrament of confirmation is more objective than its Reformation counterpart. For all forms of the rite within the
Roman Catholic tradition, "Confirmation perfects baptismal grace."[34] It is
a strengthening rite, not simply a rite that ratifies one's faith (though profession of faith is a component).[35] *The Catechism of the Council of Trent*, following the canons of the council, declares that confirmation must not be

---

at an age deferred from infancy, when a child shows some maturity" (Turner, "Confusion
over Confirmation," 540).

32. Turner, "Confusion over Confirmation," 539–41. On the validity of baptism in non-
Catholic contexts see "*Unitatis redintegratio*: Decree on Ecumenism," in Doctrinal Decrees of
the Second Vatican Council 5.3.3.17 (1962–1965; *CCFCT* 3:649).

33. Turner explains the meaning of "adult" as follows: "In [canon] law, children of catechetical age are considered adults as far as baptism is concern. Only if they are too young
to learn the significance of these rites do we welcome them not as catechumens, but with
the rite of infant baptism" ("Confusion over Confirmation," 539).

34. *CCC*, 1316 [367]. Commenting on the relative authority of the *CCC*, Joseph Ratzinger
writes, "What significance the Catechism [*CCC*] really holds for the common exercise of
teaching in the Church may be learned by reading the Apostolic Constitution *Fidei depositum*,
with which the Pope promulgated it on October 11, 1992 … : 'I acknowledge it [the Catechism]
as a valid and legitimate tool in the service of ecclesiastical communion, as a sure norm for
instruction in the faith.' " See Joseph Cardinal Ratzinger, "The Author of the Catechism and
Its Authority," in *Introduction to the Catechism of the Catholic Church*, Joseph Cardinal Ratzinger
and Christoph Schönborn (San Francisco: Ignatius, 1994), 26. The *CCC* was originally intended
to be a short catechism when it was proposed at Vatican II. Ultimately the *CCC* was produced
as a large catechism, like its forebear *The Catechism of the Council of Trent* (1566). This was done
in order to allow regional and local bishops to produce small catechisms that were attentive
to the specific needs of their area. Cf. Jane E. Regan, *Exploring the Catechism* (Collegeville,
MN: Liturgical, 1994), 40, 54–56.

35. The *RCIA* describes this strengthening as a strengthening for witness to those outside
the body and ministry to those within the body. In the *RCIA* liturgy the rite is administered
via the laying on of hands and with chrismation (233–35 [145–47]).

reduced to catechetical instruction; rather, "The name [confirmation] has been derived from the fact that by virtue of this Sacrament God confirms in us the work He commenced in Baptism, leading us to the perfection of solid Christian virtue."[36]

According to the Catechism of the Catholic Church, the perfecting of baptismal grace in confirmation "gives the Holy Spirit in order to root us more deeply in the divine filiation, incorporate us more firmly into Christ, strengthen our bond with the Church, associate us more closely with her mission, and help us bear witness to the Christian faith in words accompanied by deeds."[37]

Though more objective than Calvin's version of confirmation,[38] Catholic confirmation exhibits a subjective dynamic that distinguishes it from its Eastern counterpart. Catholic confirmation is separated in time from infant baptism and is not given "until the child reaches a more mature age."[39] The delay is intended to allow certain dispositions and capacities to develop. The Catechism of the Catholic Church delineates the following preparatory measures: "To receive Confirmation one must be in a state of grace. One should receive the sacrament of Penance in order to be cleansed for the gift of the Holy Spirit. More intense prayer should prepare one to receive the strength and graces of the Holy Spirit with docility and readiness to act."[40] Though in cases of exigency it may be administered apart from catechesis, catechesis is normally prerequisite to receiving confirmation.[41]

> Preparation for Confirmation should aim at leading the Christian toward a more intimate union with Christ and a more lively familiarity with the Holy Spirit—his actions, his gifts, and his biddings—in

---

36. *CCT*, 221.

37. *CCC*, 1316 [367]. Cf. *CCT*, 221.

38. This is demonstrable in the fact that Roman Catholic confirmation retains its status as a sacrament, its close connection to reception of the Spirit, its unrepeatable character, and its indelible effect on the recipient (e.g., *CCC*, 1316, 1317 [367]).

39. Turner, "Confusion over Confirmation," 540.

40. *CCC*, 1310 [365].

41. "In danger of death children should be confirmed even if they have not yet attained the age of discretion" (*CCC*, 1307 [364-65]). Paul Turner illustrates the numerous internal inconsistencies within the Catholic tradition that are created by the separation of confirmation from infant baptism. Chief among these inconsistencies is the formal requirement of catechesis and the willingness to confirm individuals who request it at the end of their lives and apart from catechesis (cf. Turner, "Confusion over Confirmation," 537-45, esp. introduction).

order to be more capable of assuming the apostolic responsibilities of Christian life. To this end *catechesis for Confirmation* should strive to awaken a sense of belonging to the Church of Jesus Christ, the universal Church as well as the parish community. The latter bears special responsibility for the preparation of confirmands.[42]

The necessity of preconfirmation catechesis is underscored by the requirements that the confirmand be able to "profess the faith," "have the intention of receiving the sacrament" (which assumes knowledge of the same), and "be prepared to assume the role of disciple and witness to Christ, both within the ecclesial community and in temporal affairs."[43] Thus, while the Roman Catholic tradition anathematizes those who reduce confirmation to catechization and personal profession, the tradition normally requires catechesis and personal profession prior to confirmation. In so doing, the Roman Catholic tradition in its process of entrance for those baptized in infancy exemplifies a key subjective element of the retrospective model that distinguishes it from the baptism model.[44]

REORDERING THE SACRAMENTS OF INITIATION: SOFT PAEDOCOMMUNION

To this point, the sequence of baptism-confirmation-Eucharist has been presupposed when considering examples of the retrospective model within the Roman Catholic tradition. This move is not without warrant. Among the sacraments of initiation—baptism, confirmation, and Eucharist—baptism has a well-established position as the first sacrament (both inside and outside the Roman Catholic tradition). Though the practice of allowing first

---

42. *CCC*, 1309 [365], emphasis added.

43. *CCC*, 1319 [367].

44. Quinn identifies three possible meanings that may be communicated (intentionally or unintentionally) through the word "confirmation." The latter two illustrate the subjective turn of the retrospective model: "Some will think of the postbaptismal, episcopal rites which conclude baptism; they will emphasize either handlaying or anointing. Others will immediately understand confirmation to refer to the medieval sacrament, with its emphasis on anointing or moral strengthening, or to the rite of the churches of the Reformation which completed one's religious education and admitted the confirmand to the communion table. *Twentieth century catechists have bolstered the medieval and Reformation views by comparing confirmation to a coming of age or puberty rite*" (Quinn, "Confirmation Reconsidered," 225–26, emphasis added).

Communion prior to confirmation is considered permissible, it is not the normative, confessional ordering.

The normative, confessional ordering for the Roman Catholic Church remains baptism, confirmation, and Eucharist.[45] J. P. Kenny notes, "When canonists and theologians, councils or popes publish lists of the sacraments, the order is monotonously: baptism, confirmation, Eucharist, etc. ... ; confirmation is always put in front of the Eucharist."[46]

Confessionally, the Eucharist is given the ultimate position among the sacraments of initiation and with it the greatest emphasis. The Catechism of the Catholic Church states, "The holy Eucharist *completes* Christian initiation. Those who have been raised to the dignity of the royal priesthood by *Baptism* and configured more deeply to Christ by *Confirmation* participate with the whole community in the Lord's own sacrifice by means of the *Eucharist.*" The catechism also affirms that the Eucharist is "the source and summit of the Christian life."[47] As such, the Eucharist is the center of the life of the church in its internal and external ministries.

The Catholic tradition applies the term "Eucharistic assemblies" to its gatherings, signifying "that all who eat the one broken bread, Christ, enter into communion with him and form but one body in him" (cf. 1 Cor 10:16–17). The term "Eucharistic assemblies" is an apt description of the Catholic Church's understanding of visible fellowship "because the Eucharist is celebrated amid the assembly of the faithful, the visible expression of the Church."[48] With soaring language, the catechism asserts, "The Eucharist *makes* the Church"; it explains, "Those who receive the Eucharist are united more closely to Christ. Through it Christ unites them to all the faithful in one body—the church. Communion renews, strengthens, and deepens this

---

45. Boniface Luykx states, "It is impossible ... to justify either theologically or canonically the abuse of conferring confirmation after first Communion. ... Communion before confirmation is a liturgical contradiction for which it is very difficult to find any justification." As quoted approvingly by J. P. Kenny, "The Age of Confirmation," *Worship* 35 (1960): 9. Cf. *RCIA*, general introduction, 2 [xiv].

46. Kenny, "Age of Confirmation," 5. Cf. Dogmatic Decrees of the Council of Trent 7, Canons on the Sacraments in General, can. 1 (*CCFCT* 2:840).

47. *CCC*, 1322 [368], emphasis added.

48. *CCC*, 1329 [370]. For an extended development of this idea, see Dulles, "Chapter 4: The Church as Sacrament," in *Models of the Church* (New York: Doubleday, 1978). Dulles succinctly describes the progressive interrelation between the sacraments of initiation (reflecting the order of baptism-confirmation-Eucharist) on 215.

incorporation into the Church, already achieved by Baptism. In Baptism we have been called to form but one body. The Eucharist fulfills this call."[49] While baptism incorporates one into the body, the Eucharist manifests one's incorporation fully. In all these affirmations, the Eucharist is placed at the apex of initiation and functions as the sine qua non of full entrance into the visible church.

Yet, the practice of inverting the order of confirmation and Eucharist (baptism-first Communion-confirmation) has manifested at times in the Roman tradition.[50] Kenny observes that such an inversion is defended on the following logic: "The Eucharist is supernatural food, whereas confirmation is supernatural growth; but food precedes, and is the cause of, growth; therefore the Eucharist should come first."[51] This alternate ordering affects the logical relationships between the sacraments of initiation. Insofar as each sacrament is required for full initiation into the church, the sacrament in the ultimate position receives the superlative emphasis because initiation remains incomplete until it is administered. Thus, administering confirmation last means that confirmation, not the Eucharist, marks the completion of initiation.[52]

---

49. CCC, 1396 [391], emphasis added. The RCIA calls first Communion "the culminating point of … Christian initiation." First-time communicants "with the entire community … share in the offering of the sacrifice and say the Lord's Prayer, giving expression to the spirit of adoption as God's children that they have received in baptism" (RCIA, 217 [125]).

50. Similar examples can be found in other traditions. For example, Keith T. Littler, Leslie J. Francis, and T. Hugh Thomas, "The Admission of Children to Communion before Confirmation: A Survey among Church in Wales Clerics," Contact 139 (2002): 24–38, which found 67 percent of its 224 responding clergy to favor admission to first Communion prior to confirmation (p. 29). For examples of those advocating the practice see Alan Ward, "Communion before Confirmation: A Response to 'Admitting Children to Holy Communion' in Churchman 113/4 (1999)," Churchman 114.4 (2000): 295–99; Carl E. Braaten, "Communion before Confirmation," Dialog 1.3 (1962): 61–62. Paul Nelson notes that while the traditional order of baptism, confirmation, and first Communion is common among European Lutherans, Communion before confirmation is the lived experience "for most Lutherans in North America." See "Lutheran Worship," in Bradshaw, New SCM Dictionary, 294.

51. Kenny, "Age of Confirmation," 5. Cf. Kenny's counterargument on the basis of an ex opere operato view of the sacraments (5n5). While Thomas Aquinas allows for either ordering (Summa Theologica 3.2–3), in reply to the specific logic quoted by Kenny, Aquinas gives priority to the confirmation-Eucharist ordering. This is stated directly ("Of the remaining three, it is clear that Baptism which is a spiritual regeneration, comes first; then Confirmation, which is ordained to the formal perfection of power; and after these the Eucharist which is ordained to final perfection"; Summa Theologica 3.2) and implicitly in his discussion of the supremacy of the Eucharist among the seven sacraments (Summa Theologica 3.3).

52. Analogously, G. W. H. Lampe rightly argues that separating confirmation from adult baptism makes confirmation the rite of supreme importance: a rite completing baptism (Seal

The alternate sequence above fits within the category of soft paedocom-munion introduced in the previous chapter. In soft paedocommunion, a simple confession or affirmation of faith by a child baptized in infancy is all that is required to participate in the Supper; a fuller confession is made at a rite of confirmation subsequent to first Communion. The question that we must raise and answer at this point is, Does soft paedocommunion warrant its own model within this book's proposed framework? Though it is per-haps not confessionally normative, does the logic of this sequence require a new model to explain what is happening in this expression of initiation?

The alternate sequence—baptism, Eucharist, confirmation—does not warrant its own model for at least two reasons. First, placing confirma-tion at the apex of initiation is at odds with the great emphasis placed on the Eucharist in the confessional statements above. Recalling the wording of the Catechism of the Catholic Church, "The holy Eucharist *completes* Christian initiation." Further, local churches are described as "Eucharistic assemblies," not "confirmed assemblies."[53] The prominent position of the Eucharist in confessional materials points to the exceptional nature of the alternate ordering.

Second, the nature of confirmation fails to manifest visible, corporate fellowship in the same way that the Eucharist does. Confirmation signi-fies a once-for-all action that is understood to be indelible.[54] Once given, confirmation cannot be taken back or readministered. Conversely, the Eucharist, as the only repeatable sacrament of initiation, is able to mani-fest visible fellowship in an ongoing manner. Similarly, the Eucharist is the only sacrament of initiation that can be withheld at a later point in order to disfellowship an individual. Thus, the Eucharist, not confirmation, is ground zero for the action of excommunication. Unless an entirely differ-ent meaning and nature is given to confirmation, it simply cannot bear the weight of being the *sine qua non* of visible fellowship, as can the Eucharist.

---

of the Spirit, 316). Though commenting on and from within the Anglican tradition, Lampe's judgment applies equally to the Catholic structure. From within the Catholic tradition, Hans Küng writes, "If the eucharist is a sacrament for initiated persons—and no one questions this—and confirmation belongs to initiation as seems undeniable, then it is illogical to confirm someone after his or her first communion." See Küng, "Confirmation as the Development, Re-affirmation and Completion of Baptism. II," *Colloquium* 8.2 (1976): 6.

53. *CCC*, 1322, 1329 [368, 370], emphasis added.

54. *CCC*, 1304. Baptism and ordination are also understood to leave an indelible imprint on the soul (*CCC*, 1272 and 1582).

The inverted order has two possible side effects on the status of confirmation, both of which can be explained without the use of a new model within the framework proposed in this book. The reason a new model is not required is that the logic of the resultant structure (baptism-first Communion-confirmation) can be explained by one of the four proposed models of this study.

On the one hand, the alternate order may functionally demote confirmation from its status as a rite of initiation. In this case full initiation to visible fellowship is fulfilled in first Communion, and confirmation is simply a *personal* rite of spiritual growth. The demotion of confirmation in this case is similar to the demotions that occur in each of the independent models. For example, the catechesis model demotes water baptism, removing it from the process of entrance and making it a rite of personal growth. Similarly, the baptism model demotes catechesis from the process of entrance. One is baptized and administered the Eucharist (though in some cases at a later point) apart from a fully confirmed, personal confession of faith. Though catechesis would certainly come later, that catechesis is not tied to the entrance process in the baptism model.

On the other hand, the alternate order could be understood to mean that there are functionally two "first" Communions. On this explanation, the second "first Communion" occurs after confirmation. With regard to entrance into visible fellowship, this explanation is problematic because the confirmand receives no real visible change in liturgical status, only a one-time marker. Within a congregational polity, it is possible for voting eligibility to be tied to this later confirmation.[55] Nonetheless, even here, the eucharistic sign of fellowship remains unchanged. Therefore, in this latter scenario it is not clear how confirmation would change (i.e., increase) the visible fellowship that existed before its administration. If two first Communions are affirmed, the logic is similar to the retrospective model.

---

55. For example, the Reformed Church in America allows infant-baptized, unconfirmed children to participate in the Supper. Confirmation may be delayed and brings with it full rights of membership, which in this denomination includes voting rights. We should note that Reformed Church in America churches reflect Presbyterian polity structures and are therefore not congregational in a traditional sense, but the cited document mentions voting rights as an aspect of membership. As such it offers an analogous example of how this approach might be applied within a congregational polity. See "Baptized Non-communicants" (1977 and 1984 respectively); esp. 1977, 11; 1984, section 3. Cf. Reformed Church in America Theological Commission, "Baptized Children and the Lord's Table," 1990.

Full entrance occurs only after a confirmation of personal faith that is subsequent to baptism.

As noted above, there are logical deficiencies with the soft-paedocommunion structure since it is unclear how confirmation changes or increases the visible fellowship that existed before its administration. Therefore, whether confirmation is demoted to a personal rite of growth or two "first Communions" are posited, it is best to interpret this alternate sequence as an exceptional pattern that borrows its logic from the other models developed in this study.

ORIENTATION OF CATECHESIS
TO BAPTISM: RETROSPECTION

There is a sense in which all catechesis is retrospective; for catechesis always looks back to the person, work, and teachings of Jesus Christ. The catechist's motto is aptly summed in Paul's declaration about the gospel in 1 Corinthians 15:3: "For I handed down [παρέδωκα] to you as of first importance what I also received [παρέλαβον]" (emphasis added). Paul taught what he "also received." Such a handing over echoes a statement in Jesus' high-priestly prayer: "for the words which You gave [δέδωκάς] Me I have given [δέδωκα] to them" (John 17:8). Further, Jesus commands his disciples to make disciples by "teaching them to follow all that I commanded you" (Matt 28:20, emphasis added).

The term "retrospective," therefore, properly applies to all forms of Christian catechesis. Nonetheless, in the present and subsequent chapter the issue is specifically how catechesis is oriented to baptism in the *process of entrance*. In this sense, the question becomes, Does catechesis look back to baptism or forward to it? Does baptism ground catechesis or vice versa?

BAPTISM'S PEDAGOGICAL FUNCTION

In the retrospective model catechesis as a means of entrance looks back to baptism, on which it is grounded. This retrospective dynamic emphasizes a key pedagogical function of baptism found in Paul.

The apostle Paul uses baptism as a pedagogical sign at several points in his letters.[56] That is, he uses baptism to teach his readers about specific

---

56. Much of this section has appeared in published form in my article "The Ongoing Use of Baptism: A Hole is the Baptist (Systematic) Baptistry," *Southwestern Journal of Theology*, 61 (Fall 2018): 3–27. It is used here with permission.

realities, especially their union with Christ and its implications for sanctification and the Christian life (e.g., Gal 3; Rom 6; Col 2–3).

For example, in Romans 6, the apostle Paul anticipates an antinomian distortion to the message of grace he has expounded in the preceding chapters: "What shall we say then? Are we to continue in sin so that grace may increase?" (Rom 6:1). He responds by citing the meaning of baptism and its ethical implications:

> Far from it! How shall *we who died to sin* [οἵτινες ἀπεθάνομεν τῇ ἁμαρτίᾳ] still live in it? Or do you not know that *all of us who* [ὅσοι] have been baptized into Christ Jesus have been baptized into His death? Therefore *we have been buried* [συνετάφημεν] with Him through baptism into death, so that, just as Christ was raised from the dead through the glory of the Father, so *we too may walk* [ἡμεῖς ... περιπατήσωμεν] in newness of life. For if *we have become* [γεγόναμεν] united with Him in the likeness of His death, certainly *we shall* also *be* [ἐσόμεθα] in the likeness of His resurrection, knowing this, that our old self was crucified with Him, in order that our body of sin might be done away with, so that we [ἡμᾶς] would no longer be slaves to sin; for he who has died is freed from sin. (Rom 6:2–7)

The first-person plural clauses of these verses indicate Paul's assumption that his hearers are baptized. George Beasley-Murray rightly notes that these phrases "self-evidently ... include Paul and *all* his readers, otherwise his argument against the allegedly antinomian effect of the doctrine of justification by faith falls to the ground."[57] Further, not only is baptism an assumed common experience, but Paul uses baptism as a pedagogical sign or paradigm of Christian identity. That is, baptism functions here to teach or communicate the realities and pattern of the Christian life, a life rooted and shaped by Christ's person and work.

In Romans 6, Paul recalls the baptismal imagery of the past and connects it to the present tense of Christian living. He presents the baptismal imagery as the way in which believers are to understand their new

---

57. George Beasley-Murray, "Baptism," in *Dictionary of Paul and His Letters* (Downers Grove, IL: InterVarsity, 1993), 60, emphasis original. He notes similar assumptions by Paul concerning his Christian audience in Gal 3:26–28; Col 2:12; 2:20–3:15; 1 Cor 12:13.

identity in Christ: "So you too, consider [λογίζεσθε] yourselves to be dead to sin, but alive to God in Christ Jesus" (Rom 6:11). The imperative "consider" is in the present tense. Thus, it is to be an ongoing way of thinking, and baptism is the sign that summarizes the truth of such thinking.[58] In other words, baptism is a pedagogical sign that Paul uses to remind his readers of their identity.

John Mueller, a Lutheran theologian, picks up on this pedagogical function, noting that while baptism is not to be administered more than once, it is to be in constant use by the Christian. "Baptism," writes Mueller, "should comfort and exhort the believer through his life (1 Pet 3:21; Gal 3:26–27; Rom 6:3)."[59] He continues, "For this reason the apostles in the New Testament again and again remind Christians of their Baptism ... and urge them to heed not only its sweet comfort, but also its great significance for sanctification. *Baptismus semper exercendus est* [Baptism is always practiced]."[60]

The Westminster Larger Catechism exemplifies the pedagogical function of baptism when it speaks of "improving" one's baptism. Question 167 asks, "How is our baptism to be improved by us?" It responds,

> The needful but much neglected duty of improving our baptism, is to be performed by us all our life long, especially in the time of temptation, and when we are present at the administration of it to others; by serious and thankful consideration of the nature of it [i.e., baptism], and of the ends for which Christ instituted it, the privileges and benefits conferred and sealed thereby, and our solemn vow made therein; by being humbled for our sinful defilement, our falling short of, and walking contrary to, the grace of baptism, and our engagements; by growing up to assurance of pardon of sin, and of all other blessings sealed to us in that sacrament; by drawing strength from the death and resurrection of Christ, into whom we are baptized, for the mortifying of sin, and quickening of grace; and by endeavouring to live by faith, to have our conversation in

---

58. Douglas J. Moo, *The Epistle to the Romans*, New International Commentary on the New Testament (Grand Rapids: Eerdmans, 1996), 380.

59. John Mueller, *Christian Dogmatics: A Handbook of Doctrinal Theology for Pastors, Teachers, and Laymen* (St. Louis: Concordia, 1934), 496, prooftext formats modified.

60. Mueller, *Christian Dogmatics*, 496. E.g., 1 Cor 1:13; Eph 4:5; Col 2:12; 1 Pet 3:21.

holiness and righteousness, as those that have therein given up their names to Christ; and to walk in brotherly love, as being baptized by the same Spirit into one body.[61]

By "improving" baptism, the catechism does not mean adding new things to baptism, but rather it intends that the individual live out more fully the grace benefits signified and sealed in baptism. To do so, this baptism must be recalled "by serious and thankful consideration."[62] This recollection is specific, not generic; for the believer is to recall its "nature," "ends," "privileges and benefits," and "solemn vow made therein." Baptism and all it represents is here portrayed as a resource for living the Christian life.

The improvement of baptism envisioned within the Westminster Larger Catechism is not specific to the process of initiation, for it "is to be performed by us all our life long." There is, therefore, a sense in which all models of the conceptual framework are compatible with this notion *following entrance*. Yet, within the retrospective model the confirmation process leading to first Communion is undoubtedly included in and a significant step toward improving one's baptism. The catechesis *leading to entrance* within the retrospective model is instrumental in this improvement.

RECALLING AND AFFIRMING BAPTISMAL VOWS

The retrospective model makes confirmation the capstone of catechesis. The projected practice of confirmation within this model, however, illustrates the retrospective orientation of catechesis to baptism.

When confirmation is practiced as a separate rite from infant baptism (and prior to first Communion), the baptismal vows spoken over an individual in infancy are renewed and joined with a personal profession of the faith. For example, the Catechism of the Catholic Church states,

> When Confirmation is celebrated separately from Baptism, as is the case in the Roman Rite, the Liturgy of Confirmation begins with *the renewal of baptismal promises and the profession of faith by the confirmands*. This clearly shows that Confirmation follows Baptism. When

---

61. Westminster Larger Catechism, q. 167 (*RC*, 217, 219).
62. Westminster Larger Catechism, q. 167 (*RC*, 217, 219).

adults are baptized, they immediately receive Confirmation and participate in the Eucharist.[63]

A similar requirement for renewal and profession is evident within the Anglican confirmation rite.[64] The Anglican Catechism, which is often appended to the Book of Common Prayer, manifests both dynamics. Concerning profession, the catechism is titled "A Catechism, That is to say, An instruction, to be learned of every person before he be brought to be confirmed by the bishop."[65] Framed in this way, the content of the catechism is intended to provide the content of the confirmand's profession of faith.

Concerning the renewal of baptismal promises, the confirmand begins by giving his or her name, reporting that this name was given them at their baptism, and affirming that in that baptism they were "made a member of Christ, the child of God, and an inheritor of the kingdom of heaven."[66] The confirmand further recounts what was promised on his or her behalf in that baptism: "First, that I should renounce the devil and all his works, the pomps and vanity of this wicked world, and all the sinful lusts of the flesh. Secondly, that I should believe all the Articles of the Christian Faith.[67] And, thirdly, that I should keep God's holy will and commandments, and walk in the same all the days of my life."[68] The confirmand then recites, via interrogation, the Apostles' Creed, Ten Commandments, and the Lord's

---

63. *CCC*, 1298 [362], emphasis added.

64. It should be noted that practice within the Anglican tradition is not as clear with regard to the sequence of baptism, confirmation, and Eucharist. Communion before confirmation is a known practice. Gregory Dix highlights how the medieval development of the practice of confirmation as a separate rite (in time) from baptism seems to be based on Peter Lombard's *Sentences*. Citing specific examples, he argues that this work depends largely on a compilation by Gratian Lombard, which was largely dependent on false or forged sources. Dix, with a tone of lament, calls into question the Anglicans' inheritance of this medieval tradition. Cf. Dix, *The Theology of Confirmation in Relation to Baptism* (London: Dacre, 1946), esp. part 3.

65. Anglican Catechism (1549, 1662), in Schaff, *Creeds of Christendom* 3:517.

66. Anglican Catechism (1549, 1662), in Schaff, *Creeds of Christendom* 3:517.

67. "All the Articles of the Christian Faith" refers primarily to the Apostles' Creed. The creed is quoted in full in the interrogation of the sponsors, in which they are asked whether they—on behalf of the infant—believe. Cf. "Public Baptism of Infants," in *Book of Common Prayer and Other Rites and Ceremonies of the Church, according to the Use of the Church of England* (London: John Bill, Thomas Newcomb, and Henry Hills, 1681), 3.

68. Anglican Catechism (1549, 1662), in Schaff, *Creeds of Christendom* 3:517.

Prayer, explaining the meaning of the component parts of each symbol respectively. The catechism also covers the doctrines of the sacraments[69] and, in so doing, signals the intention that the rite will prepare one to participate fully in the visible fellowship and corporate worship of the church.

RECALLING BAPTISM ITSELF

The recounted content from the infant baptismal liturgy above is theologically dense, including renunciations, confession of the creed, and promise of obedience. Apart from these aspects, however, the theological density *of baptism itself* functions as the foundation for the retrospection of this model.

For example, the Catechism of the Council of Trent states,

> Whoever reads the Apostle [Paul] carefully will unhesitatingly conclude that a perfect knowledge of Baptism is particularly necessary to the faithful. For not only frequently, but also in language the most energetic, in language full of the Spirit of God, he *renews the recollection of this mystery, declares its divine character, and in it places before us the death, burial and Resurrection of our Lord as objects both of our contemplation and imitation.* Pastors, therefore, can never think that they have bestowed sufficient labor and attention on the exposition of this Sacrament. ... Each person, reading a lesson of admonition in the person of him who is receiving Baptism, *will call to mind the promises by which he bound himself to God when he was baptized,* and *will reflect whether his life and conduct have been such as are promised by the profession of Christianity.*[70]

All Christians are here called to recall their baptism. The chief example proffered is that of the apostle Paul, who "not only frequently, but also in language the most energetic, in language full of the Spirit of God ... *renews the recollection of this mystery.*" Such a recollection is centered on the "divine character" of baptism and "the death, burial and Resurrection of our Lord" depicted therein "as objects both of our contemplation and imitation."[71]

---

69. Anglican Catechism (1549, 1662), in Schaff, *Creeds of Christendom* 3:521–22.

70. *CCT,* 169, emphasis added. The *RCIA* states, "Baptism recalls and makes present the paschal mystery itself, because in baptism we pass from the death of sin into life" (general introduction, 6 [xv]).

71. *CCT,* 169.

Standing at the headwaters of the Reformation, Martin Luther illustrates a retrospective focus on baptism itself when he writes,

> In baptism ... every Christian has enough to study and practice all his or her life. Christians always have enough to do to believe firmly what baptism promises and brings—victory over death and the devil, forgiveness of sin, God's grace, the entire Christ, and the Holy Spirit with his gifts. In short, the blessings of baptism are so boundless that if our timid nature considers them, it may well doubt whether they could all be true.[72]

Despite points of disagreement that some traditions would have with Luther's baptismal theology (e.g., baptismal regeneration), traditions across the denominational spectrum will agree with Luther that the theological mysteries of baptism (even in the variety of ways in which they are understood) are inexhaustible. That is, the ongoing use of baptism is not simply a remembrance of one's identification with Jesus as his disciple; it is a remembrance of the entirety of the Christian faith and all that God has done for one in salvation. There is a theological depth to baptism that suits it for its ongoing pedagogical function. This theological depth can be illustrated in six brief observations that touch major loci of systematic theology, specifically theology proper, Christology (person and work), salvation (objective and subjective), the Christian life, ecclesiology, and eschatology.

First, relating to theology proper, baptism is Trinitarian. In the Gospel according to Matthew, the apostles, and by extension the church, are commanded to make disciples by "baptizing ... in the name of the Father and the Son and the Holy Spirit" (Matt 28:19).[73] Further, Jesus' baptism in the Jordan by John stands in the background of all Christian baptism (Matt 3:13–17).[74]

---

72. Luther, *Large Catechism* (1529; *BC*, 461). A similar example is found in the Roman tradition: "Baptism is justly called by us the Sacrament of faith, by the Greeks, the mystery of faith, because it embraces the entire profession of the Christian faith" (*CCT*, 240).

73. Even baptism administered in Jesus' name only, so long as it is within an orthodox frame of reference, is inherently Trinitarian. Michael Reeves aptly notes, "When you proclaim Jesus, the Spirit-anointed Son of the Father, you proclaim the Triune God." See Reeves, *Delighting in the Trinity* (Downers Grove, IL: IVP Academic, 2012), 37–38.

74. While in one sense we do not see a clear statement connecting the baptism of Jesus and Christian baptism, there is strong reason for seeing a connection. For example, note the way in which baptism bookends the presentation of Jesus' public ministry in Matthew: it begins with his baptism (3:16–17) and ends with his command to baptize (28:19). We see a similar pattern elsewhere. It is common for the apostolic summary of the gospel to begin

Here the Spirit descends (v. 16), resting on Jesus, and the Father declares from heaven, "This is My beloved Son, with whom I am well pleased" (Matt 3:17). Thus, apart from any assertion of sacramental efficacy, the Trinitarian background and formula of baptism alone indicates the theological depth of this rite.

Second, relating to Christology, baptism displays core aspects of Christ's person and work. On the one hand, the rite as a whole puts forward the atoning work of Christ: his death, burial, and victorious resurrection over sin, death, and the devil. Connecting these realities to baptism, Paul writes: "having been buried with Him in baptism, in which you were also raised with Him through faith in the working of God, who raised Him from the dead" (Col 2:12; see v. 15 for the aspect of triumph). On the other hand, baptism also recalls truths of Christ's *person*. The theological themes of death and burial connected to baptism presuppose Christ's incarnate person, for God alone is immortal (1 Tim 1:17; 6:16) and only mortal humans may die. The theological theme of resurrection connected to baptism affirms his incarnation as well, for he was raised bodily from the dead. This theme is emphasized by the mode of immersion. Drawing from the imagery of Romans 6, Luther writes that the act of immersion and emersion signify the "slaying of the old Adam and the resurrection of the new creature, both of which must continue in us our whole life through.[75] Though many traditions within the West practice other modes, immersion enjoys a long tradition in the church. For example, the Eastern Orthodox Church across

---

with the baptism of Jesus (see Mark 1; Acts 10:32–48; note the criteria for selecting Judas' replacement in Acts 1:21–22) and end with a call to be baptized (Acts 10:48; 2:38 [explicit command]; cf. 8:12 [inferred command]). If apostolic summaries and preaching of the gospel began with Jesus' baptism and ended with a call to respond through baptism, then the connection between these baptisms seems so fundamental and presuppositional that it would not have needed direct mention. For an alternative view, see John Hammett, *Forty Questions about Baptism and the Lord's Supper* (Grand Rapids: Kregel Academic, 2015), 71–72, 75. Even if one disagrees with the position taken here, the Trinitarian shape of Christian baptism stands on the foundation of Matt 28 alone. Nonetheless, I doubt that Matthew's compositional strategy fails to bring Jesus' baptism and Christian baptism into close relation. See Gregory S. Thellman, "The Narrative-Theological Function of Matthew's Baptism Command (Matthew 28:19b)," *Anafora* 6 (2019): 81–106.

75. Luther, *Large Catechism* (1529; BC, 465). The fuller quote reads as follows: "These two parts, being dipped under the water and emerging from it, point to the power and effect of baptism, which is nothing else than the slaying of the old Adam and the resurrection of the new creature, both of which must continue in us our whole life long. Thus a Christian life is nothing else than a daily baptism, begun once and continuing ever after."

its history has practiced triple immersion, and many credobaptist traditions have practiced single immersion. The baptismal actions of this mode—immersion (placing under) and emersion (drawing out)—display core aspects of Christ's person and work.[76] Whether or not one is an immersionist, the connection between Christ's death, burial, and resurrection and baptism are readily acknowledged by all Christian traditions. As such, the point being made here stands: the person and work of Christ are intimately linked with baptism.

Third, relating to the doctrine of salvation, baptism is a visible portrayal of conversion (subjective) and union and identification with Christ (objective). As an act of obedience, baptism clearly manifests one's conversion and discipleship unto Christ. Submission to baptism visibly affirms Jesus' declaration, "All authority in heaven and on earth has been given to Me" (Matt 28:18). Commenting on baptism in the name of Jesus as found in Acts, Beasley-Murray notes that when connected to such a formula "submi[ssion] to [baptism] becomes a confession of trust in Him."[77] Moreover, baptism is a command of the risen Christ (Matt 28:19). While there is evidence that Jesus and his disciples baptized persons during his ministry,[78] the command to be baptized as a means of becoming a disciple is not given until *after* Jesus' resurrection. The postresurrection timing of his command to be baptized is significant for recognizing that baptism is itself a form of profession. To request and receive baptism in response to the command of

76. Immersion is commonly argued for on the basis of its correspondence with the meaning of baptism. E.g., David Allen, " 'Dipped for Dead': The Proper Mode of Baptism," in *Restoring Integrity in Baptist Churches*, ed. Thomas White, Jason G. Duesing, and Malcolm B. Yarnell III (Grand Rapids: Kregel, 2008), 104-5. At the conclusion of his lengthy review of documentary and archaeological evidence within the first five centuries of the church, Everett Ferguson concludes that the normative mode of administration was "immersion with exceptions" (*Baptism in the Early Church*, 857-60).

77. George Beasely-Murray, *Baptism in the New Testament* (Grand Rapids: Eerdmans, 1962), 101.

78. The Synoptics omit what John's Gospel includes: that there was a practice of baptism in Jesus' ministry (John 3:22-24; 4:1-2) at least for a time (though R. T. France has argued that this extended across Jesus' ministry): "After these things Jesus and His disciples came into the land of Judea; and there He was spending time with them and baptizing" (John 3:22); "So then, when the Lord knew that the Pharisees had heard that He was making and baptizing more disciples than John (although Jesus Himself was not baptizing; rather, His disciples were) ..." (John 4:1-2). See France, "Jesus the Baptist?," in *Jesus of Nazareth: Lord and Christ; Essays on the Historical Jesus and New Testament Christology*, ed. Joel B. Green and Max Turner (Grand Rapids: Eerdmans, 1994), cf. 105-6.

the *risen* Christ, to whom "all authority in heaven and on earth has been given" (Matt 28:18), is to profess one's faith in his resurrection and the legitimacy of his lordship.

Further, baptism signifies one's cleansing from sin and union with Christ. Beasley-Murray notes, "Cleansing is the primary meaning of baptism in all religious groups that have practiced it."[79] Similarly, Hammett observes, "While it is worded in slightly different ways, cleansing or purification or forgiveness of sins is one of the most widely agreed upon aspects of the meaning of baptism, included in Catholic, Lutheran, Reformed, and Baptist formulations."[80] As it relates to union with Christ, Paul writes, "For you are all sons *and daughters* of God through faith in Christ Jesus. For all of you who were baptized into Christ have clothed yourselves with Christ" (Gal 3:26–27). Thomas Schreiner comments, "Verse 26 says we know we are Christ's if we have faith. And v. 27 says that those who are baptized have clothed themselves with Christ. In other words, baptism signifies that one is united to Christ."[81] The baptismal actions (immersion and emersion) administered to the particular individual signify that person's union with Christ. Baptism is not merely a reenactment of *Christ's* death, burial, and resurrection, but it demonstrates the *identification and solidarity (i.e., union) of the baptizand with Christ and vice versa.*[82]

Through its visible portrayal of union with Christ, baptism displays the profound truth of the glorious exchange between Christ and the new disciple. Luther, speaking of the benefits that follow faith, describes this exchange vividly: "[Faith] unites the soul with Christ as a bride is united with her bridegroom. ... It follows that everything they have they hold in

---

79. Beasely-Murray, *Baptism in the New Testament*, 104; cf. Hammett, *Forty Questions*, 117–18.

80. Hammett, *40 Questions*, 117; cf. 1 Pet 3:21; Acts 2:38; 22:16. How the rite of baptism is related to this cleansing is of course not a matter of consensus across denominations.

81. Thomas R. Schreiner, "Baptism in the Epistles," in Schreiner and Wright, *Believer's Baptism*, 89.

82. The "vice versa" of this statement applies on the basis of Matt 10:32–33 (cf. Luke 12:8), where Jesus declares, "Therefore, everyone who confesses Me before people, I will also confess him before My Father who is in heaven. But whoever denies Me before people, I will also deny him before My Father who is in heaven." This logic will be worked out differently between various denominations. For example, paedobaptist traditions will affirm this proleptically on covenantal grounds, whereas credobaptist traditions will understand baptism to signify the identification and solidarity with Christ as a present reality for the baptizand. See also John 15:5–6; Gal 2:20 for the idea of mutual indwelling and Christ's union with the believer.

common, the good as well as the evil. Accordingly, the believing soul can boast of and glory in whatever Christ has as though it were its own, and whatever the soul has Christ claims as his own."[83] In depicting union with Christ, baptism illustrates the exchange of the baptizand's sin, condemnation, and death with the righteousness, acceptance, and life of Christ. What is declared of Christ at the Jordan is true for all who are united with him by faith: "This is My beloved Son, with whom I am well pleased" (Matt 3:17). This approbation is true of the disciple not inherently but derivatively by virtue of the disciple's union with Christ. As Donald Fairbairn so aptly describes it, "Christ is the natural, only-begotten Son of God, and in a way that is both similar and different, Christians become adopted sons and daughters of God, thus sharing by grace in the fellowship the Son has with the Father by nature."[84]

Fourth, the Christian life and its ethics are a reality signified in baptism. Beasley-Murray writes, "It is surely significant that the longest exposition of baptism in Paul's letters is given for an ethical purpose. Romans 6:1–14 is filled with appeals for life consonant with participation in the redemption of Christ that lies at the heart of baptism."[85] Paul writes, "Therefore we have been buried with Him through baptism into death, so that, just as Christ was raised from the dead through the glory of the Father, so we too may walk in newness of life" (Rom 6:4).

Paul's use of baptismal imagery to illustrate and teach his readers about the new, ethical reality of the Christian life is not limited to Romans 6. In fact, Beasley-Murray notes that Paul's appeal for a life shaped by the reality signified in baptism is "most extensively developed in Colossians 2:20–3:13."[86] Paul reminds the believers in Colossae that they "[have] been *buried*

---

83. Martin Luther, *On the Freedom of a Christian*, in *Three Treatises*, 286.

84. Donald Fairbairn, *Life in the Trinity: An Introduction to Theology with the Help of the Church Fathers* (Downers Grove, IL: IVP Academic, 2009), 9. Fairbairn develops this distinction in a variety of ways across his work. For example, following Cyril of Alexandria, he highlights two kinds of unity: a unity of (1) substance and (2) fellowship. The unity of substance is unique between the Father and Son; it is incommunicable. The unity of fellowship is something that is shared with us (36). He concludes, "The heart of Christian faith is the eternal relationship that has characterized the persons of the Trinity, and Jesus explicitly describes the relationship between God the Father and himself [e.g., John 17:20–24], God the Son. ... Our sharing in the Father-Son relationship is at the center of what it means for us to participate in God" (37).

85. Beasley-Murray, "Baptism," 64.

86. Beasley-Murray, "Baptism," 64.

with Him in baptism, in which you were also *raised with Him* through faith in the working of God" (Col 2:12, emphasis added). On the basis of their baptism into Christ's death ("If you have died with Christ ..."; v. 20), Paul admonishes believers to avoid new regulations such as "Do not handle, do not taste, do not touch!" (v. 21). Further, utilizing baptismal-resurrection imagery, he exhorts, "Therefore if *you* have been *raised up with Christ*, keep seeking [ζητεῖτε] the things *that are* above, where Christ is, seated at the right hand of God" (Col 3:1). As in Romans 6:11, where believers are told to consider themselves dead to sin, the main verb, ζητεῖτε (keep seeking), is a present active indicative second-person plural, indicating the ongoing, *corporate* nature of the action (i.e., "you all keep seeking"). Paul here calls the Colossian believers to an *ongoing* manner of life lived *together* that is shaped by baptism.

In light of the new ethical reality signified in baptism, Paul continues, "Therefore treat [lit. 'put to death'][87] the parts of your earthly body as dead *to* sexual immorality, impurity, passion, evil desire, and greed" (Col 3:5). Because of the execution of the old man and resurrection of the new man, believers are to "rid yourselves of" (NASB), "get rid of" (NRSV; cf. NIV), "put ... away" (ESV), or "put off" (KJV; Col 3:8; ἀπόθεσθε) the practices of the old self, and "put on" (Col 3:10; ἐνδυσάμενοι) the practices of the new self (cf. Col 3:8–17). Thus, this new ethical reality is summed in the baptismal sign, a sign that plays an ongoing pedagogical role in the life of believers. Baptism is a sign of these realities, and it is to be used by the believer to remember those realities and subsequently live them out.

Fifth, baptism manifests the baptizand's union with the body of Christ, the church, and its mission in the world. The close association of baptism with entrance into the communion of the local church is seen in Acts 2:41–42, where "those who had received [Peter's] word were baptized; and that day there were added about three thousand souls" (Acts 2:41). Subsequently, we see these persons living in community, "continually devoting themselves to the apostles' teaching and to fellowship, to the breaking of bread and to prayer" (Acts 2:42). Historically speaking, Christian churches have

---

87. The word νεκρώσατε, translated "treat ... as dead" by the NASB , is different from that used in Rom 6:11 for "consider [λογίζεσθε] yourselves." The NRSV, ESV, and NIV all render νεκρώσατε as "put to death"; similarly, the KJV renders it "mortify."

not and do not practice self-baptism (i.e., se-baptism or auto-baptism).[88] Rather, a local church or parish administers baptism to persons as a means of making them disciples (Matt 28); as such, it is a rite to be received.[89] Thus, the doctrine of the church—its fellowship and obedient mission in the world—is bound up with this rite as well.[90]

Finally, baptism signifies the eschatological hope of the gospel. Here we begin by recalling what was previously said about Paul's discussion of baptism in Colossians 2-3. Baptism as a sign of future resurrection bears eschatological weight. Nonetheless, Schreiner sees eschatological significance in baptism's association with the washing with and pouring out of the Holy Spirit (Titus 3:5 with Ezek 11:19; 36:25-27; Titus 3:6 with Joel 2:28-29; Isa 44:3), union with Christ the seed of Abraham (Gal 3:15-4:7, especially 3:27-28), and victory over sin (Rom 6:3-4, 9-10).[91] He summarizes, "Baptism, therefore, functions as a reminder of the new eschatological reality that has been obtained with the death and resurrection of Christ."[92] This eschatological reality of resurrection is already present in the life of the believer, but it is also a reality that has not yet been fully realized. As such baptism signifies the already-but-not-yet tension of the Christian life: a life bathed in eschatological hope.

While each of these elements could be developed at length, and others could be added to them, the preceding examples are intended simply to illustrate the theological density of baptism. The retrospective model *grounds* its initiatory catechesis on this dense theological foundation. The preceding discussion will also be important for understanding the prospective model in the next chapter, which draws on the dense theological

---

88. John Smyth's se-baptism is a notable deviation from this norm. For a discussion of Smyth's se-baptism, see Jason K. Lee, *Theology of John Smyth* (Macon, GA: Mercer University Press, 2003), 71-74.

89. The main verb of Matt 28:19-20 is μαθητεύσατε (aorist active imperative plural), "to make a disciple of, teach." According to Daniel Wallace, the participles βαπτίζοντες ("baptizing") and διδάσκοντες ("teaching") are best understood as participles of means, i.e., "the means by which the disciples were to make disciples was to baptize and then to teach." See Wallace, *Greek Grammar beyond the Basics*, 645.

90. For helpful and succinct summary of this point, see Hammett, *Forty Questions*, 119-20.

91. Schreiner, "Baptism in the Epistles," 87-89. For more discussion on the association of baptism with the gift of the Holy Spirit, see Schreiner's discussion of 1 Cor 12:13 ("Baptism in the Epistles," 71-73).

92. Schreiner, "Baptism in the Epistles," 89.

properties of baptism for its catechesis. The retrospective model, however, uniquely makes baptism an existential grounding for catechesis. On the retrospective model, the triune God expounded in pre-*entrance* catechesis is the God who, by the hands of the minister, has already baptized them.

CATECHESIS AS MYSTAGOGY

In a generic sense, the catechesis of the retrospective model is mystagogical in nature.[93] Mystagogy is the "study or explanation of mysteries." Mystagogical catechesis is a form of catechesis typically associated with the early church in which newly baptized persons were debriefed on their experience of the sacraments and rites of initiation.[94]

While some church fathers would give explanations of baptism, chrismation, Eucharist, and other attendant practices (e.g., exorcism, renunciation, anointing[s], etc.) *prior* to their administration (e.g., Theodore of Mopsuestia and John Chrysostom), the majority practice was to instruct participants *after* receiving them (e.g., Ambrose of Milan and Cyril of Jerusalem).[95] The majority practice of administering mystagogy following the sacraments of initiation is exemplified by the Rite of Christian Initiation of Adults, which defines "mystagogy" as "postbaptismal catechesis." The rationale for this sequence is rooted in the conviction that "the new, personal experience of the sacraments and the community" give this catechesis a "distinctive spirit and power."[96] Thus, in the majority practice, the one who is being instructed in the faith is being instructed

---

93. The intention here is not to make a one-to-one correlation between patristic mystagogical catechesis and the catechesis of the retrospective model. In addition to differences in content, technically, the former occurred only after first Communion and therefore was subsequent to entrance. Thus, the correlation between patristic mystagogy and the catechesis of the retrospective model noted here is more about orientation and function than it is about content.

94. Cf. Maxwell E. Johnson, "Mystagogical Catechesis," in Bradshaw, *New SCM Dictionary*.

95. A distinction exists here between catechesis that expounds the Christian faith and catechesis that expounds on the sacraments of initiation (i.e., baptism, anointing[s], etc.); "mystagogy" refers to the latter. For example, Cyril of Jerusalem places five of his twenty-three lectures after baptism and the other rites of initiation. These last five lectures explain these rites or "mysteries." Cf. Jeffrey P. Baerwald, "Mystagogy," in *The New Dictionary of Sacramental Worship*, 2nd ed., ed. Peter E. Fink (Collegeville, MN: Liturgical, 1990); Johnson, "Mystagogical Catechesis," 330; Cyril of Jerusalem, *The Catechetical Lectures of S. Cyril*, in *Cyril of Jerusalem, Gregory Nazianzen*, NPNF² 7:1–157.

96. *RCIA*, 244, 247 [151].

regarding something that happened to him or her. Understood in this way, the content of the instruction is essentially an exposition of this previous experience, and as a result the experience becomes part of a foundation for the instruction.

The retrospective model exemplifies a mystagogical orientation of catechesis to baptism, for its catechesis is essentially a debriefing of the meaning of the baptism previously received. Thus, it is not too much to say that the state of being baptized is integral *to the catechesis* of this model, for it is the foundation on which its instruction is given.

BAPTISM AND FAITH

The retrospective model projects a cause-effect orientation between baptism and faith. In this model, baptism is an instrumental cause of faith. Faith is here understood as an objective gift of God conveyed through baptism. While there are distinctive ways in which this conveyance is construed, the effect is the same: baptism is an instrumental cause of the faith prerequisite for entrance.

In what follows, three key examples of this orientation will be noted: infused faith, future faith, and infant faith. This section will also highlight the objective-subjective flexibility of the retrospective model. A mediating position (infant faith) has been included and treated more fully than the others because of its theoretical and heuristic usefulness in exploring catalytic possibilities in chapter 5.

INFUSED FAITH

As with the baptism and catechesis models surveyed in chapter 2, the retrospective model accommodates an objective-subjective continuum. The Roman Catholic tradition offers a more objective understanding of the baptism-faith relationship, in which faith is a gift coming through the baptismal action of the church (*ex opere operato*).[97] The Catechism of the Council

---

97. The CCC emphasizes the action of Christ in the sacraments, but it also makes clear that Christ's action in the sacraments is mediated through the priesthood of the church. It states, "The ordained priesthood guarantees that it really is Christ who acts in the sacraments through the Holy Spirit for the Church. The saving mission entrusted by the Father to his incarnate Son was committed to the apostles and through them to their successors: they receive the Spirit of Jesus to act in his name and in his person. The ordained minister is the sacramental bond that ties the liturgical action to what the apostles said and did and, through them, to

of Trent describes the sacraments as "signs instituted not by man but by God, which we firmly believe *have in themselves the power of producing the sacred effects of which they are the signs.*" Further, it describes baptism as "a sign which indicates the infusion of divine grace into our souls."[98]

Three of the Canons on Sacraments in General from the seventh session of the Council of Trent highlight the inherent power of the sacraments to produce faith. Canon 6 asserts that the sacrament itself contains and communicates grace apart from active faith.[99] Canon 7 asserts the infallibility of this communication of grace. Finally, canon 8 affirms, "If anyone says that grace is not conferred by the sacraments of the new law *through the sacramental action itself* [*ex opere operato*], but that faith in the divine promise is by itself sufficient for obtaining the grace: let him be anathema."[100] Commenting on these canons (especially canon 6), Pope John Paul II in his Instruction on Infant Baptism (*Pastoralis actio*) states,

---

the words and actions of Christ, the source and foundation of the sacraments" (*CCC*, 1120 [317]). Thus, while this sacramental action is closely connected to the work of the priest, the work of the priest is understood to be intermediate. Commenting on the meaning of *ex opere operato*, the catechism likewise emphasizes the work of Christ. It reads, "Celebrated worthily in faith, the sacraments confer the grace that they signify. They are efficacious because in them Christ himself is at work: it is he who baptized, he who acts in his sacraments in order to communicate the grace that each sacrament signifies. ... This is the meaning of the Church's affirmation that the sacraments act *ex opere operato* (literally: 'by the very fact of the action's being performed'), i.e., by virtue of the saving work of Christ, accomplished once for all. It follows that 'the sacrament is not wrought by the righteousness of either the celebrant or the recipient, but by the power of God.' From the moment that a sacrament is celebrated in accordance with the intention of the Church, the power of Christ and his Spirit acts in and through it, independently of the personal holiness of the minister. Nevertheless, the fruits of the sacraments also depend on the disposition of the one who receives them" (*CCC*, 1127-28 [319]). As the *Oxford Dictionary of the Christian Church* summarizes, "To say, therefore, that a sacrament confers grace 'ex opere operato' is to assert in effect that the sacrament itself is an instrument of God, and that so long as the conditions of its institution are validly fulfilled, irrespective of the qualities or merits of the persons administering or receiving it, grace is conferred." See "Ex Opere Operato," in *Oxford Dictionary of the Christian Church*, 3rd ed. rev., ed. F. L. Cross and E. A. Livingstone (New York: Oxford University Press, 2005), 592.

98. *CCT*, 152, 154, emphasis added.

99. "If anyone says that the sacraments of the new law do not contain the grace which they signify; or do not confer that grace on those who place no obstacle in the way, as if they were only external signs of grace or justice received by faith, and some kind of mark of the Christian profession by which believers are distinguished from unbelievers in the eyes of people: let him be anathema" (Council of Trent, session 7, Canons on Sacraments in General, can. 6 [*CCFCT* 2:840]).

100. Council of Trent, session 7, Canons on Sacraments in General, cans. 7-8, emphasis added.

In accordance with the teaching of the Council of Trent on the sacraments, Baptism is not just a sign of faith but also *a cause of faith.* It produces in the baptized "interior enlightenment," and so the Byzantine liturgy is right to call it the sacrament of enlightenment, or simply enlightenment, meaning that the faith received pervades the soul and causes the veil of blindness to fall before the brightness of Christ (2 Cor 3:15–16).[101]

The infused, enlightening grace of baptism leads to faith, but this only takes place within the context of the church's faith. As the Catechism of the Council of Trent states, "It may not be doubted that in Baptism infants receive the mysterious gifts of faith." It immediately qualifies, however, "Not that they believe with the assent of the mind, but they are established in the faith of their parents, if the parents profess the true faith."[102] Similarly, while the Catechism of the Catholic Church calls baptism "the sacrament of faith," it also qualifies that "faith needs the community of believers. It is only within the faith of the Church that each of the faithful can believe." In the baptismal ceremony, "The catechumen or the godparent is asked: 'What do you ask of God's Church?' The response is: 'Faith!' "[103] The faith of the church precedes the faith of the individual and is its nurturer: "It is the Church that believes first, and so bears, nourishes and sustains my faith. Everywhere, it is the Church that first confesses the Lord: ... It is through the Church that we receive faith and new life in Christ by Baptism."[104]

On the infused-faith understanding, the grace of baptism is infused or implanted in the heart of the infant like a seed. As the parents and sponsors (along with the church) water this seed through catechesis, the seed

---

101. Instruction on Infant Baptism (*Pastoralis actio*) (Rome: 1980), 18, http://www.vatican.va/roman_curia/congregations/cfaith/documents/rc_con_cfaith_doc_19801020_pastoralis_actio_en.html. " 'This bath is called enlightenment, because those who receive this [catechetical] instruction are enlightened in their understanding' ... [Justin Martyr, *Apology*, 1.61.12]. Having received in Baptism the Word, 'the true light that enlightens every man,' the person baptized has been 'enlightened,' he becomes a 'son of light,' indeed, he becomes 'light' himself" (CCC, 1216 [342]).

102. *CCT*, 188.

103. *CCC*, 1253 [351].

104. *CCC*, 168 [52].

of faith grows and bears fruit. Though catechesis helps it grow and form, the Catechism of the Catholic Church describes this growth as beginning in baptism: "For all the baptized, children or adults, faith must grow after Baptism. For this reason the Church celebrates each year at the Easter Vigil the renewal of baptismal promises. Preparation for Baptism leads only to the threshold of new life. *Baptism is the source of that new life in Christ from which the entire Christian life springs forth.*"[105]

The inherent grace of the sacrament is highlighted by the assertion that baptism is a nonrepeatable sacrament. Due to its "nature and efficacy" baptism is "on no account to be reiterated."[106] Thus, alongside the following views (future faith and infant faith), the infused faith view bases baptismal *validity* on the objectivity of the sacrament, not the personal faith of the baptizand.[107]

In sum, on the infused-faith account, baptism gives the grace necessary for saving faith. All subsequent catechesis, including that leading to entrance, finds an objective point of reference for its faith-forming and faith-shaping enterprise in the inherent, infused grace of baptism.

FUTURE FAITH

Second, a more subjective view is found among the Reformed who see in baptism the promise of future faith for infants.[108] The emphasis within the Reformed confessions is squarely on baptism as a sign of God's electing,

---

105. *CCC*, 1254 [351], emphasis added. The *CCC* closely links the ongoing catechesis of members to the church's liturgy, even calling this ongoing catechesis mystagogy, as we have already discussed in this chapter: " 'The liturgy is the summit toward which the activity of the Church is directed; it is also the font from which all her power flows.' It is therefore the privileged place for catechizing the People of God. 'Catechesis is intrinsically linked with the whole of liturgical and sacramental activity, for it is in the sacraments, especially in the Eucharist, that Christ Jesus works in fullness for the transformation of men.' " It continues, "Liturgical catechesis aims to initiate people into the mystery of Christ (It is 'mystagogy.') by proceeding from the visible to the invisible, from the sign to the thing signified, from the 'sacraments' to the 'mysteries' " (*CCC*, 1074-75 [303]).

106. *CCT*, 200.

107. In a statement similar to Luther's definition of baptism and grounding of baptismal validity in his 1529 catechisms, the *CCC* states: "Hence Baptism is a bath of water in which the 'imperishable seed' of the Word of God produces its life-giving effect (1 Pet 1:23; cf. Eph 5:26). St. Augustine says of Baptism: 'The word is brought to the material element, and it becomes a sacrament' " (*CCC*, 1228 [346]). It is important to remember in these views that while a sacrament must be valid to be effective, adherents typically qualify that a valid sacrament is *not automatically* effective.

108. As will be noted in the subsequent section, this is consistent with Lutheran thought as well.

covenantal love. The baptismal sign is one that leads to faith and assurance (albeit not inevitably).

Though baptism is clearly distinguished from the infused faith or *ex opere operato* understanding, the Heidelberg Catechism views baptism as a "divine pledge and sign" through which "[God] may assure us that we are spiritually cleansed from our sins as really as we are externally washed with water."[109] Similarly, the Westminster Confession states, "Baptism is a sacrament ... [that is] to be unto [the party baptized] a sign and seal of the covenant of grace, of his ingrafting into Christ, of regeneration, of remission of sins, and of his giving up unto God, through Jesus Christ, to walk in the newness of life."[110] The sign and seal of baptism are abiding and the sacrament is not to be repeated.[111] The function of baptism as an abiding, objective sign of God's saving disposition toward the baptizand is not limited to confessing adults.

Representative of the broader tradition, the Heidelberg Catechism defends infant baptism on the grounds that infants, "as well as the adult, are included in the covenant and church of God; and since redemption from sin by the blood of Christ, and *the Holy Ghost, the author of faith, is promised to them no less than to the adult.*" It is through baptism, "as a sign of the covenant, [that they are] also admitted into the Christian church, and ... distinguished from the children of unbelievers."[112] Thus, the benefits of the covenant, including the promise of "the Holy Spirit, the author of faith," are pledged in baptism categorically to those within the covenant, including infants.

The gift of the faith-authoring Spirit is not necessarily conferred at the time of baptism. As the Westminster Confession makes clear,

> The efficacy of baptism is not tied to that moment of time wherein it is administered; yet, notwithstanding, by the right use of this ordinance, the grace promised is not only offered, but really exhibited, and conferred, by the Holy Ghost, to such (whether of age or

---

109. Heidelberg Catechism, q. 73 (1563; *RC*, 218).

110. Westminster Confession 28.1 (1647; *RC*, 217), emphasis added; cf. Westminster Shorter Catechism, q. 94, and Westminster Larger Catechism, q. 165.

111. "Baptism once received does continue all a man's life, and is a perpetual sealing of our adoption unto us" (Second Helvetic Confession 20.2 [1566; *RC*, 216]). Cf. Belgic Confession 34; Westminster Confession 28.7.

112. Heidelberg Catechism, q. 74 (1563; *RC*, 220), emphasis added.

infants) as that grace belongeth unto, according to the counsel of God's own will, in His appointed time.[113]

Importantly, it is the right *use* of the sacrament, not the sacrament itself, through which the Spirit conveys the grace offered therein.[114] The timing of this faith is left undefined (simply the "appointed time" of God). While infant faith is theoretically possible according to this statement ("whether of age or infants"), the initial sentence looms large over the timing of faith for baptized infants, for the "efficacy of baptism is not tied to that moment of time wherein it is administered."[115]

As an abiding pledge and sign of God's grace, baptism is framed as a faith-producing instrument of the Spirit. Here infant baptism is understood to be a sanctified tool used by the Spirit to produce and sustain faith long after its administration.[116] The unrepeatability of baptism bears witness to its latent effectiveness as an instrumental cause of faith.[117]

INFANT FAITH

Finally, a mediating view between the more objective infused-faith (or *ex opere operato*) and future-faith views is infant faith (*fides infantium*). Concerning timing, the concept of infant faith is closer to the *ex opere operato* view, since faith is given in the baptismal event.[118] However, with the

---

113. Westminster Confession of Faith 28.6 (1647; RC, 217, 219).

114. As is evident in discussions of the Lord's Supper within Reformed sacramental theology, a spiritual interpretation regarding the sacramental action (esp. regeneration) is evident here. The water of baptism is not efficacious in itself, "for the blood of Jesus Christ only, and the Holy Ghost cleanse us from all sin" (Heidelberg Catechism, q. 72 [1563; RC, 218]). For similar statements on the parallel action of the Spirit alongside (not in) the water of baptism, see Belgic Confession 34; Westminster Confession of Faith 28.5.

115. Westminster Confession of Faith 28.6 (1647; RC, 217, 219).

116. This accords with Calvin's position as expressed in the *Institutes*: "The objection [that baptism should be preceded by faith] is easily disposed of by the fact, that children are baptized for *future* repentance and faith. Though these are not yet formed in them, yet *the seed of both lies hid in them* by the secret operation of the Spirit. This answer at once overthrows all the objections which are twisted against us out of the meaning of baptism" (Calvin, *Institutes* 4.16.20 [trans. Beveridge], emphasis added).

117. Cf. Westminster Confession of Faith 28.7 (1647; RC, 219).

118. Luther and the Lutheran tradition, however, are staunchly opposed to an *ex opere operato* (or *opus operatum*) understanding of the sacraments (i.e., view that the sacraments are *effective* merely "by the work done" apart from the proper disposition by the recipient). "It is simply a Judaistic opinion to think that we are justified through ceremonies without a proper disposition in the heart, that is, apart from faith" (Apology of the Augsburg Confession 221.18). See also Augsburg Confession (BC 70–71.29); Apology of the Augsburg Confession

future-faith view, the infant-faith view understands baptism as a kind of visible form of God's word. Jaroslav Pelikan notes that Augustine's notion of the sacraments as the "visible Word of God" "became a primary mark of Protestant sacramental thought."[119] Pelikan's full discussion of the forms of God's word in Luther (oral, written, and visible) helpfully shows the ways in which each form interacts with and depends on the others.[120] Put briefly, the visible form of God's word (the sacraments) prevents the oral form (proclamation) and written form of God's word (Scripture) from becoming abstract and impersonal; and the oral and written forms prevent the visible form from becoming magical superstition.

With this close connection between word and sacrament in the background, baptism is thus cast as a proclamation of God's word through which a baptizand may hear and respond to God's work in Jesus Christ. This hearing and responding is mysterious. While Calvin was willing to entertain the possibility of infant knowledge and faith,[121] more developed examples of this view are found within the theology of Luther.

Though there is scholarly debate about the constancy of an infant-faith view in Luther's thought, he indisputably argues for its possibility and reasonableness in his polemics against credobaptists.[122] In arguing for the plausibility of infant faith Luther places the burden of proof on his opponents.

(*BC* 151–52.207; 190.12; 191.25; 222.23; 259.11–12; 268–69.59). Nonetheless, even a scholar sympathetic to Luther's theology admits, "Baptism [for Luther] possesses such an objective reality, that it seems to take on an *ex opere operato* character." See David P. Scaer, "Luther, Baptism, and the Church Today," *Concordia Theological Quarterly* 62.4 (1998): 265.

119. Jaroslav Pelikan, *Luther's Works: Luther the Expositor; Introduction to the Reformer's Exegetical Writings Companion Volume* (St. Louis: Concordia, 1959), 219–20. See Augustine, *Tractates on the Gospel according to St. John* 80.3 (*NPNF*¹ 7:344).

120. Pelikan, *Luther the Expositor*, 219–36.

121. Calvin, *Institutes* 4.16.19 (trans. Beveridge): "I would not rashly affirm that [infants] are endued with the same faith which we experience in ourselves or have any knowledge at all resembling faith, (this I would rather leave undecided); but I would somewhat curb the stolid arrogance of those men who, as with inflated cheeks affirm or deny whatever suits them." Calvin's discussions of infant faith have a very different feel from those of Luther. Calvin does not ground his discussion on the close connection of word and sacrament (as will soon be discussed) but rather God's sovereign ability to reveal himself and regenerate in other ways: "But what I have said again and again I now repeat, that, for regenerating us, doctrine is an incorruptible seed, if indeed we are fit to perceive it; but when, from nonage, we are incapable of being taught, God takes his own methods of regenerating" (Calvin, *Institutes* 4.16.31 [trans. Beveridge]); cf. Lewis Bevens Schenck, *The Presbyterian Doctrine of Children in the Covenant*, Yale Studies in Theology 12 (New Haven: Yale University Press, 1940), 21–22.

122. Luther did not argue for infant faith at every point in his career. For example, early in his career Luther asserted vicarious or "inpoured faith" (e.g., *Babylonian Captivity* [1520; *LW* 36:73]).

When [those who deny infant baptism] say, "Children cannot believe," how can they be sure of that? Where is the Scripture by which they would prove it and on which they would build? They imagine this, I suppose, because children do not speak or have understanding. But such a fancy is deceptive, yea, altogether false, and we cannot build on what we imagine.[123]

Against the line of attack that infants cannot believe and therefore should not be baptized, Luther finds both exegetical and theological warrant for the possibility and reasonableness of infant faith in baptism.

Luther finds exegetical warrant for the possibility of infant faith in passages that speak of infants as "innocents" (e.g., Ps 106:37; Matt 2:16), children as inheritors of the kingdom (Matt 19:14), and the account of John the Baptist's in utero response to Jesus (Luke 1:41). Such passages "tell us that children may and can believe, though they do not speak or understand."[124]

Drawing from John the Baptist's leaping in the womb, Luther makes a theological argument for the reasonableness of infant faith:

We can hardly deny that the same Christ is present at baptism and in baptism, in fact is himself the baptizer, who in those days came in his mother's womb to John. In baptism he can speak as well through the mouth of the priest, as when he spoke through his mother. Since then he is present, speaks, and baptizes, why should not his Word and baptism call forth spirit and faith in the child as then it produced faith in John? He is the same one who speaks and acts then and now. Even before, he had said through Isaiah [55:11], "His word shall not return empty. ..." I have cited these many verses showing

---

Nonetheless, it is generally accepted that by 1522 Luther shifted from vicarious faith (i.e., alien faith) to *fides infantium* as a primary accent, even if for only a season. See Bernhard Lohse, *Martin Luther's Theology: Its Historical and Systematic Development*, ed. and trans. Roy A. Harrisville (Minneapolis: Fortress, 1999), 304; cf. Luther, *Defense and Explanation of All Articles* (1520; LW 32:14). Jonathan Trigg asserts that the doctrine "first advanced, and later receded." See Trigg's summary of the debate over the constancy of Luther's shift in Trigg, *Baptism in the Theology of Martin Luther* (New York: Brill, 1994), 103n193.

123. Luther, *Concerning Rebaptism* (1528; LW 40:241–42); cf. Trigg, *Baptism in the Theology*, 103.

124. Luther, *Concerning Rebaptism* (LW 40:242).

that they can believe, and that it is reasonable to hold that they do believe.[125]

His argument echoes themes central to his broader baptismal theology: Christ is present, Christ baptizes, Christ speaks, and through his word Christ brings about faith in the child. These themes are apparent in Luther's definition and explanation of baptism especially as found in his 1529 catechisms.

Luther's definition of baptism in his *Small Catechism* delineates three parts to the sacrament. Baptism is "[1] water enclosed in [2] God's command and connected with [3] God's Word."[126] Notably, all three of these parts are objective realities distinct from the baptizand.

First, baptism is understood as water baptism. Importantly, the water is not by itself. It is not a mere external washing; it is "enclosed in God's command and connected with God's Word."[127] For Luther, word and sacrament are inseparable. Apart from the word of God, there is no salvation. In his treatise *The Freedom of a Christian* (1520) Luther lauds the role of God's word in salvation: "Let us then consider it certain and firmly established that the soul can do without anything except the Word of God and that where the Word of God is missing there is no help at all for the soul."[128] Paul Althaus, summarizing this robust relation of word, sacrament, and salvation in Luther's theology, writes, "God confronts us in his word. We receive and accept his word in faith. God deals with men within the context

---

125. Luther, *Concerning Rebaptism* (LW 40:242–43). Luther adds the following to the quote above: "Now it is up to you to bring forth a single Scripture verse which proves that children cannot believe in baptism. I have cited these many verses showing that they can believe, and that it is reasonable to hold that they do believe. *I grant that we do not understand how they do believe, or how faith is created.* But that is not the point here" (emphasis added). The explanation provided prior to this qualifying statement provides at least a partial explanation about *how* infants believe, namely, by the presence, action, and speech of Christ. Unless Luther is attempting to walk back his entire paragraph (which is improbable), his statement is a recognition that the doctrine has not been circumscribed in his preceding explanation and remains mysterious.

126. Luther, *Small Catechism* (1529; BC, 359.1–2). A similar definition appears in his Smalcald Articles (1537): "Baptism is nothing other than God's Word in the water, commanded by God's institution, or, as Paul says, 'washing by the Word'" (BC 319:5.1).

127. Luther, *Small Catechism* (1529; BC, 359.1–2).

128. Martin Luther, "On the Freedom of a Christian," in *Three Treatises*, 279.

of this correlation between the promise of the gospel and faith. And Luther understands the sacraments within this context."[129]

For Luther, the sacraments play an instrumental role in producing faith precisely because of their intimate connection to God's word. The value of the external sign of water baptism rests in the fact that the water is not alone; it has been "enclosed in God's command and connected with God's Word."[130] Answering the claim that only faith is needed for salvation and not the sacramental sign of baptism, Luther writes, "Faith must have something to believe—something to which it may cling and upon which it may stand. Thus faith clings to the water and believes it to be baptism, in which there is sheer salvation and life, not through the water ... but through its incorporation with God's Word and ordinance and the joining of his name to it."[131] In the *Small Catechism* Luther asks, "How can water do such great things?" To this he replies, "Clearly the water does not do it, but the Word of God, which is with and alongside the water, and faith, which trusts this Word of God in the water."[132] In all this it is clear that for Luther, baptism is water joined with the word of God.

Second, for Luther, the "command" of baptism is the command to be baptized, specifically as found in the Great Commission (Matt 28:19).[133]

---

129. Paul Althaus, *The Theology of Martin Luther* (Philadelphia: Fortress, 1966), 345.

130. Luther, *Small Catechism* (1529; BC, 359.1–2). Robert Kolb asserts, "Baptism is a good example of Luther's ontology of the Word: God speaks, and the reality of salvation takes place in the life of God's chosen people." See Kolb, " 'What Benefit Does the Soul Receive from a Handful of Water?': Luther's Preaching on Baptism, 1528–1539," *Concordia Journal* 25.4 (1999): 352. As noted earlier, the Roman Catholic tradition at times uses similar word-sacrament language as Luther (*CCC*, 1228 [346]). Whereas on the Roman view baptism could be wrecked by postbaptismal sins to which the grace of penance must be added (a "second plank," as Jerome calls it), Luther understood penance or repentance as "nothing else than a return and approach to baptism, to resume and practice what has earlier been begun but abandoned" (*Large Catechism* [1529; BC, 466.79]).

131. Luther, *Large Catechism* (1529; BC, 460.29).

132. Luther, *Small Catechism* (1529; BC, 359.9–10). This understanding echoes in Melanchthon's Apology of the Augsburg Confession (1530), "And God moves our hearts through the word and the rite at the same time so that they believe and receive faith just as Paul says [Rom 10:17], 'So faith comes from what is heard.' For just as the Word enters through the ear in order to strike the heart, so also the rite enters through the eye in order to move the heart. The word and the rite have the same effect. Augustine put it well when he said that the sacrament is a 'visible word,' because the rite is received by the eyes and is, as it were, a picture of the Word, signifying the same thing as the Word. Therefore both have the same effect" (Apology of the Augsburg Confession [1531; BC, 219–220.5; cf. 270–71.70]). Just prior to this, the number of sacraments was defined as three: the Lord's Supper, baptism, and absolution. Cf. Augustine, *Tractates on John* 80.3 (on John 15:3; NPNF¹ 7:344).

133. As quoted in the *Small Catechism* (1529; BC, 359.4).

God's command gives baptism a "divine origin" and makes baptism a divine action. The divine origin of baptism means it cannot be dismissed as human invention. "It is solemnly and strictly commanded," Luther writes, "that we must be baptized or we shall not be saved, so that we are not to regard it as an indifferent matter, like putting on a new red coat." Further, Luther argues that baptism is God's act. He supports this with the observation that baptism is in God's name. "To be baptized in God's name," he writes, "is to be baptized not by human beings but by God himself. Although it is performed by human hands, it is nevertheless truly God's own act."[134]

Finally, the "word" to which baptism is "connected" is the promise of the gospel. Luther finds this promise succinctly expressed in Mark 16:16, "Whoever believes and is baptized will be saved, but whoever does not believe will be damned."[135] The benefit of the promise connected to baptism is salvation itself. In the *Large Catechism*, Luther writes, "The power, effect, benefit, fruit, and purpose of baptism is that it saves. ... To be saved ... is nothing else than to be delivered from sin, death, and the devil, to enter into Christ's kingdom, and to live with him forever." The command, gospel promise, and name of God connected to the water of baptism make it of inestimable worth; indeed, it is a "treasure ... greater and nobler than heaven and earth."[136]

Though counterintuitive and mysterious, infant faith finds peculiar possibility within Luther's baptismal theology precisely because the faith-producing word of God is "with and alongside the water."[137] As Kenneth Craycraft notes, "The Word makes the element the sacrament and the sacrament brings the Word to the individual."[138] The water of baptism is thus a delivery mechanism for the life-giving, faith-producing word of God, and it may function in this way even for infants. Pelikan observes,

---

134. Luther, *Large Catechism* (1529; BC, 457.6, 9–10).

135. As quoted in *Small Catechism* (1529; BC, 359.7–8).

136. Luther, *Large Catechism* (1529; BC, 458.16; 459.24); cf. *Small Catechism* (1529; BC, 359.5–6).

137. Luther, *Small Catechism* (1529; BC, 359.9–10). See also John Mueller's approving discussion of Luther's infant faith view in *Christian Dogmatics* (332–33, 502–5). Though some of the Lutheran baptismal interrogations are directed at infants, Mueller finds these anticipatory of the faith that is wrought in the moment of baptism. Baptism, after all, is the sacrament, not the human ceremonies that precede it. "Baptism is indeed a *medium iustificationis*, or the means of regeneration, by which faith is engendered" (503).

138. Kenneth R. Craycraft, "Sign and Word: Martin Luther's Theology of the Sacraments," *Restoration Quarterly* 32.3 (1990): 147.

"In his exegesis of passages on Baptism [Luther] took the position that the unique need of the infant was uniquely met by the distinctive quality of Baptism and by no other form of the Word of God. Thus God addressed His Word of redemption to the infant through Baptism."[139] While *fides infantium* seems odd to critics, one should recognize that the address of God in baptism makes infant faith a plausible assertion for Luther.

Additionally, the nature of faith also makes infant faith plausible for Luther. Faith is God's work and gift. In the treatise *Babylonian Captivity of the Church* (1520), Luther writes, "*Faith is a work of God, not of man*, as Paul teaches [Eph. 2:8]. The other works he works through us and with our help, but this one alone he works in us and without our help."[140] Luther maintained that faith is the work of God throughout his career. Preaching on John 3:4 in 1538, Luther states that that Holy Spirit is given in baptism and that he "works faith in us."[141] For Luther, faith is not simply a human response that originates from within the individual apart from God, but rather, faith is the work and gift of God.

The objective nature of faith and of baptism combined with the unpretentious state of infants leads Luther to conclude that infant baptism is the surest form of baptism. In his treatise *Concerning Rebaptism* (1528) Luther writes, "I maintain ... that the most certain form of baptism is child baptism. For an adult might deceive and come to Christ as Judas and have himself baptized. But a child cannot deceive." Infants do not bring their own works, but rather come to Christ "that his Word and work might be effective in them, move them, and make them holy, because his Word and work cannot be without fruit. ... Were [his word and work] to fail here it would fail everywhere and be in vain, which is impossible."[142]

Importantly, though he argued for the possibility of infant faith, Luther did not hinge the validity of baptism on an individual's faith, whether

---

139. Pelikan, *Luther the Expositor*, 230.

140. Luther, *Babylonian Captivity* (*LW* 36:62), emphasis added.

141. Luther, *Sermons on the Gospel of St. John* (*LW* 22:285). In his preface to the book of Romans (1546), Luther writes, "Faith ... is a divine work in us which changes us and makes us to be born anew of God, John 1[:12–13]. It kills the old Adam and makes us altogether different men, in heart and spirit and mind and powers; and it brings with it the Holy Spirit." See Martin Luther, "Preface to the Epistle of St. Paul to the Romans [1546]" (*LW* 35:370).

142. Luther, *Concerning Baptism* (1528; *LW* 40:244); cf. statement in his postil in *LW* 40:229.

infant or adult; rather, faith represents the proper *use* of baptism.[143] In his *Large Catechism*, Luther writes, "We do not put the main emphasis on whether the person baptized believes or not, for in the latter case baptism does not become invalid. Everything depends upon the Word and commandment of God."[144] Regardless of the faith of the recipient, baptism "remains forever."[145] All one needs to do to make proper use of one's baptism is to believe the command of God that encloses it and the word of God connected to it. Though an infant may believe in the baptismal event, even if he or she does not, the validity of baptism remains, as does the possibility of future faith.[146] "We bring the child with the intent and hope that it may believe, and we pray God to grant it faith. But we do not baptize on this basis, but solely on the command of God."[147]

---

143. Luther allowed for faith to save apart from baptism in cases of necessity. "Faith is such a necessary part of the sacrament that it can save even without the sacrament" (*Babylonian Captivity of the Church*, 190). Althaus notes, "In 1533, Luther still maintains this relationship between word and sacrament [i.e., that the word can save without the sacrament]. 'For the word can exists without the sacrament, but the sacrament cannot exist without the word. And in case of necessity, a man can be saved without the sacrament, but not without the word; this is true of those who desire baptism but die before they can receive it." See Paul Althaus, *The Theology of Martin Luther* (Philadelphia: Fortress, 1966), 349n19; cf. D. Patrick Ramsey, "*Sola Fide* Compromised? Martin Luther and the Doctrine of Baptism," *Themelios* 34.2 (2009), section 3, http://themelios.thegospelcoalition.org/article/sola-fide-compromised-martin-luther-and-the-doctrine-of-baptism. One must not, however, despise the sacrament and neglect it when it is available: "Whoever rejects baptism rejects God's Word, faith, and Christ, who directs and binds us to baptism" (Luther, *Large Catechism* [*BC*, 460.31]).

144. Luther, *Large Catechism* (1529; *BC*, 463.52–53). In his 1528 treatise "Concerning Rebaptism" Luther argues that baptism administered on the basis of one's faith is uncertain, for Luther was convinced that one's faith was never complete ("Always something is lacking in faith"; *LW* 40:253). Further, only God can discern the hearts of men. Thus, reasons Luther, "Whoever bases baptism on faith and baptizes on chance and not on certainty that faith is present does nothing better than he who baptizes him who has no faith" (*LW* 40:239–40).

145. "Therefore baptism remains forever. Even though someone falls from it and sins, we always have access to it so that we may again subdue the old creature" (Luther, *Large Catechism* [1529; *BC*, 466.77]).

146. "Even if infants did not believe—which, however, is not the case, as we have proved—still the baptism would be valid and no one should rebaptize them. Similarly, the sacrament is not vitiated if someone approaches it with an evil purpose. Moreover, that same person would not be permitted on account of that abuse to take it again the very same hour, as if not having truly received the sacrament the first time. That would be to blaspheme and desecrate the sacrament in the worst way. How dare we think that God's Word and ordinance should be wrong and invalid because we use it wrongly" (Luther, *Large Catechism* [1529; *BC*, 463.55]).

147. Luther, *Large Catechism* (1529; *BC*, 464.57).

PRELIMINARY IMPLICATIONS

In sum, Luther's position that infant faith is possible offers an interesting example of the retrospective model's projected view of baptism as a cause of faith. While *fides infantium* is a minority view, it is theoretically important because it stands as the most objective Protestant version of baptism and mediates the objective and subjective examples examined above (infused- and future-faith views respectively). Here, faith is conveyed to an infant through the word of God *in* baptism. Catechesis is, therefore, not simply an activity that looks back to baptism for its content; rather, *baptism is the first catechetical lesson.* As Pelikan aptly describes it, "God addresse[s] His Word of redemption to the infant through Baptism."[148] Luther says that it is this first word that one must "study and practice all his or her life."[149]

All three views sketched in this section project a view of baptism as an instrumental cause of faith. Though variously described, faith begins and is grounded in baptism. Importantly, all three views deny that personal faith grounds baptismal validity. Rather, baptism is objectively, not subjectively, grounded and is under no circumstances to be repeated. Since baptism is understood to be the starting point of faith, the catechesis leading to entrance is an unfolding or unpacking of the word of God first spoken to the individual in baptism. Thus, in the logic of the retrospective model, the catechesis that follows baptism and leads to entrance draws on the content and existential reality (i.e., "you are baptized") of baptism.

PROJECTED VIEW OF THE CHURCH

The retrospective model projects a two-tier or mixed-body (*corpus permixteum*) view of the church composed of communicant and noncommunicant members. The first class of members is fully initiated and visibly manifests this initiation through ongoing participation at the Lord's Supper. The second class of members is living in the liminal space between baptism and first Communion. These individuals have received the objective sign of baptism but have not yet given a public profession of faith officially recognized by the church. They are considered members, but they do not manifest this membership visibly through the Lord's Supper.

---

148. Pelikan, *Luther the Expositor*, 230.
149. Luther, *Large Catechism* (1529; BC, 461).

The model also projects a Christendom view of church and society, because it assumes sufficient societal structures in which the faith of noncommunicant members can be grown and formed. Commenting on the separation of confirmation from infant baptism, a pattern consonant with the retrospective model, Aidan Kavanagh argues that such a model "presupposes a sustained Catholic birthrate and functioning forms of religious education such as the parochial school."[150] Similarly, Paul Covino identifies what he calls the "environmentalist school" of Roman Catholic thought on infant baptism. One author who Covino puts forward as an exemplar of this school, Nathan Mitchell, writes, "The church ... is more than a community of transformed adults. It is also a nurturing environment that encourages gradual growth in faith for individuals and groups of all conditions, including children."[151] Because of its protraction of the initiation process, the retrospective model projects a Christendom or environmentalist view of the church. Here, the church through baptism plants seeds of faith, and then through its fellowship and catechesis supplies an environment conducive to the formation and growth of faith in the initiate. Members pass through a metamorphosis from noncommunicant immaturity to communicant maturity.

SUMMARY

This chapter has sketched the major contours of the retrospective model. Regarding entrance, the retrospective model, along with the prospective model to follow, affirms credocommunion: only those are admitted to the Lord's Supper who have reached an age of discretion and are able to examine and prepare themselves.

Baptism is here given an objective validity that is grounded in the command to baptize and the faith of the church (both its confession of faith and collective subjective faith), not the faith of the baptizand. Though faith can be related to baptism in a variety of ways (e.g., infused, infant, or future), the model makes baptism an instrumental cause of faith. Importantly, the faith brought about through baptism is prerequisite for entrance.

---

150. Kavanagh, *Shape of Baptism*, 196–97.

151. Nathan Mitchell, "The Once and Future Child: Towards a Theology of Childhood," *Living Light* 12 (1975): 429–30, as cited by Paul F. X. Covino, "The Postconciliar Infant Baptism Debate in the American Catholic Church," *Worship* 56.3 (1982): 252.

Catechesis in this model leads to an examination of the catechumen's faith prior to entrance. This examination is often accomplished through a formal sacrament or rite of confirmation, which serves as a capstone to the catechetical process leading to entrance. Because confirmation is separated in time from baptism and preceded by catechesis, it is given a subjective dynamic that distinguishes it from that found in the baptism model. Additionally, the retrospective model grounds the catechesis required for entrance on the theological density of baptism. As will be discussed in the subsequent chapter, the prospective model also draws from the dense theology of baptism for its catechesis. The retrospective model, however, uniquely makes baptism an *existential* grounding for catechesis. On the retrospective model, the triune God expounded in pre-*entrance* catechesis is the God who, by the hands of the minister, has already baptized the catechumen.

The retrospective model is readily illustrated by the practice of infant baptism in combination with credocommunion. This fact raises questions regarding the exploratory catalyst question that chapter 5 will address. For example, is the theological catalyst that gives rise to the use of the retrospective model simply the age of the person being baptized? In chapter 5 I will argue that the matter is not so simply resolved. Nonetheless, even if the later exploratory discussion leaves the reader unconvinced, the models developed in chapters 2–4 hold explanatory power for mapping the liturgical logic of major models of Christian initiation. Before turning to the heuristic exploration (ch. 5), we need to develop the fourth model of our framework, the prospective model. It is to this task that we now turn.

4

—

PROSPECTIVE MODEL

When the person being baptized goes down into the water, he who baptizes him, putting his hand on him, shall say: "Do you believe in God, the Father Almighty?" And *the person being baptized shall say: "I believe."* Then holding his hand on his head, he shall baptize him once.

And then he shall say: "Do you believe in Christ Jesus, the Son of God, who was born of the Holy Spirit and the Virgin Mary, and was crucified under Pontius Pilate, and was dead and buried, and rose again the third day, alive from the dead, and ascended into heaven, and sat down at the right hand of the Father, and will come to judge the living and the dead?" And *when the person says: "I believe,"* he is baptized again.

And again the deacon shall say: "Do you believe in the Holy Spirit, in the holy church, and in the resurrection of the body?" *Then the person being baptized shall say: "I believe,"* and he is baptized a third time.[1]

With these words, the Apostolic Tradition (ca. 215) describes an early Christian baptismal liturgy. The approach here illustrates key elements of a different baptismal model that this chapter will unpack, a model we will here call the prospective model.

The previous chapter examined the first of two interdependent models that make both baptism and catechesis prerequisites for entrance into the visible fellowship of the church as it is expressed at the Communion Table. There I sought to show that on the retrospective model catechesis as a means of entrance looks back to baptism, on which it is grounded. Baptism

---

1. Apostolic Tradition 21.12–18 (*CCFCT* 1:61), emphasis added.

on that model can in many ways be understood as the chief catechetical lesson of which all subsequent catechesis is essentially an unpacking. The prospective model is the next interdependent model to be examined.

Category	Independent	Prerequisite(s) of entrance? Baptism or catechesis or both?	Interdependent			Prerequisite(s) of entrance? Baptism or catechesis or both?	Independent
Model	Baptism		Retrospective	Orientation of catechesis to baptism	Prospective		Catechesis
Sequence	Baptism ↓ **Entrance** ↓ Catechesis		Baptism ↓ Catechesis ↓ **Entrance**		Catechesis ↓ Baptism ↓ **Entrance**		Catechesis ↓ **Entrance** ↓ (Baptism)

←————— OBJECTIVE   SUBJECTIVE —————→

The prospective model marks a shift in its first position from baptism to catechesis. This distinguishes it from the two models to its left—the baptism model and retrospective model—which place baptism in the first position of their initiatory patterns of entrance. Moving from left to right on the framework, the last two models, the prospective model and catechesis model, place catechesis in the first position. In placing catechesis at the start of the initiatory process, the latter two models are decidedly more subjective than their counterparts. The present chapter provides a profile of the prospective model that will fill out the remaining slot of the explanatory framework. Once we have completed the construction of the typology in this chapter, we will work through a heuristic and exploratory analysis in the subsequent chapter. As was the case with chapter 3, I will give more attention to the prospective model in order to help fund some of the heuristic work that will follow. Specifically, we will explore the possibility of a theological catalyst that gives rise to one interdependent model over the other.

DEFINITION

The prospective model is an interdependent model in which baptism and catechesis are both prerequisites for entrance. Catechetical preparation, whether formal or informal, prior to baptism and entrance is a key mark of this model. Here, however, catechesis anticipates baptism and grounds baptismal administration. The catechetical process concludes with examination of some sort that is connected to baptism.

Historically, this model finds expression in various forms of a catechumenate that lead to baptism and first Communion. In contrast to the catechesis model (ch. 2), the prospective model examined in this chapter makes baptism prerequisite to entrance. Thus, the prospective model gives a stronger corporate aspect to baptism than does the catechesis model.

BAPTISM AND ENTRANCE

As noted in the previous chapter, the first three models of the framework (left to right)—baptism, retrospective, and prospective models—make water baptism prerequisite to entrance. The prospective model places baptism and first Communion in close relation, removing the liminal space between baptism and entrance that is characteristic of the retrospective model. The close proximity of baptism and first Communion is similar to that found in the baptism model; however, the prospective model makes catechesis and examination a prerequisite for both baptism and first Communion.

Again moving left to right, the last three models of the framework—retrospective, prospective, and catechesis models—affirm credocommunion. The term "credocommunion" (lit. "believers' Communion") refers to the practice of only administering the Lord's Supper to those who have given a credible profession of faith and manifested a capacity for self-examination prior to reception.[2] However, only the last two models—prospective and catechesis models—require similar capacities as well as a personal profession of faith prior to or in *baptism*.

Notable examples of this pattern appear early in the Christian tradition. For example, the Didache (ca. 60–150) states, "Before the baptism, let the one baptizing and the one who is to be baptized fast, as well as any others who are able. Also, you must instruct the one who is to be baptized to fast for one or two days beforehand."[3] Such instruction implies that the baptizand can receive and follow it.

---

2. See previous chapter for a fuller discussion of the biblical support for and confessional examples of credocommunion.

3. Didache 7.4 (*CCFCT* 1:42).

Additionally, in his *First Apology* (AD 155), Justin Martyr describes the practice of Christian baptism and its connection to instruction. He writes,

> As many as are persuaded and believe that the things we teach and say are true, and undertake to live accordingly, are instructed to pray and ask God with fasting for the remission of their past sins, while we pray and fast with them. Then they are brought by us where there is water, and are born again in the same manner of rebirth by which we ourselves were born again, for they then receive washing in water in the name of God the Father and Master of all, and of our savior, Jesus Christ, and of the Holy Spirit.[4]

Justin goes on to call the washing of baptism "illumination" because "those who learn these things [i.e., remission of sins through Jesus Christ] are illuminated in the mind. And he who is illuminated is washed in the name of Jesus Christ, who was crucified under Pontius Pilate, and in the name of the Holy Spirit, who through the prophets foretold all the things about Jesus."[5] Importantly, the illumination of the mind through the teaching and instruction of the church leads one to the washing of baptism. The baptism of infants is not mentioned, nor does it matter for the point in view. Here, the distinctive pattern of instruction leading to baptism is evident.

Similarly, recall the Apostolic Tradition (ca. 215) quotation with which we opened this chapter. This liturgy evinces the practice of baptismal examination and, by extension, prebaptismal instruction. Here the baptizand is interrogated regarding specific doctrinal or creedal content that follows ("Do you believe in ...") and is not baptized until affirming personal faith in these teachings ("I believe"). This dialogue presupposes catechesis and personal faith that has led to and is now being expressed in baptism.

I do not adduce the above examples to build a case for the existence or propriety of credobaptism over paedobaptism, but rather to note the prebaptismal orientation that instruction took (at least at times) in the liturgy and disciple-making practices of the early church.

---

4. Justin Martyr, *First Apology* 1.61.2–3 (*CCFCT* 1:46).
5. Justin Martyr, *First Apology* 1.61.12–13 (*CCFCT* 1:47).

BAPTISM AND FAITH

The prospective model places catechesis before baptism. In so doing, the model grounds baptismal administration on the personal faith of the baptizand in a way that distinguishes it from the retrospective model. On the logic of the prospective model, personal faith is prerequisite for baptism and in some cases is understood to be actualized through baptism. While there are differing ways in which faith is related to baptism in this sequence, the effect is the same: baptism is a sanctified instrument whereby the personal faith (*fides qua creditur*) in the content of the Christian faith (*fides quae creditur*) is manifested to the church and to the world.[6] Faith leads to baptism, and baptism administered on this condition leads to entrance.

In what follows, I will note three key examples of this orientation: (1) sacramental adult baptism,[7] (2) credobaptism, and (3) conversion-baptism. These examples highlight the objective-subjective flexibility of the prospective model. A mediating position (conversion-baptism) has been included and treated more fully than the others because of its theoretical usefulness in considering catalytic possibilities in chapter 5.

SACRAMENTAL ADULT BAPTISM:
FAITH AS RECEPTOR FOR BAPTISMAL GRACE

The most objective form of the prospective model is found in the adult baptism of the Roman Catholic and Eastern Orthodox traditions.[8] Here, baptismal grace is conveyed *ex opere operato* ("from the work performed").

---

6. For example, the *RCIA* states, "The faith of those to be baptized is not simply the faith of the Church, but the personal faith of each one of them and each one of them is expected to keep it a living faith" (*RCIA*, 211 [124]). *Fides qua creditor* = "The faith by which one believes." *Fides quae creditor* = "The faith which is believed." For discussion of these terms see Pelikan, *Credo*, 49.

7. The term "sacramental" may be misleading in that conversion-baptism also claims to be sacramental. A key distinction between these categories as used here is their differing grounds for baptismal validity. Sacramental adult baptism as used here refers to all forms of adult baptism that are considered valid regardless of any disquieting dispositions or lack of understanding that might come to light later. For example, should a man baptized as an adult later reveal that he had requested baptism in order to win approval as a suitor of a young woman, the church would not require him to be baptized again (e.g., Cyril of Jerusalem, *Procatechesis* 4–5, in *Catechetical Lectures* [*NPNF*² 7:2]). This sort of objective validity is characteristic of both *ex opere operato* baptismal theology (Roman Catholic and Eastern Orthodox) and sacramental Protestant baptismal theology (e.g., Lutheran, Anglican, Presbyterian, Methodist, and in certain streams of Baptist tradition). Conversion-baptism, as will be shown below, grounds baptismal validity on a more subjective footing.

8. "Adult baptism" is the typical term used to refer to the baptism of noninfants (e.g., *CCC*, 1247 [350]: "Since the beginning of the Church, *adult Baptism* is the common practice where

Commenting on the meaning of *ex opere operato*, the Catechism of the Catholic Church emphasizes the work of Christ as mediated through the church. It states,

> Celebrated worthily in faith, the sacraments confer the grace that they signify. They are efficacious because in them Christ himself is at work: it is he who baptized, he who acts in his sacraments in order to communicate the grace that each sacrament signifies. ... This is the meaning of the Church's affirmation that the sacraments act *ex opere operato* (literally: "by the very fact of the action's being performed"), i.e., by virtue of the saving work of Christ, accomplished once for all. It follows that "the sacrament is not wrought by the righteousness of either the celebrant or the recipient, but by the power of God." From the moment that a sacrament is celebrated in accordance with the intention of the Church, the power of Christ and his Spirit acts in and through it, independently of the personal holiness of the minister. Nevertheless, the fruits of the sacraments also depend on the disposition of the one who receives them.[9]

In its canons on the sacraments in general, the Council of Trent states, "If anyone says that grace is not conferred by the sacraments of the new law through the sacramental action itself, but that faith in the divine promise is by itself sufficient for obtaining the grace, let him be anathema."[10] In short, *ex opere operato* refers to the inherent effectiveness and validity of a sacrament apart from personal faith. While faith is needed to receive fully the grace of the sacrament, the sacrament contains grace apart from personal faith.

Eastern Orthodoxy also holds to an *ex opere operato* view. John Kamiris notes, "The completeness, the wholeness, of the sacraments is contingent

---

the proclamation of the Gospel is still new. The catechumenate (preparation for Baptism) therefore occupies an important place. This initiation into Christian faith and life should dispose the catechumen to receive the gift of God in Baptism, Confirmation, and the Eucharist" [emphasis added]). Paul Turner explains, "In [canon] law, children of catechetical age are considered adults as far as baptism is concern. Only if they are too young to learn the significance of these rites do we welcome them not as catechumens, but with the rite of infant baptism" ("Confusion over Confirmation," 539).

9. *CCC*, 1127–28 [319].

10. *Dogmatic Decrees of the Council of Trent*, session 7, Canons on the Sacraments in General, 8 (*CCFCT* 2:840).

upon their divine order and institution by the Lord, who is the invisible celebrant and our 'initiator.' It is contingent also upon the canonical position of the officiating clergy and upon the effect, both *ex opere operato* and *ex opere operantis* ['from the work of the worker']."[11] Thus, for both traditions (East and West), God through the church and its sacraments dispenses grace. Baptism stands as the gateway to sacramental grace "since the other Sacraments are accessible through Baptism only."[12]

While emphasizing the objectivity of the sacraments, the Roman and Eastern Orthodox traditions do relate faith to baptism. In these traditions faith is the receptor by which baptismal grace is received personally in its fullness. For example, in his *Reply* (1576) to the Augsburg Confession (1576), the Eastern Orthodox Jeremias II, ecumenical patriarch, affirms the necessity of faith for receiving the saving grace of baptism and the other sacraments of initiation. The initiatory sacraments do not save automatically or mechanically; rather, they must be accompanied by active faith. Commenting on the fourth article of the Augsburg Confession ("Justifying Faith"), Jeremias writes,

> [Concerning the remission of sins] you contend that, as you believe, the remission of sins is granted mainly by faith alone. But the catholic church demands a living faith, which is made evident by good works; for as James says, "faith without works is dead." Furthermore, Basil the Great says: "The grace from above does not come to the one who is not striving. But both of them, the human endeavor and the assistance descending from above through faith, must be mixed together for the perfection of virtue."[13]

Later, agreeing with the thirteenth article of the Augsburg Confession, Jeremias writes, "Thus we, too, condemn those who think that without faith they have the forgiveness of sins and benefit from the sacred ceremonies.

---

11. Karmiris, "Concerning the Sacraments," 22. F. E. Mayer observes that the *ex opere operato* view is less prominent in the Eastern Church (*Religious Bodies of America*, 17). The emphasis on mystery within the Eastern Orthodox Church may have something to do with this. In fact, the sacraments are called "mysteries" in the East (cf. 16).

12. *CCT*, 189. Cf. *CCC*, 1213 [342].

13. Jeremias II, *Reply of Ecumenical Patriarch* (*CCFCT* 1:401). For quotations see Basil of Caesarea, *Short Rules* (PG 31:1085). Jeremias makes similar statements in a subsequent section ("The Ministry of the Word"; *CCFCT* 1:402).

For whatever does not proceed from faith is sin."[14] The sacraments are administered, he concludes, "so that *those who believe* may be sanctified by them, receive the forgiveness of sins, the inheritance of the kingdom, and similar blessings."[15]

In both the Roman and Eastern Orthodox traditions, faith is a prerequisite for adults seeking baptism. For example, the Catechism of the Council of Trent states, "Besides a wish to be baptized, in order to obtain the grace of the Sacrament, faith is also necessary. Our Lord and Saviour has said: 'He that believes and is baptized shall be saved' [Mark 16:14]."[16] Further, the Catechism of the Catholic Church calls baptism "the sacrament of faith."[17] The faith required for baptism, however, is not a "perfect and mature faith, but a beginning that is called to develop." This development takes place in the context of the church. This understanding is manifested in the liturgy of baptism, in which "the catechumen or the godparent is asked: 'What do you ask of God's Church?' the response is: 'Faith!' "[18] Faith, therefore, leads to baptism, and baptism leads to faith.[19]

On this view, prebaptismal catechesis forms the faith that receives sacramental, baptismal grace. For example, the Catechism of the Catholic Church states,

> Since the beginning of the Church, adult Baptism is the common practice where the proclamation of the Gospel is still new. The catechumenate (preparation for Baptism) therefore occupies an important place. This initiation into Christian faith and life [i.e.,

---

14. Jeremias II, *Reply of Ecumenical Patriarch* (*CCFCT* 1:428).

15. Jeremias II, *Reply of Ecumenical Patriarch* (*CCFCT*, 1:428–29), emphasis added.

16. *CCT*, 191. The *RCIA* also reiterates the importance of faith for baptism, stating, "In their renunciation of sin and profession of faith those to be baptized express their explicit faith in the paschal mystery that has already been recalled in the blessing of water and that will be connoted by the words of the sacrament soon to be spoken by the baptizing minister. ... The faith of those to be baptized is not simply the faith of the Church, but the personal faith of each one of them and each one of them is expected to keep it a living faith" (*RCIA*, 211 [124]).

17. *CCC*, 1253 [351]; cf. *RCIA*, 50 [22].

18. *CCC*, 1253 [351].

19. "For all the baptized, children or adults, faith must grow after Baptism. For this reason the Church celebrates each year at the Easter Vigil the renewal of baptismal promises. Preparation for Baptism leads only to the threshold of new life. *Baptism is the source of that new life in Christ* from which the entire Christian life springs forth" (*CCC*, 1254 [351], emphasis added).

the catechumenate] should dispose the catechumen *to receive the gift of God in Baptism, Confirmation, and the Eucharist.*[20]

The catechumenate, therefore, prepares one to receive the grace of baptism and the subsequent sacraments of initiation.

While the catechumenate was at times quite lengthy (three to five years),[21] at minimum, catechetical instruction must be given prior to adult baptismal administration. The Catechism of the Council of Trent speaks of "catechetical instruction" given in the litany of ceremonies leading to baptism. Once the baptismal candidate has entered the church, but prior to coming to the font, the priest "first instructs [the baptizands] in the doctrines of the Christian faith, of which a profession is to be made in Baptism."[22] The rationale for this "brief" instruction is grounded on Matthew 28:19–20. The Tridentine catechism states, "From this command we may learn that Baptism is not to be administered until, as least, the principal truths of our religion are explained."[23]

Given its close relation to instruction about and confession of the person and work of Christ, baptism is called "illumination" or "enlightenment" within the broader Catholic tradition.[24] Justin Martyr states, "And this washing [of baptism] is called 'illumination,' as those who learn these things are illuminated in the mind. And he who is illuminated is washed in the name of Jesus Christ, who was crucified under Pontius Pilate, and in the name of the Holy Spirit, who through the prophets foretold all the things about Jesus."[25] The learning spoken of here refers to that which has preceded baptism through the teaching of the church. Earlier Justin writes, "As many as are persuaded and believe that the things we teach and say are true, and undertake to live accordingly, are instructed to pray and ask God with fasting for the remission of their past sins, while we pray

---

20. *CCC*, 1247 [350].

21. Alan Kreider, "Baptism, Catechism, and the Eclipse of Jesus' Teaching in Early Christianity," *The Mennonite Quarterly Review* 72 (1998): 10; cf. *RCIA*, 76 [38].

22. *CCT*, 205.

23. *CCT*, 205.

24. See Jensen, *Baptismal Imagery*, 91–135.

25. Justin Martyr, *First Apology* 1.61.12–13 (*CCFCT* 1:47). Cf. *CCC*, 1216 [342].

and fast with them." Only upon this giving and receiving of instruction is baptism administered.[26]

Building on the passages from Justin, the Catechism of the Catholic Church asserts, "Having received in Baptism the Word, 'the true light that enlightens every man,' the person baptized has been 'enlightened,' he becomes a 'son of light,' indeed, he becomes 'light' himself."[27] Baptism thus functions as a brightening of the light of the catechesis and concomitant faith that has led one to request baptism.[28]

CREDOBAPTISM: FAITH SIGNIFIED IN BAPTISM

The administration of baptism on the basis of a prior personal profession of faith is variously called "believers' baptism" or "credobaptism."[29] Charles Deweese offers a succinct definition of the view when he affirms that "conversion precedes baptism—that voluntary belief and commitment to Christ *must happen prior* to immersion."[30]

Believers' baptism has a strong confessional tradition within the Radical and English Reformations. For example, Michael Sattler's well-known Schleitheim Confession (1527) makes a strong connection between baptism and prebaptismal instruction:

> Baptism shall be given to all those who have learned repentance and amendment of life, and who believe truly that their sins are taken away by Christ, and to all those who walk in the resurrection of Jesus Christ, and wish to be buried with Him in death, so that they may be resurrected with him, and to all those who with this significance request it [baptism] of us and demand it for themselves. This excludes all infant baptism, the highest and chief abominations

---

26. Justin Martyr, *First Apology* 1.61.2–3 (*CCFCT* 1:46).

27. *CCC*, 1216 [342].

28. Cf. *CCT*, 191, 207.

29. A distinction is made here between the terms "credobaptism" and "credobaptist." "Credobaptism" here designates the administration of baptism on the basis of a personal profession of faith by the baptizand. A credobaptist, however, is one who *only* administers baptism on the basis of a personal profession of faith.

30. Charles W. Deweese, "Believer's Baptism Is Covenant," in *Defining Baptist Convictions: Guidelines for the Twenty-First Century*, ed. Deweese (Franklin, TN: Providence House, 1996), 103, emphasis added.

of the pope. In this you have the foundation and testimony of the apostles. Mt. 28, Mk. 16, Acts 2, 8, 16, 19.[31]

Here we read that only those who have been catechized in the gospel truths of Jesus' death, burial, and resurrection, as well as the theological and ethical meanings of *baptism*, are eligible to receive it. Indeed, unless they personally request it "with this significance"—namely, with the desire "to be buried with him in death, so that they may be resurrected with him"—they are not eligible to receive it. Similarly, the Mennonite Waterland Confession (1580) reserves baptism for "those who hear, believe and freely receive in a penitent heart the doctrine of the holy gospel; for such Christ commanded to be baptized, but by no means infants."[32]

The Particular Baptist London Confession (1644) affirms, "Baptisme is an Ordinance of the NT, given by Christ, to be dispensed onely upon persons professing faith or that are Disciples, or taught, who upon pro-fession of faith, ought to be baptized."[33] The Second London Confession (1677) states that "the only proper subjects" of baptism are "those who do actually profess repentance towards God, faith in, and obedience, to our Lord Jesus."[34] The English, General Baptist Orthodox Creed (1678) denies the legitimacy of infant baptism and affirms that water baptism is "a sign of our entrance into the covenant of grace, and ingrafting into Christ, and into the body of Christ, which is his church." It goes on to state that bap-tism is a prerequisite for church membership ("None ought to be admit-ted into the visible church of Christ, without being first baptized") and, in language similar to the Second London Confession, that it is to be given only to "those which do really profess repentance towards God, and faith in, and obedience to our Lord Jesus Christ."[35]

The Baptist Faith and Message, the current confessional statement of the Southern Baptist Convention, most recently revised in 2000, illustrates

---

31. Schleitheim Confession (1527; *BCF*, 25), emphasis added.
32. Waterland Confession 31 (1580; *BCF*, 60).
33. London Confession 39 (1644; *BCF*, 155).
34. Second London Confession 29.2 (1677; *BCF*, 291).
35. Orthodox Creed 28 (1678; *BCF*, 317–18).

the credobaptist placement of saving faith prior to baptism. The statement on baptism is unchanged from its 1963 predecessor and reads,

> Christian baptism is the immersion *of a believer* in water in the name of the Father, the Son, and the Holy Spirit. It is an act of obedience *symbolizing the believer's faith* in a crucified, buried, and risen Saviour, *the believer's* death to sin, the burial of the old life, and the resurrection to walk in newness of life in Christ Jesus. It is a *testimony to his faith* in the final resurrection of the dead.[36]

Here, baptism is described as "an act of obedience *symbolizing*" saving faith.[37] This faith precedes baptism and is the basis for it. Additionally, the emphasis in this statement is on the subjective elements of the ordinance. Baptism is defined as "an act of obedience." Further, it "symbolizes *the believer's faith ... the believer's death* to sin, [*the believer's*] *burial* of the old life, and [*the believer's*] *resurrection* to walk in newness of life in Christ." Further, baptism "is a testimony to *his* [*i.e., the believer's*] *faith* in the final resurrection of the dead."[38]

In sum, credobaptism symbolizes faith, conversion, and salvation that are already a reality in the baptizand's life. It manifests the reality, but it does not bring the reality into effect either as an efficient cause or as an instrumental one. Better, baptism is an effect of saving faith and conversion. One is baptized because one has already been converted, and it stands as a sign of this conversion.

CONVERSION-BAPTISM: FAITH ACTUALIZED IN BAPTISM

The two major views within Protestant thought on the faith-baptism relationship have historically been credobaptism and paedobaptism. Credobaptism places the personal, saving faith of the baptizand *prior* to baptismal administration, making baptism a symbol of faith.[39] Paedobaptism

---

36. Baptist Faith and Message 7 (2000; *BCF*, 516), emphasis added.

37. Baptist Faith and Message 7 (2000; *BCF*, 516), emphasis added.

38. Baptist Faith and Message 7 (2000; *BCF*, 516), emphasis added.

39. Credobaptism, if understood as baptism administered to a believer, may be applied quite broadly. The notion of personal faith leading to baptism is not unique to those who administer baptism exclusively to believers (Baptists or credobaptists). While distinctions of how grace and the sacramental sign exist, the same movement is evident in virtually all versions of discriminate adult baptism, whether Protestant, Catholic, or Eastern Orthodox.

places the personal, saving faith of the baptizand *after* baptism, making baptism (in some sense) a cause of faith.[40]

Another major option regarding the faith-baptism relationship places the personal, *saving* faith of the baptizand *in* the act of baptism. On this view, baptism is understood to be the means of expressing, even actualizing,[41] personal, saving faith. Though most adherents admit exceptions, baptism is normally a necessary condition of saving faith, conversion, and salvation. This view of baptism has been variously called "conversion-baptism," "conversion-initiation," "mission baptism," "converts' baptism," or "faith-baptism."[42]

This mediating view of faith's relation to baptism is represented notably by R. E. O. White, George Beasley-Murray, and James D. G. Dunn, and, more recently, Anthony N. S. Lane and Anthony R. Cross, to name but a few.[43] On the denominational level, a form of conversion-baptism exists within the Stone-Campbell Restoration Movement.

A. B. Caneday traces articulations of baptism within the denomination.[44] He notes diversity within this movement on the issue of how baptismal regeneration occurs.[45] The Stone-Campbell Restoration Movement stridently opposes creeds and confessions of faith, making it particularly

---

The distinction among these views of baptism is thus not whether baptism signifies the faith of the baptizand, but the degree to which and how baptism effects what it signifies.

40. For further discussion, see the previous chapter.

41. Dunn states, "Baptism properly performed is for the NT essentially the act of faith and repentance—*the actualization of saving faith* without which, usually, commitment to Jesus as Lord does not come to its necessary expression. As the Spirit is the vehicle of saving grace, so baptism is the vehicle of saving faith." See James D. G. Dunn, *Baptism in the Holy Spirit: A Re-examination of the NT Teaching on the Gift of the Spirit in Relation to Pentecostalism Today* (Philadelphia: Westminster, 1970), 227, emphasis added.

42. Cf. Cross, *Recovering the Evangelical Sacrament*, 40–95.

43. E.g., R. E. O. White, *The Biblical Doctrine of Initiation* (London: Hodder & Stoughton, 1960); Beasley-Murray, *Baptism in the New Testament* (cf. 274n2 for list of scholars of various denominations contemporary to Beasley-Murray who held to a form of convert-baptism); Dunn, *Baptism in the Holy Spirit*; Lane, "Dual-Practice Baptism View," in Wright, *Baptism: Three Views*, 139–71; Cross, *Recovering the Evangelical Sacrament*.

44. A. B. Caneday, "Baptism in the Stone-Campbell Restoration Movement," in Schreiner and Wright, *Believer's Baptism*, 284–328. For an excellent overview of baptism in the Stone-Campbell Movement see Douglas A. Foster, Paul M. Blowers, and D. Newell Williams, "Baptism," in *The Encyclopedia of the Stone-Campbell Movement*, ed. Foster, Blowers, and Williams (Grand Rapids: Eerdmans, 2004), 57–67.

45. Caneday, "Baptism in the Stone-Campbell Restoration Movement," 327.

susceptible to diversity of this sort.[46] In the absence of a confessional corpus
to analyze, Caneday specifically focuses on Alexander Campbell's baptismal theology as articulated in his last major work, *Christian Baptism*, and
demonstrates that Campbell and the more careful receivers of his teaching
maintain a distinction between faith as the efficient cause of regeneration
and baptism as an instrumental cause of regeneration. Campbell explains,

> The influence which baptism may have upon our spiritual rela-
> tions is, therefore, not because of any merit in the act as our own;
> *not as a procuring cause, but merely as an instrumental and concurring
> cause,* by which we "put on Christ," and are united to him formally
> as well as in heart, entering into covenant with him, and uniting
> ourselves to him in his death, burial, and resurrection. ... While,
> then, baptism is ordained for remission of sins, and for no other
> specific purpose, *it is not as a procuring cause, as a meritorious or effi-
> cient cause, but as an instrumental cause, in which faith and repentance
> are developed and made fruitful and effectual* in the changing of our
> state and spiritual relations to the Divine Persons whose names are
> put upon us in the very act.[47]

As I will discuss below, this distinction articulated here between faith as
the efficient cause of regeneration and baptism as an instrumental cause
of regeneration is a key mark of the conversion-baptism view.

---

46. Antipathy toward creeds lies at the headwaters of this movement. Thomas Campbell,
the founder of the movement, sets forth thirteen propositions in his *Declaration and Address*
(1809). In proposition 3, he asserts, "Nothing ought to be inculcated upon Christians as articles of faith; nor required of them as terms of communion; but what is expressly taught,
and enjoined upon them, in the word of God. Nor ought any thing be admitted, as of divine
obligation, in their church constitution and managements, but what is expressly enjoined by
the authority of our Lord Jesus Christ and his apostles upon the NT church; either in express
terms, or by approven precedent." See Campbell, *Declaration and Address* [1809], 3 (*CCFCT*
3:220). Pelikan, commenting on the force of Campbell's propostions, observes with some irony,
"Various 'denominational statements' or explanations of the Disciples that occasionally came
from one or another individual or group within what was called simply 'the Brotherhood'
did not, and *by definition* could not, carry the force and authority of a creed or confession"
(*CCFCT* 3:726, emphasis added).

47. Alexander Campbell, *Christian Baptism, with Its Antecedents and Consequents* (Bethany,
VA: 1851), 205, emphasis added. Cf. John Mark Hicks, "Stone-Campbell Sacramental Theology,"
Restoration Quarterly 50 (2008): 35–48.

Key Features

Several features of the conversion-baptism view should be noted. First, the conversion-baptism view argues that baptism is a part of gospel proclamation. For example, Cross contends, "*Baptism was a part of the kerygma, the apostolic preaching of the gospel.*"[48] Peter's response in Acts 2:38 provides the key evidence for this assertion. When asked, "What are we to do?" (v. 37), Peter replies, "*Repent, and each of you be baptized* in the name of Jesus Christ for the forgiveness of your sins; and you will receive the gift of the Holy Spirit" (v. 38). Cross then charts similar repentance-baptism responses to the apostles' teaching throughout the book of Acts (e.g., Acts 8:12–13; 8:36–38; 9:17–18; 16:14–15, 31–33). From his survey, he concludes that baptism was integral to the response of those receiving the gospel in faith because it was part of the proclamation of the apostles, particularly as the *prescribed* response for which they called.[49]

Second, the conversion-baptism view considers conversion to be a process that is complex, not simple. For example, Cross argues, "Faith, water baptism, and the gift of the Spirit (Spirit-baptism) form one experience."[50] Cross contends that in the New Testament baptism fits within a larger complex of conversion or initiation. While some make much of the variable sequences between faith, repentance, baptism, and reception of the Spirit found in the book of Acts, Cross argues that the components are all assumed even when absent and that baptism often serves as a "synecdoche" for the entire conversion process.[51] In this, he follows R. E. O White

---

48. Cross, *Recovering the Evangelical Sacrament*, 40, emphasis added.

49. Cross, *Recovering the Evangelical Sacrament*, 40n3. Cross follows other scholars in seeing the call for baptism as integral to apostolic preaching. E.g., Donald Guthrie, *New Testament Theology* (Leicester: Inter-Varsity, 1981), 736–37; W. F. Flemington, *The New Testament Doctrine of Baptism* (London: SPCK, 1948), 73.

50. Cross, *Recovering the Evangelical Sacrament*, 46. Cf. Dunn, *Baptism in the Holy Spirit*, 4.

51. Cross, *Recovering the Evangelical Sacrament*, 72–83. The concept of baptism as synecdoche is important for his argument and is developed at length several times within the work. Cross cites a variety of authors who support the close connection of faith, repentance, baptism, and reception of the Spirit. For example, F. F. Bruce, *The Epistle of Paul to the Galatians: A Commentary on the Greek Text*, New International Greek Testament Commentary (Exeter: Paternoster, 1982), 186, states "If it is remembered that repentance and faith, with baptism in water and reception of the Spirit, followed by first communion, constituted one complex experience of Christian initiation, then what is true of the experience as a whole can in practice be predicated of any element in it. The creative agent, however, is the Spirit."

and Robert H. Stein, who find multiple facets of conversion inseparably clustered together.[52] White contends, "The full rite of Christian initiation emerges from Luke's account as comprising the hearing of the gospel, repentant acceptance of God's word, baptism, reception of the Spirit, entrance to the church and to the New Age of eschatological fulfillment."[53] Similarly, Stein argues, "In the experience of becoming a Christian, five integrally related components took place at the same time, usually on the same day: repentance, faith, confession, receiving the gift of the Holy Spirit, and baptism."[54] The conversion-baptism view interprets this data to mean that baptism functions as the visible marker not of a conversion that has or will happen but of conversion itself.

Third, the conversion-baptism view prioritizes faith in the faith-baptism relationship. Beasley-Murray summarizes the relation of faith and baptism (especially in Paul), giving the accent to faith: "The hearing of the Gospel in faith goes *before* baptism; faith receives the gift of God *in* baptism; and faith is the constitutive principle of the Christian life *after* baptism. There is not a line in Paul's writings that justifies a reversal of this emphasis in the relationship between faith and baptism."[55] For Beasley-Murray faith has priority, but faith that refuses baptism is a foreign concept.[56]

Fourth, the conversion-baptism view trades on the currency of a significant overlap between and close connection of the effects of faith and the effects of baptism. Beasley-Murray finds that similar effects are associated with both faith and baptism in the New Testament, including but not limited to the following:

1. Forgiveness of sins (*baptism*: Acts 2:38; *faith*: 1 John 1:9; Acts 15:9)

---

52. Cross, *Recovering the Evangelical Sacrament*, 45.

53. White, *Biblical Doctrine of Initiation*, 199–200.

54. Robert H. Stein, "Baptism in Luke-Acts," in Schreiner and Wright, *Believer's Baptism*, 52. Stein elsewhere dedicates more space to supporting this thesis within the NT canon. Cf. Stein, "Baptism and Becoming a Christian in the New Testament," *The Southern Baptist Journal of Theology* 2 (1998): 6–17. For other examples of this position among conversion-baptism adherents, see Dunn, *Baptism in the Holy Spirit*, 4; Lane, "Dual-Practice Baptism View," 141.

55. George R. Beasley-Murray, *Baptism Today and Tomorrow* (New York: St. Martin's, 1966), 40–41.

56. Beasley-Murray stops short of making baptism absolutely necessary for salvation. While the NT provides grounds for formulating a "normative doctrine," God is free to work around circumstances to save (*Baptism Today and Tomorrow*, 39).

2. Union with Christ (*baptism*: Gal 3:26ff.; Col 2:12; Rom 6:1–11; *faith*: Eph 3:18; Col 2:12)

3. Possession of the Spirit (*baptism*: Acts 2:38; *faith*: Gal 3:2, 14; John 1:12; 20:30ff.)

4. Membership in the church (*baptism*: 1 Cor 12:13; *faith*: Acts 2:41; terms that describe the church as body of believers, e.g., Acts 4:32; Gal 6:16)

5. Inheritance of the kingdom (*baptism*: John 3:3–5; *faith*: John 3:14); regarding John 3:14, he takes "eternal life" to be "a shorthand expression for life in the eternal kingdom of God"[57]

From these observations, Beasley-Murray concludes, "It is evident that God's gift to baptism and to faith is one: it is his salvation in Christ. There is no question of his giving one part in baptism and another to faith, whether in that order or in the reverse. He gives *all* in baptism and *all* to faith."[58]

Finally, regarding sacramental effectiveness, the conversion-baptism view affirms that baptism is an instrumental cause of conversion, not its efficient cause. Drawing his conclusions from the overlapping benefits of faith and baptism, Beasley-Murray states, "God's gracious giving to faith belongs to the context of baptism, even as God's gracious giving in baptism is to faith. Faith has no merit to claim such gifts and baptism has no power to produce them." Faith is here framed as the efficient cause and baptism the instrumental cause of conversion. Later, commenting on Galatians 3:26–27 ("In Christ Jesus you are all sons *and daughters* of God through faith. For all you who were baptized to Christ have clothed yourselves with Christ"), Beasley-Murray concludes, "I cannot see how the force of [these verses] can be justly preserved other than by recognizing that Paul views baptism as the moment of faith in which the adoption to sonship in Christ is *realized*."[59] Baptism is here understood as a sanctified instrument through

---

57. Cf. Beasley-Murray, *Baptism Today and Tomorrow*, 27–36; Beasley-Murray, "The Authority and Justification for Believers' Baptism," *Review and Expositor* 77 (1980): 65; Anthony N. S. Lane, "Baptism in the Thought of David Wright," *Evangelical Quarterly* 78.2 (2006): 145n6. Cross makes a similar point but enumerating several other common aspects (*Recovering the Evangelical Sacrament*, 55n58 and, especially, his chart on 60).

58. Beasley-Murray, *Baptism Today and Tomorrow*, 37, emphasis original.

59. Beasley-Murray, *Baptism Today and Tomorrow*, 37, 54, emphasis added.

which faith is manifested or "realized."[60] Similarly, Dunn affirms, "The NT writers would never say, for example, that the 'sign (of baptism) is or effects what it signifies.' Spirit-baptism and water-baptism remain distinct and even antithetical, the latter being a preparation for the former and the means by which the believer actually reaches out in faith to receive the former."[61] Thus, on the conversion-baptism view, faith and baptism are interdependent in conversion. Similarly, "Baptism," writes Cross, "does not just belong to the beginning of the Christian life, initial justification, but is an integral and inseparable dimension of faith that cannot be separated from faith without changing what it is."[62]

Implications

Since baptism is construed as an instrument used by faith, conversion-baptism projects a view of conditional or subjective baptismal validity. Here, as with credobaptism, baptismal validity is determined by the state of understanding and disposition of the baptizand. Thus, a baptism received in a state of ignorance or hypocrisy is invalid. For example, Cross denies baptismal validity where faith is absent: "According to the NT, there is no baptism without personal faith."[63] Similarly, Dunn states, "Baptism properly performed is for the NT essentially the act of faith and repentance—the *actualization of saving faith* without which, usually, commitment to Jesus as Lord does not come to its necessary expression. As the Spirit is the vehicle of saving grace, so *baptism is the vehicle of saving faith*." He concludes, "Faith demands baptism as its expression; Baptism demands faith for its validity."[64]

---

60. Beasley-Murray also calls baptism a "trysting place of the sinner with his Saviour" (*Baptism in the New Testament*, 305). This word picture also emphasizes the instrumentality of baptism as a means of salvation: faith meets Christ in baptism, "but in the last resort [baptism] is only a *place*" (*Baptism in the New Testament*, 305).

61. Dunn, *Baptism in the Holy Spirit*, 227.

62. Cross, *Recovering the Evangelical Sacrament*, 69. Cross views the development of a catechumenate as a credobaptist corruption of this principle and "the development, ascendency, and eventual dominance of infant baptism" as the paedobaptist corruption of it (69n100).

63. Cross, *Recovering the Evangelical Sacrament*, 64. Cross, however, is not a rigorist regarding baptismal regeneration. Cross remains open regarding the freedom of God to save those baptized in infancy (*Recovering the Evangelical Sacrament*, 64n78). Cf. R. T. France, "Exegesis in Practice: Two Samples," in *New Testament Interpretation: Essays on Principles and Methods*, ed. I. Howard Marshall (Carlisle: Paternoster, 1977), 278.

64. Dunn, *Baptism in the Holy Spirit*, 227–28, emphasis added. While Dunn's description offers an accurate description of the conversion-baptism construal of faith's relation to

Thus, as it does with baptismal effectiveness, conversion-baptism joins its credobaptism counterpart on the issue of baptismal validity: always faith with baptism and baptism with faith—baptism is not baptism without faith.

At first blush the conversion-baptism view may appear to be inimical to the prospective model, which makes catechesis antecedent to baptism. Does the urgency and immediacy of baptismal administration cut off the practice of prebaptismal catechesis? Unquestionably, there is an antipathy among conversion-baptism advocates to the notion of a prebaptismal catechumenate: an extended period of instruction leading to baptism. For example, Cross avers, "In the period of the NT any catechumenate was post baptism, which was administered immediately."[65] Similarly, Beasley-Murray argues that a prolonged, prebaptismal catechumenate is alien to the narratives of Acts. He writes,

> In the earliest years the confession must have been very simple and instruction confined to the elements of the Gospel. Of every baptism recorded in the Acts of the Apostles, the circumstances are such as to exclude the possibility that a long period of catechetical instruction preceded them; the baptisms were administered as soon as faith was professed. Not that the primitive Christian communities considered instruction unnecessary, but the teaching was given after baptism, just as the baptized converts of Pentecost "continued in the instruction of the Apostles, in the fellowship, in the breaking of bread and in the prayers" (Acts 2:42).[66]

So, representatively, Beasley-Murray and Cross argue that extended instruction prior to baptism is a foreign concept in the New Testament. Importantly, however, Beasley-Murray does not deny that instruction preceded baptism, only that it was not complex or protracted. This observation

---

baptism, Dunn emphasizes the reception of the Holy Spirit as the most significant marker of conversion. Baptism, argues Dunn, is "the right of acceptance by the local Christians or congregation as representative of the world-wide Church; but otherwise it is not a channel of grace, and neither the gift of the Spirit nor any of the spiritual blessings which he brings may be inferred from or ascribed to it." He continues, "A recall to the beginnings of the Christian life in the NT is almost always a recall not to baptism, but to the gift of the Spirit, or to the spiritual transformation his coming effected" (*Baptism in the Holy Spirit*, 228).

65. Cross, *Recovering the Evangelical Sacrament*, 86n169.

66. Beasley-Murray, *Baptism in the New Testament*, 285, emphasis original.

offers a clue to the appropriateness of placing conversion-baptism within the bounds of the prospective model.

A key concern of the conversion-baptism view is the separation of faith from baptism evident in both credobaptism and paedobaptism. The former places saving faith *before* the baptismal event; the latter places saving faith *after* the baptismal event. As Beasley-Murray observes, "The Baptist stresses the significance of baptism as testifying to an appropriation of salvation by an already accomplished act of faith, as the Paedobaptist ... emphasizes the hope of a future appropriation by faith of that which has been claimed for the baptized by his sponsors." In contrast, conversion-baptism makes faith, baptism, and conversion (or "the appropriation of salvation") concurrent. Beasley-Murray writes, "God's gift to baptism and to faith is one: it is salvation in Christ. There is no question of his giving one part in baptism and another to faith, whether in that order or in reverse. He gives *all* in baptism and *all* to faith." Regarding the nature of baptism, he concludes, "Baptism is administered to converts. ... Conversion and baptism are inseparable, if not indistinguishable. In the primitive apostolic Church baptism was 'conversion-baptism.'" Baptism, on the conversion-baptism view, is one's faith-response to the apostles' preaching. Faith, baptism, and conversion are "inseparable, if not indistinguishable."[67]

While the conversion-baptism view argues for immediate baptism as the appropriate response to gospel proclamation, the view is not antithetical toward prebaptismal catechesis of every sort. After all, this view is predicated on a full understanding of the gospel. Further, baptism is the appropriate response of faith and repentance that have come from hearing the gospel proclaimed (Acts 2:38; Rom 10:17). Such an affirmation implies that evangelistic preaching—the proclamation of the gospel—is inherently doctrinal (leading to faith) and moral (leading to repentance) in content. Such preaching we contend is *catechetical* in nature.

The gospel message has specific doctrinal content. "The gospel" that Paul "delivered ... as of first importance" was "that Christ died for our sins according to the Scriptures, and that He was buried, and that He was raised on the third day according to the Scriptures" (1 Cor 15:3–4). The phrase repeated in verses 3 and 4, "according to the Scriptures" (κατὰ τὰς γραφάς), indicates the connection of this message with the larger message of the

---

67. Beasley-Murray, *Baptism Today and Tomorrow*, 26, 37–38.

Scriptures. Indeed, Jesus was the fulfillment of Old Testament messianic prophecy and anticipation. Further, in addition to the explicit recounting of Christ's atoning death, his burial, and resurrection, Paul's summary assumes the person of "Christ," the reality and humiliation of the incarnation (for one must be human to die), and the exaltation of Christ's second coming and the resurrection it would bring (1 Cor 15:51–52). Indeed, the Christian hope is bound up with this message (1 Cor 15:19). While more might be said, these observations are sufficient to indicate the doctrinal thickness of the gospel message.

Additionally, the doctrinal content of the gospel is irreducibly complex.[68] There is a certain amount of knowledge that must be apprehended by personal faith to be saving faith. In other words, a person by personal faith (*fides qua creditur*) must take hold of the Christian faith, "the faith that was once for all *time* handed down to the saints" (Jude 3; *fides quae creditur*) in order to be saved. Francis Schaffer highlights this aspect when he identifies the Christian message as a system of doctrine:

> It is a system in that the person who accepts Christ as his Savior must do so in the midst of the understanding that *prior to the creation of the world a personal God on the high level of trinity existed.* And if they "accept Christ as their Savior" and do not understand that *God exists as an infinite-personal God* and do not understand that *man has been made in the image of God and has value,* and do not understand that *man's dilemma is not metaphysical because he is small but moral because man revolted against God in a space-time Fall,* in all probability they are not saved.[69]

Reception of Jesus Christ as God's Son and one's Savior is rightly understood to presuppose a definite body of doctrinal knowledge; such knowledge is prerequisite for faith and confession. Gospel proclamation is essentially

---

68. This term is borrowed from intelligent-design theorist Michael Behe: "By irreducibly complex I mean a single system composed of several well-matched, interacting parts that contribute to the basic function, *wherein the removal of any one of the parts causes the system to effectively cease functioning.*" See Behe, *Darwin's Black Box: The Biochemical Challenge to Evolution* (New York: Simon & Schuster, 1998), 39, emphasis added. Carl Trueman speaks of the "ineradicable complexity" of Christian doctrine, creeds, and confessions in the same sense as that used here. See Trueman, *The Creedal Imperative* (Wheaton, IL: Crossway, 2012), 170; also 18, 175.

69. Francis A. Schaeffer, *Two Contents, Two Realities* (Downers Grove, IL: InterVarsity, 1975), 9–10, emphasis added.

catechetical at this point, for it is concerned with communicating *fides quae creditur* (the Christian faith) so that those who hear it might have *fides qua creditor* (personal faith).

While dramatically different in its scope when compared with the catechumenates of Cyril of Jerusalem, Augustine, or other patristic catechists, even conversion-baptism admits catechesis in its most basic form prior to baptism. If it did not, the core affirmations of the conversion-baptism view about faith using baptism as an instrument become specious, because faith would then be reduced to a nonpropositional notion. In other words, if the catechetical nature of evangelistic preaching is denied, the personal faith leading to baptism has no connection to "the faith that was once for all *time* handed down to the saints" (Jude 3). Therefore, though the conversion-baptism view compresses the prebaptismal catechesis into gospel proclamation, conversion-baptism affirms with the other views of the prospective model (i.e., adult sacramental baptism and credobaptism) that catechesis, even in its simplest form, *must* precede baptism.

In sum, though each of the preceding views differs in the way in which faith is related to baptism in the process of entrance, the effect is the same: baptism is a sanctified instrument whereby personal faith (*fides qua creditur*) in the content of the Christian faith (*fides quae creditur*) is manifested to the church and to the world. Faith leads to baptism, and baptism administered on this condition leads to entrance.

ORIENTATION OF CATECHESIS
TO BAPTISM: PROSPECTION

Just as we noted in the previous chapter that all catechesis has a sense in which it is retrospective, looking back at what God has done for us in the sending of his Son and the sending of his Spirit, there is also a sense in which all catechesis is prospective. All catechesis is prospective in that it anticipates growth in understanding, repentance, faith, and, ultimately, greater conformity to the image of Christ in the lives of those instructed. Paul exemplifies this prospective nature of catechesis in his letter to the Colossians:

> For this reason we also, since the day we heard *about it*, have not
> ceased praying for you and asking that you may be filled with the

knowledge of His will in all spiritual wisdom and understanding, so that you will walk in a manner worthy of the Lord, to please *Him* in all respects, bearing fruit in every good work and increasing in the knowledge of God. (Col 1:9–10)

Paul prays that they will "be filled with the knowledge of [God's] will in all spiritual wisdom and understanding." Further, he is aiming for a knowledge of God that is "increasing" and fruitful. Given the robust instruction that follows, such growth in knowledge and understanding is clearly his aim in providing *more* instruction.

The kind of knowledge for which Paul aims, however, is not merely head knowledge. He desires that they "walk [περιπατῆσαι] in a manner worthy of the Lord, to please *Him* in all respect, bearing fruit in every good work" (v. 10). In other words, Paul desires that they *live* this knowledge. The final clause indicates that this learning process is unending, for he is praying that they will continue "increasing [αὐξανόμενοι] in the knowledge of God" (v. 10). Paul reveals the goal of his teaching later in the chapter: "We proclaim Him [i.e., Christ], admonishing every person and teaching [διδάσκοντες] every person with all wisdom, *so that we may present every person complete in Christ*" (1:28). Catechesis is, therefore, carried out in hope for future growth and conformity to the image of Christ.

The previous section on the relationship between faith and baptism noted the irreducible complexity of the gospel message. Such complexity points to the ongoing teaching ministry of the church and the prospective dynamic explored here. J. I. Packer notes that this complexity necessitates the ongoing teaching ministry of the church. He writes,

[The gospel] was a message of some complexity, needing to be learned before it could be lived, and understood before it could be applied. It needed, therefore, to be *taught*. Hence Paul, as a preacher of it, had to become a teacher. He saw this as part of his calling; he speaks of "the gospel: whereunto I am appointed a preacher ... *and a teacher*" [1 Tim 4:11]. And he tells us that teaching was basic to his evangelistic practice; he speaks of "Christ ... whom we preach ... *teaching every man* in all wisdom" [Col 1:28]. In both texts the reference to teaching is explanatory of the reference to preaching. In other words: it is by teaching that the gospel preacher fulfills his ministry. To *teach* the gospel is his first responsibility: to reduce it to its simplest essentials, to analyse it point by point, to fix its meaning by positive and negative definition, to show how each part of the message links up with the rest—and to go on explaining it till he is quite sure that his listeners have grasped it.[70]

As Packer notes, learning the gospel precedes living out its implications. Instruction in the fundamental elements of the faith, its doctrine and ethics,[71] is an activity that spans the life of a believer. It is introduced in one's first exposure to the gospel, intensified through further instruction (formal or informal, especially in preparation for baptism or confirmation or both, depending on the tradition), and reiterated within the proclamation of the Scriptures in corporate worship as well as other educational activities of the church.

The term "prospective," therefore, properly applies to all forms of Christian catechesis. Nonetheless, in the present chapter the issue is specifically how catechesis is oriented to baptism in the process of entrance. The previous chapter showed how the retrospective model grounds the catechesis leading to entrance upon baptism. There, catechesis looked back to baptism as its existential grounds and point of reference. In contrast, the prospective model grounds baptism on catechesis. Here, catechesis anticipates baptismal profession, administration, and baptismal life as it will be lived out both in and outside the baptismal community of the church. The following subsections will examine these key areas of anticipation.

---

70. J. I. Packer, *Evangelism and the Sovereignty of God* (Downers Grove, IL: InterVarsity, 1961), 47, emphases original.

71. Doctrine and ethics are commonly noted as a twofold objective of catechesis. Broadly, Paul's typical movement from theology to ethics within his epistles justifies this assertion. Cyril of Jerusalem summarizes these parts: "For the method of godliness consists of these two things, pious doctrines, and virtuous practice: and neither are the doctrines acceptable to God apart from good works, nor does God accept the works which are not perfected with pious doctrines" (*Catechetical Lectures* 7.18).

CATECHESIS AS ANTICIPATION OF BAPTISMAL PROFESSION

Verbal Baptismal Profession

The catechesis of the prospective model anticipates baptismal profession and subsequent life as a confessor. Personal faith (*fides qua creditur*) must coincide with corporate faith (*fides quae creditur*; "the faith that was once for all time handed down to the saints," Jude 3) if it is to be Christian faith. Catechesis seeks to hand down this faith to those who would follow after the risen Lord Jesus Christ so that they might know and obey all that he commands (Matt 28:18–20).

Historically, baptism has functioned as the initial, liturgical nexus of personal and corporate faith. Hans Lietzmann asserts, "It is indisputable that the root of all creeds [*Regulae fide*] is the formula of belief [*Glaubensformel*] pronounced by the baptizand, or pronounced in his hearing and assented to by him, before his baptism."[72] Similarly, in his introduction to his *Creeds of the Churches*, John Leith affirms, "Creedal statements were from the beginning associated with baptism. The importance of this rite for the development of creeds is very considerable."[73]

The close association of baptism and creed within Christian history is undeniable. For example, Jaroslav Pelikan observes that the Apostles' Creed (ca. 753), itself an expansion of the Roman Symbol (second century),

---

72. Hans Lietzmann, "Die Anfänge des Glaubensbekenntnisses," in *Festgabe für D. Dr. A. von Harnack ... zum siebzigsten Geburtstag dargebracht von Fachgenossen und Freunden* (Tübingen: Mohr Siebeck, 1921), 226; cf. Jaroslav Pelikan, "Introduction," *CCFCT* 1:15. When a creed is recited by a baptizand it is described as declarative; when creedal statements are spoken to the baptizand, who then assents to them, the creed is called interrogatory. For example, the Creed of Marcellus (340) begins, "I believe in God, All Governing [*pantokratora*]; And [I believe] in Christ Jesus His only begotten Son, our Lord, ... And [I believe] in the Holy Spirit" (Creed of Marcellus [340], in Leith, *Creeds of the Churches*, 23). The Interrogatory Creed of Hippolytus (ca. 215) contains similar content, but it begins each of its sections with the words, "Do you believe ... ?" (Interrogatory Creed of Hippolytus [ca. 215], in Leith, *Creeds of the Churches*, 23).

73. John H. Leith, "Creeds and Their Role in the Church," in *Creeds of the Churches*, 6. Leith goes on to note that the interpolation of Philip's interrogation and the Ethiopian eunuch's response in Acts 8:37 ("And Philip said, 'If you believe with all your heart, you may.' And he replied, 'I believe that Jesus Christ is the Son of God' ") underscores the "importance of baptism in creedal development" (*Creeds of the Churches*, 7). More will be said of this passage in what follows. Leith supports his claim by noting the interrogatory nature of early creedal confession such as that found in the Apostolic Tradition of Hippolytus (ca. 215; Leith, *Creeds of the Churches*, 23).

"remains the most common baptismal formula in Western Christian churches."[74] Similarly, in Eastern Orthodox churches, the unrevised form (non-
filioque form) of the Niceno-Constantinopolitan Creed (381) is required
of candidates of baptism and recited in the liturgy.[75] While the phenomenology of a verbal profession of faith in the baptismal event is undeniable,
some have questioned the originality of such profession.

Objections to Verbal Profession in Baptism

Two objections to the originality of a verbal baptismal profession should
be noted: one textual and one historical. Textually, an objection may be
raised on the basis that the New Testament provides no explicit recounting of a baptismal liturgy in which a verbal baptismal profession of faith
is given. If original to the New Testament, the most explicit account of a
verbal profession of faith in the baptismal event would be Acts 8:37.[76] With
its surrounding context, the passage reads:

> Then Philip opened his mouth, and beginning from this Scripture
> he preached Jesus to him. As they went along the road they came
> to some water; and the eunuch said, "Look! Water! What prevents
> me from being baptized?" [And Philip said, "If you believe with all
> your heart, you may." And he answered and said, "I believe that Jesus
> Christ is the Son of God."] And he ordered the chariot to stop; and

---

74. Pelikan, "The Apostles' Creed" (*CCFCT* 1:667); cf. the Roman Symbol (second century;
CCFCT 1:681–82). " 'I believe' (*Apostles' Creed*) is the faith of the Church professed personally
by each believer, principally during Baptism" (*CCC*, 167 [52]).

75. Cf. Liturgy of John Chrysostom (*CCFCT* 1:285). Pelikan notes that Chrysostom's author-
ship of the liturgy is dubious, as is its exact date (*CCFCT* 1:269). For a full discussion of the
history and background of this liturgy that is still in use today, see Robert F. Taft, *The Diptychs*,
vol. 4 of *A History of the Liturgy of St. John Chrysostom* (Rome: Pontificium Institutum Studiorum
Orientalium, 1991). On the unrevised form of the creed being required of candidates for
baptism, see, for example, question 291 of the Longer Catechism of the Orthodox, Catholic,
Eastern Church (1890), which reads, "What is required of him that seeks to be baptized?" It
answers, "Repentance and faith; for which cause, also, before Baptism the? [*sic*] recite the
Creed. Repent, and be baptized every one of you in the name of Jesus Christ for the remis-
sion of sins, and ye shall receive the gift of the Holy Ghost (Acts 2:38). He that believeth and
is baptized shall be saved (Mark 16:16)" (cf. Schaff, *Creeds of Christendom* 2:492). Here, "the
Creed" is the Niceno-Constantinopolitan Creed, as stated in question 67 (Schaff, *Creeds of
Christendom* 2:456).

76. Paul F. Bradshaw, "The Profession of Faith in Early Christian Baptism," *Evangelical
Quarterly* 78.2 (2006): 102. The "Western" reading is supported by Irenaeus, *Against Heresies*
3.12.8.

they both went down into the water, Philip as well as the eunuch, and he baptized him. (Acts 8:35–38)

While Oscar Cullmann argues that verse 37 is the earlier reading, the prevailing scholarly consensus on the issue is that it is a later scribal interpolation.[77] Thus, the uncertain originality of Acts 8:37 raises questions about the only explicit biblical evidence for verbal confession in the baptismal event.[78]

Additionally, Paul Bradshaw raises a *historical* objection to the notion of verbal baptismal profession. Bradshaw argues that the profession of faith was originally only a prerequisite to the baptismal event and not actually a part of the event itself. He writes,

That in the ancient Syrian tradition the profession of faith did not originally occur in close conjunction with the moment of immersion but some time before it suggests that its relation to baptism was viewed somewhat differently than in those parts of the West where ... the two actions took place concurrently. The profession of faith here [i.e., the Syrian tradition] appears as the moment of decision for the convert, and symbolizes a change of ownership and allegiance from the devil to Christ, especially in the more dramatic forms that it took in several fourth-century rites, when the candidate faced west to renounce the devil and then turned towards the east for the act of adherence to the person of Christ. It was the occasion of final commitment to Christ's service, which then admitted

---

77. Oscar Cullmann finds "traces of an ancient baptismal formula" in the question "What prevents [κωλύει] me from being baptized?" Further, he believes "it is probably an error to regard verse 37 as a later addition, though it is only attested by the Western Text and from this reaches the Antiochean Text." Among other things, he finds this credible on the basis that the confession is in the simple (non-Trinitarian) form. See Oscar Cullmann, "Traces of an Ancient Baptismal Formula in the New Testament," in *Baptism in the New Testament*, Studies in Biblical Theology 1/1 (London: SCM, 1950), 71. Cf. Bruce M. Metzger, *A Textual Commentary on the Greek New Testament*, 2nd ed. (Stuttgart: Deutsche Bibelgesellschaft, 1994), 315–16.

78. This is not, however, to say that the "Western text" is wholly without value. Everett Ferguson states, "Even if not original the verse must go back to an early edition of the Acts and retains importance as historical testimony to Christian practice at least as early as the second century. Baptism was preceded by a confession from the candidate that 'Jesus Christ is the Son of God.'" See Ferguson, *Baptism in the Early Church* (Grand Rapids: Eerdmans, 2009), 173. In Ferguson's view, the Western text thus provides strong *historical* evidence that baptismal interrogation and response was common in the early church.

the believer to the inner circle of his disciples where he or she would learn the deep truths of the Christian faith that were hidden from unbelievers. Only after this teaching had been vouchsafed to the elect, would they go on to the final stage of baptism and incorporation into the number of the faithful. Thus, ritually speaking, the three stages of transition—pre-liminal, liminal, and post-liminal—are quite clearly differentiated here, and the profession of faith or act of adherence marks the movement from the pre-liminal to the liminal stage, and not from the liminal to the post-liminal.[79]

While Bradshaw affirms that a personal profession of faith was prerequisite to baptism (better: to final, prebaptismal catechesis), he argues that such a profession most likely did not occur in the event of baptism itself within the early centuries of the church. For example, he observes that the Didache (ca. 60–150) omits any mention of baptismal interrogation or profession: a fact that is striking given the details it includes about baptismal preparation and administration.[80] The Didache prescribes baptism in the Trinitarian formula. It allows for pouring, but prefers immersion in cold, running water. It also indicates that instruction for certain preparations should be given to the one being baptized. "And before the baptism, let the one baptizing and the one who is to be baptized fast, as well as any others who are able. Also, you must instruct the one who is to be baptized to fast for one or two days beforehand."[81] In the company of such great detail, the omission of instructions about interrogation or confession is striking.[82]

---

79. Bradshaw, "Profession of Faith," 104. Here "pre-liminal" refers to a preinitiatory or precatechumenate status, "liminal" to a learner or catechumenate status, and "post-liminal" to those who have received baptism and its attendant rites.

80. Bradshaw, "Profession of Faith," 103.

81. Didache 7.4 (*CCFCT* 1:42). Cf. Paul F. Bradshaw, "The Gospel and the Catechumenate in the Third Century," *Journal of Theological Studies* 50 (1999): 143–52; Maxwell E. Johnson, "From Three Weeks to Forty Days: Baptismal Preparation and the Origins of Lent," *Studia Liturgica* 20 (1990): 185–200.

82. While we are allowing the objection to have its full weight for the sake of the argument, the fact remains that interrogatory baptismal creeds have a long and wide history. Malcolm Yarnell observes: "The earliest evidence we have of the interrogatory [baptismal formula] dates from the late second century and has been found in six versions in four different languages—Arabic, Ethiopic, Coptic, and Latin—spanning almost the entirety of

Taken together or separately, the textual and historical objections above raise suspicion. Is the notion of a verbal baptismal profession, especially as it appears in the baptismal use of declarative or interrogatory creeds, a later liturgical development? Is it a practice foreign to the primitive church?

Even if both the textual and historical objections are granted, the assertion that the catechesis of the prospective model anticipates baptismal profession can be safely defended. This is so because a verbal profession of faith simply makes explicit in the baptismal event what is already implicit there. Beasley-Murray aptly observes,

> Baptism is an overt, public act that expresses inward decision and intent; since it is performed in the open, and not in secret, it becomes by its nature a confession of a faith and allegiance embraced. If baptism "in the name of Jesus" is a baptism "with respect to Jesus," and so distinguished from all other kinds of baptism by its relation to Him, then to submit to it becomes a confession of trust in Him. It is but natural that what is involved in the event should be brought to explicit mention and that the confession, "Jesus is Lord," be *uttered* by the one baptized.[83]

With Beasley-Murray's observation the reader should recall all that was said in the previous chapter regarding the theological density of baptism. As Luther states, "In baptism ... every Christian has enough to study and practice all his or her life."[84] Similarly, the Roman Catechism states, "Baptism is justly called by us the Sacrament of faith, by the Greeks, the mystery of faith, because it embraces *the entire profession of the Christian faith.*"[85]

---

the known Christian world." See Malcolm B. Yarnell III, *The Formation of Christian Doctrine* (Nashville: B&H Academic, 2007), 191; cf. R. H. Connolly, "On the Text of the Baptismal Creed of Hippolytus," *Journal of Theological Studies* 25 (1924): 135. In several of the earliest texts of the baptismal creed the repetition of "I believe" combined with a separate immersion after each statement only strengthens the notion of baptismal profession (cf. Connolly, "On the Text," 132).

83. Beasley-Murray, *Baptism in the New Testament*, 101. The practice of private baptism or baptism out of the sight of the larger congregation was likely related to the early church practice of baptizing in the nude. This resulted in baptisteries that were separate from the sanctuary (see Dudley, "Baptistry," 55; Davies, *Architectural Setting of Baptism*).

84. Luther, *Large Catechism* (1529; BC, 461).

85. CCT, 240, emphasis added.

Baptism is a theologically dense ordinance; as such, it is inherently confessional. Thus, the person requesting and receiving baptism joins the church in confessing what the church confesses when it administers baptism. Receiving baptism, even apart from a verbal profession in the event, is, therefore, a tacit affirmation of the baptismal formula pronounced over the baptizand. At minimum such a formula, even from the earliest days of the church, involves the proclamation that "Jesus Christ is Lord" (contra the pagan "Caesar is Lord"). In its fuller form, the baptismal formula is explicitly Trinitarian, following the pattern of words found in Matthew 28:19, "baptizing them in the name of the Father and the Son and the Holy Spirit." To request and receive baptism in either of these ways is to give one's assent to the church's pronouncement and with it one's profession of faith.

Commenting on baptism in the name of Jesus, Beasley-Murray notes that when connected to such a formula "submi[ssion] to [baptism] becomes a confession of trust in Him."[86] Moreover, baptism is a command of the risen Christ (Matt 28:19). While there is evidence that Jesus and his disciples baptized persons during his ministry (John 3:22; 4:1–2),[87] the command to be baptized as a means of becoming a disciple is not given until *after* Jesus' resurrection. The postresurrection timing of his command to be baptized is significant for the argument that baptism is itself a form of profession. To request and receive baptism in response to the command of the risen Christ is to profess one's faith in his resurrection and present legitimacy of his lordship. In sum, even if the practice of an explicit, verbal baptismal profession is called into question, the notion of baptism *as profession* remains.

The catechesis of the prospective model anticipates the profession of baptism, preparing the baptizand, at minimum, to understand the confessional significance of the approaching event, and, in a fuller sense, to prepare the baptized to give an explicit, verbal profession of faith. In many traditions this profession takes the form of a creedal confession.

---

86. Beasley-Murray, *Baptism in the New Testament*, 101.

87. "After these things Jesus and His disciples came into the land of Judea; and there He was spending time with them and baptizing" (John 3:22); "So then, when the Lord knew that the Pharisees had heard that He was making and baptizing more disciples than John (although Jesus Himself was not baptizing; rather, His disciples were)" (John 4:1–2). Interestingly, R. T. France has argued that this extended across Jesus' ministry ("Jesus the Baptist?," in *Jesus of Nazareth*, 94–111; cf. 105–6).

CATECHESIS AS ANTICIPATION OF BAPTISMAL ADMINISTRATION

Not only does the catechesis of the prospective model anticipate baptismal profession, but it anticipates baptismal administration. The former anticipates the action of the baptizand in the baptizand's request for baptism and reception of baptism. The latter, however, refers to the action of the local church that administers baptism. As shown above, baptism is at minimum a profession of one's faith (*fides qua creditur*) in the Christian faith (*fides quae creditur*). Nonetheless, self-baptism is not the manifest practice of the Scriptures or of church history: the local church, most often as publicly represented through its ordained ministers, baptizes. Further, the corresponding action to baptismal profession is baptismal interrogation (e.g., "Do you believe ... ?"). Baptismal interrogation occasions baptismal profession. Furthermore, as discussed in the previous section, even where baptismal interrogation is not explicit, the baptismal formula itself is a kind of interrogation and profession, since the baptizand by his or her assent to baptism administered in this way tacitly affirms the pronounced baptismal formula.

The prospective model's pattern of catechesis leading to baptism projects a robust view of baptismal administration as a corporate statement. Here, baptism is more than a mere monologue of the baptizand's profession of faith, for the church leads one by means of catechesis to the baptismal waters. The reception of this catechesis is prerequisite to the reception of baptism. As such, the administration of baptism by the church is a statement to the baptizand and to all witnesses that the prerequisites for baptismal administration have been met. While the requirements for baptism are different from tradition to tradition (e.g., fasting, anointings, exorcisms, a specific regimen of catechesis, etc.), two basic requirements are ubiquitous: faith and repentance (cf. Acts 2:38, 41). The requirements of faith and repentance correspond with the two key aims of catechesis: doctrine and ethics.

By baptizing an individual upon his or her request in response to the gospel, the church is declaring to the baptizand and to the world that, as far as the church can discern, *fides qua creditur* and *fides quae creditur* have coalesced. The church witnesses that it has heard in the candidate's request for baptism a personal faith and allegiance to Christ that bears all the essential marks of a genuine knowledge of the gospel and response to the church's proclamation of the gospel. In short, baptismal *administration* is a visible, corporate confirmation of faith.

Further, in administering baptism to a person who requests it as a response to the gospel, the church also declares that the visible moral life of the individual manifests the fruit of repentance. In fact, in the context of a personal response to gospel proclamation, the request for baptism is itself an indication of penitence. Here, Peter's words reverberate: "Repent, and ... be baptized" (Acts 2:38). Those requesting baptism in this context are attesting that they in fact are penitent. Thus, baptism is united with repentance.

The placement of catechesis prior to baptism and to entrance in the prospective model makes faith and repentance prerequisite to both. The twin catechetical concerns for faith and doctrine along with repentance and ethics are evidenced early in extrabiblical church history. Justin Martyr writes,

> As many as are persuaded and believe that the things we teach and say are true, and undertake to live accordingly, are instructed to pray and ask God with fasting for the remission of their past sins, while we pray and fast with them. Then they are brought by us where there is water, and are born again in the same manner of rebirth by which we ourselves were born again, for they then receive washing in water in the name of God the Father and Master of all, and of our savior, Jesus Christ, and of the Holy Spirit.[88]

Justin notes that to be baptized one must be "persuaded and believe that the things we teach and say are true." Here, the concern for the coalescence of *fides qua creditur* and *fides quae creditur* emerges. Further, those who desire baptism must "*undertake to live accordingly*." Thus, according to Justin, doctrinal orthodoxy must be paired with a credible commitment "to live accordingly"—orthopraxy (lit. "right practice").[89]

Orthopraxy within the early church included abstaining from particular sins (e.g., vice lists)[90] and abandoning vocations that were inher-

---

88. Justin Martyr, *First Apology* 1.61.2–3 (CCFCT 1:46).

89. Similar requirements are found in Augustine, *On the Catechising of the Uninstructed* 26.50, in *Augustine: On the Holy Trinity, Doctrinal Treatises, Moral Treatises* (NPNF¹ 3:312).

90. J. D. Charles, "Vice and Virtue Lists," in *Dictionary of New Testament Background*, 1252–57, esp. 1255, identifies thirteen virtue lists and twenty-three vice lists within the NT (e.g., Col

ently sinful. For example, the Apostolic Tradition states, "If one is a brothel keeper who is a caretaker of prostitutes, either let him cease or be cast out. If he is a maker of idols or painter, let them be taught not to make idols; either let them cease or be cast out."[91] The Apostolic Tradition later requires an examination of a baptismal candidate's life for its virtue and good works prior to entering the final stage of the catechumenate that culminates in baptism.[92] Commenting on this teaching of the Apostolic Tradition, Alan Kreider writes, "The early Christians expected catechumens to behave like Christians before they had received 'new birth' in baptism; according to the Apostolic Tradition they were even expected to behave like Christians before they had 'heard the gospel.'" He continues, "They sensed that only people who had committed themselves to follow Jesus could understand that his teaching and way are practicable; only people who were already being changed by the good news could understand it. They did not think their way into a new life; they lived their way into a new kind of thinking."[93] Repentance was, therefore, evaluated on the basis of lifestyle and vocation.

While the weight of emphasis between doctrinal catechesis and moral catechesis varies from tradition to tradition, these twin concerns are readily illustrated within a variety of confessional traditions. Broadly speaking, the fact that the contents of Christian catechisms typically include expositions of the Apostles' Creed (West) or Nicene Creed (East) and the

---

3:5, 8, 12–15; Gal 5:19–23). Similar examples are found in the post-NT era. For example, the Didache (ca. 60–150), a church manual dealing with matters of Christian initiation, begins by laying out its "two ways": the way of life and the way of death. In summarizing the former, it expounds upon the Great Commandments (1.2). Regarding the latter, it states, "The way of death is this: First of all, it is wicked and thoroughly blasphemous: murders, adulteries, lusts, fornications, thefts, idolatries, magic arts, sorceries, robberies, false witness, hypocrisies, duplicity, deceit, arrogance, malice, stubbornness, greediness, filthy talk, jealousy, audacity, haughtiness, boastfulness" (5.1). At the conclusion of the "two ways" moral catechesis, the Didache states, "Give public instruction on all these points [i.e., in the 'two ways'], and then 'baptize' in running water, 'in the name of the Father and of the Son and of the Holy Spirit'" (7.1). See Teaching of the Twelve Apostles, Commonly Called the Didache, in Early Christian Fathers, ed. and trans. Cyril C. Richardson (Philadelphia: Westminster, 1953), 1:171, 173, 174.

91. Bradshaw et al., Apostolic Tradition: A Commentary, 16.2–3 [88]. See also the vocational prohibitions in Apostolic Constitutions 8.32.7–13, Canons of Hippolytus 11, and Testamentum Domini 2.2 (Bradshaw et al., Apostolic Tradition: A Commentary, 89); Clinton E. Arnold, "Early Church Catechesis and New Christians' Classes in Contemporary Evangelicalism," Journal of the Evangelical Theological Society 47 (2004): 49–50.

92. Apostolic Constitutions 20.1–2, in Bradshaw et al., Apostolic Tradition: A Commentary, 104.

93. Kreider, "Baptism, Catechism, and the Eclipse of Jesus' Teaching," 15–16. Cf. Apostolic Tradition 20.2.

Ten Commandments[94] testifies to the concern that catechumens—prior to baptism and entrance into the community—learn faith and repentance. Further, the frequent use of creedal confession and the renunciation of the devil, his works, and pomp in the baptismal liturgies of the Roman Catholic, Eastern Orthodox, Anglican, and Lutheran traditions bolster this observation as well.[95]

Specific examples of the prospective model pattern in which personal faith and repentance of the baptizand are prerequisite to baptism are readily available from a wide-ranging sample of denominations. The Roman Catechism requires of adults (which includes those attaining the age of reason) that "the Christian faith is to be proposed; and they are earnestly to be exhorted, persuaded and invited to embrace it." It goes on to add, "Should anyone desire Baptism and be unwilling to correct the habit of sinning, he should be altogether rejected."[96] The Catechism of the Catholic Church describes the catechumenate as a "preparation for Baptism" in which one is "initiat[ed] into Christian faith and life." It continues, "The catechumenate, or formation of catechumens, aims at bringing their conversion and faith to maturity."[97]

Similar requirements are found among Protestants. For example, question 95 of the Westminster Shorter Catechism asks, "To whom is Baptism to be administered?" It responds, "Baptism is not to be administered to any that are out of the visible church, till they profess their *faith* in Christ, and *obedience* to him."[98]

---

94. See Alan Kreider's full discussion of the trajectory of ethical catechesis in the West toward a focus on the OT and Decalogue and away from the NT and the teachings of Jesus ("Baptism, Catechism, and the Eclipse of Jesus' Teaching," 5-30).

95. For example, Cyril of Jerusalem reminds the newly baptized that prior to their baptism they were led to say, "I renounce thee, Satan ... and all thy works ... and all [thy] pomp" (*Catechetical Lectures* 19.4-6); cf. *RCIA*, 224 [140-41]; Anglican Catechism (1549, 1662), in Schaff, *Creeds of Christendom* 3:517; Luther, *Small Catechism* (1529; *BC*, 374.19-375.22). See Edward Yarnold's discussion of renunciation and the variety of elements renounced in early baptismal ceremonies in *The Awe-Inspiring Rites of Initiation: The Origins of the R.C.I.A.*, 2nd ed. (Collegeville: Liturgical, 1994), 19.

96. *CCT*, 188, 191.

97. *CCC*, 1247-48 [350].

98. Westminster Shorter Catechism, q. 95 (*RCH*, 217), emphasis added. The requirement of "faith" and "obedience" is also included in the Westminster Confession of Faith (28.4) and Westminster Larger Catechism, q. 166, both of which extend these requirements to one or both parents of an infant being baptized.

Doctrinal and moral prerequisites are also evinced in the Anabaptist Schleitheim Confession (1527):

Baptism shall be given to all those who have learned repentance and amendment of life, and who believe truly that their sins are taken away by Christ, and to all those who walk in the resurrection of Jesus Christ, and wish to be buried with Him in death, so that they may be resurrected with him, and to all those who with this signif-icance request it [baptism] of us and demand it for themselves.[99]

Here we read that only those who have been catechized in the gospel truths of Jesus' death, burial, and resurrection, as well as the theological and ethical meanings of *baptism*, are eligible to receive it. Indeed, unless they personally request it "with this significance"—namely, with the desire "to be buried with him in death, so that they may be resurrected with him"—they are not eligible to receive it.

Similarly, the Particular Baptist Second London Confession states that "the only proper subjects" of baptism are "those who do actually profess repentance towards God, faith in, and obedience, to our Lord Jesus."[100] The 1963 and 2000 versions of Baptist Faith and Message frame baptism as "an act of obedience symbolizing the believer's faith in a crucified, buried, and risen Saviour, the believer's death to sin, the burial of the old life, and the resurrection to walk in newness of life in Christ."[101]

The Russian Baptist Religious Doctrine of the Evangelical Christians (1884) makes explicit what is implicit within other Baptist confessions,[102] namely, the practice of examination of the baptismal candidate: "The Church has the right and duty to convince itself that the person seeking baptism by water experienced rebirth from above and consciously desires

---

99. The Schleitheim Confession (1527, Anabaptist; *BCF*, 25), emphasis added.

100. Second London Confession 29.2 (1677; *BCF*, 291). Similar wording is used in the Orthodox Creed, 28 (*BCF*, 326).

101. Baptist Faith and Message 7 (*BCF*, 413, 516). The 1963 and 2000 statements on baptism and the Lord's Supper are identical.

102. E.g., the New Hampshire Confession does not explicitly mention evaluation of a baptismal candidate's faith, but it reserves baptism for "a believer ... to show forth in a solemn and beautiful emblem, our faith in a crucified, buried, and risen Saviour" (New Hampshire Confession 14 [*BCF*, 382]).

to fulfill the commandment of the Lord (Acts 8:37)."[103] Where believers' baptism is administered discriminately, a credible profession of personal faith
that intersects sufficiently with the core elements of the gospel must be
discerned. Thus, the practice of examination of some sort is implicit to
the practice of credobaptism.

The preceding examples, to which many more could be added, make
faith and repentance prerequisite to baptism. When and where this is the
case, baptismal administration functions as a form of confirmation.[104] As
such, the very act of baptism implies that the prerequisites for administration have been met; baptismal administration is a statement to the
baptizand and to all witnesses concerning the known fitness of the candidate to receive the baptism the candidate has requested. In this context,
the catechesis of the prospective model, both in its instruction and interrogation, anticipates baptismal administration as a corporate affirmation
of the content of the baptizand's personal profession of faith and visible
fruit of repentance.

CATECHESIS AS ANTICIPATION OF BAPTISMAL LIFE

Catechesis prepares the initiate to receive baptism, and it prepares the
church for administering baptism as well. For both parties it anticipates
a unified, covenantal, baptismal life of faith and obedience that is liturgically renewed at each observance of the Lord's Supper.

In Romans 6:4, Paul describes the life inaugurated by baptism:
"Therefore we have been buried with Him through baptism into death, so
that, just as Christ was raised from the dead through the glory of the Father,
so we too may walk in newness of life [ἡμεῖς ἐν καινότητι ζωῆς περιπατήσωμεν]."
Union with Christ in his death, burial, and resurrection results in a life
that is radically different from before. Those so united with Christ have
"died to sin [ἀπεθάνομεν τῇ ἁμαρτίᾳ]" (Rom 6:2). Paul continues, "For if we
have become united with Him in the likeness of His death, certainly we
shall also be in the likeness of His resurrection, knowing this, that our old
self was crucified with Him, in order that our body of sin might be done

---

103. Religious Doctrine of the Evangelical Christians 14 (Russian, 1884; BCF, 444).

104. The projected view of confirmation as a rite within the prospective model will be
discussed below. Baptism in the prospective model, however, functions in a way similar to
the maturity-rite form of confirmation discussed in the previous chapter.

away with, so that we would no longer be slaves to sin; for the one who has died is freed from sin" (Rom 6:5–7).[105] The life spoken of here is nothing short of a life of repentance, faith, and holiness. In this teaching, Paul is heading off all forms of antinomianism that would convert grace into a motive for licentious living. With this teaching in the background, baptism, when preceded by instruction, functions as a visible marker—a formal inauguration—of new life.

Beasley-Murray notes that Paul's appeal for a life shaped by the reality signified in baptism is "most extensively developed in Colossians 2:20–3:13." The believer's burial and resurrection with Christ in baptism (Col 2:12) becomes the motif for the ethical teaching that follows. As Beasley-Murray notes, "The fact that the believer died and rose in Christ is not only a motive for Christlike living, but a basis to work out the baptismal pattern of dying to sin and rising to righteousness."[106] On this basis Paul calls the Colossian believers not to "submit ... to decrees, such as, 'Do not handle, do not taste, do not touch!' " (Col 2:20b–21), but rather to "set your mind on the things *that are* above, not on the things that are on earth" (Col 3:2), "[to put to death] the parts of your earthly body as dead to sexual immorality, impurity, passion, evil desire, and greed" (Col 3:5). These themes were developed in chapter 3. Here, however, attention is drawn to the fact that when the proclamation of the gospel and call to repentance precede baptism they anticipate the new life symbolized in baptism. Such is the pattern and anticipation created by the prospective model.

In the catechesis-baptism sequence of the prospective model, baptism is at once a personal profession of faith in the Christian faith and an act of submission to the risen Christ as Lord. In this model, the baptizand is visibly inaugurated into a life of faith and obedience, both of which are immediately displayed within the very act of baptism. The new life is baptismal in the sense displayed in Romans 6:1–14 and Colossians 2:20–3:13. Even in the variety of ways in which the objective-subjective aspects are worked out, the catechesis-baptism sequence projects baptismal life as the life of a confessor and obedient disciple within the gospel community of the local church.

---

105. Emphasis original to NASB, showing implied words and phrases.
106. Beasley-Murray, "Baptism," 64.

NATURE AND TIMING OF CONFIRMATION

Confirmation in the prospective model manifests in two ways. It is either a conjoined function of baptism or a separate rite that is given in close proximity to baptism prior to entrance. In chapter 3, three forms of confirmation were identified within the Roman Catholic tradition:

1. Rite of initiation—administered with baptism[107]

2. Rite of maturity—administered at a (varying) age of discretion

3. Rite of reception—administered to a proselyte from another Christian denomination[108]

Paul Turner explains that in the Roman tradition the initiation form of confirmation (form 1) is expressed *only* in the rite of adult baptism.[109] Within the prospective model, when confirmation is practiced as a separate rite from baptism it takes the initiation form (form 1), not the maturity-rite form (form 2).

With the baptism model, the prospective model makes confirmation concurrent with baptism either as an accompanying rite (e.g., Eastern Orthodoxy) or as a function of baptism itself (e.g., Reformed paedocommunion). The prospective model as a whole, however, is much more subjective than the baptism model. Within the prospective model, baptism is grounded on the handing down of catechesis by the church to the baptizand. As such, even where confirmation is practiced as a separate sacrament or rite following baptism, confirmation is received in the context of personal faith.

In the retrospective model, confirmation is at minimum the capstone of the catechetical process, an examination of a noncommunicant member's faith that leads to full-communicant status (i.e., entrance). While

---

107. This can apply (1) to adults or children of catechetical age or (2) to infants (in the Eastern Orthodox tradition).

108. Turner, "Confusion over Confirmation," 539–41. On the validity of baptism in non-Catholic contexts see "*Unitatis redintegratio*: Decree on Ecumenism," in Doctrinal Decrees of the Second Vatican Council 5.3.3.17 (1962–1965; CCFCT 3:649).

109. By "adult," Turner explains, "In [canon] law, children of catechetical age are considered adults as far as baptism is concern. Only if they are too young to learn the significance of these rites do we welcome them not as catechumens, but with the rite of infant baptism" ("Confusion over Confirmation," 539).

the Roman Catholic tradition would say more here, it does not say less. In contrast, the prospective model assigns the function of confirming the maturity of an initiate's faith to *baptism*. This shift in function and meaning corresponds with the preceding discussion of catechesis as an anticipation of baptismal profession and administration. Thus, the prospective model is inimical to the maturity-rite form of confirmation (form 2). Within the prospective model the rite of confirmation either collapses into baptismal profession and administration or, when practiced as a separate rite, functions as an objective sealing of the Holy Spirit.

The maturity-rite definitions of confirmation common within the traditions springing from the Reformation exemplify the collapse of confirmation into baptismal profession. On the one hand, as discussed in the previous chapter, these traditions deny confirmation's status as a sacrament.[110] Protestants typically affirm only two sacraments or ordinances: baptism and the Lord's Supper. On the other hand, where the rite is practiced within the Reformation traditions, it is typically understood to be a maturity rite given to those baptized in infancy.[111] This is reflected in the Council of Trent's anathematization of the Reformation practice of confirmation expressed by Calvin, Ursinus, Melanchthon, and others:[112] "If anyone says that confirmation of the baptized is an empty ceremony, and not rather a true and proper sacrament; or that at one time *it was nothing but a form of religious instruction* in which those approaching adolescence presented an account of their faith publicly to the church: let him be anathema."[113]

Where confirmation functions merely as a maturity rite, those receiving catechesis prior to baptism and professing their faith in baptism have

---

110. E.g., Thirty-Nine Articles 25 (1562), in Schaff, *Creeds of Christendom* 3:502–3.

111. While G. W. H. Lampe admits that the practice of confirmation as it came to be practiced in the Reformation is *not* historically or biblically warranted by direct correlation, he maintains that it is theologically correct. "Theologically ... the Reformers were right. Their development of Confirmation made it possible to retain infant Baptism along with the doctrine of justification *sola fide*. The Christian who was baptized in infancy was now able to make his necessary profession of faith after due instruction" (*Seal of the Spirit*, 314).

112. Calvin, *Institutes* 4.19.4, 13; Ursinus, *Commentary of Dr. Zacharias Ursinus*, 10; cf. 12; Melanchthon, *Loci Communes*, 141–42. See also Bucer, *De Regno Christi*, 5.

113. Dogmatic Decrees of the Council of Trent 7, can. 3.1 (1545–1563; *CCFCT* 2:842), emphasis added.

no need of a secondary rite to confirm their faith. Rather, confirmation occurs in baptism, which functions as a "wet confirmation."[114]

The Roman and Eastern Churches practice confirmation as a distinct sacrament from baptism, identifying confirmation as one of the three sacraments of initiation (baptism, confirmation, and Eucharist).[115] The Catechism of the Catholic Church compares and contrasts the practice of confirmation between the East and West as follows:

> In the first centuries Confirmation generally comprised one single celebration with Baptism, forming with it a "double sacrament," according to the expression of St. Cyprian. Among other reasons, the multiplication of infant baptisms all through the year, the increase of rural parishes, and the growth of dioceses often prevented the bishop from being present at all baptismal celebrations. In the West the desire to reserve the completion of Baptism to the bishop caused the temporal separation of the two sacraments. The East has kept them united, so that Confirmation is conferred by the priest who baptizes. But he can do so only with the "Myron" consecrated by a bishop."[116]

It is interesting to note that a difference in polity gave rise to a difference in the timing of administration. Unlike the East, where the presbyter can administer chrism (so long as it has been blessed by the bishop), the West reserves this administration of chrism for the bishop. While there is a distinction in these traditions regarding the administration of confirmation to infants, they are similar in their understanding of confirmation in relation to those who have understanding and discretion. In the latter case, confirmation follows baptism and leads to first Communion.

---

114. J. I. Packer, *Concise Theology: A Guide to Historic Christian Beliefs* (Wheaton, IL: Tyndale House, 1993), 216.

115. See previous chapter on the logic of this order as well as the inversion of this order (esp. baptism, Eucharist, and confirmation).

116. CCC, 1290 [360]. The catechism further comments on the respective emphases that emerge from these two traditions: "The practice of the Eastern Churches gives greater emphasis to the unity of Christian initiation. That of the Latin Church more clearly expresses the communion of the new Christian with the bishop as guarantor and servant of the unity, catholicity and apostolicity of his Church, and hence the connection with the apostolic origins of Christ's Church" (CCC, 1292 [360]).

Both East and West affirm confirmation to be an objective sealing of an individual and connect the sacrament to the reception of the Holy Spirit. According to the Catechism of the Catholic Church, the perfecting of baptismal grace in confirmation "gives the Holy Spirit in order to root us more deeply in the divine filiation, incorporate us more firmly into Christ, strengthen our bond with the Church, associate us more closely with her mission, and help us bear witness to the Christian faith in words accompanied by deeds."[117] Similarly, the Eastern patriarch Jeremias II states,

One should immediately anoint with the divine myrrh the one who has been baptized. For this chrism is the seal and the mark of Christ. We receive grace from it. By virtue of the chrismation, we are called Christians and are the anointed ones of the Lord. For the Lord does not deem us unworthy to be named after him because by grace he calls us sons of God and gods. And when the priest anoints the one baptized, he says: "The seal of the gift of the Holy Spirit, Amen." Therefore, it is reasonable that chrismation follows baptism and is not postponed for a time.[118]

The initiation form of confirmation is clearly in view here. Confirmation is "the seal of the gift of the Holy Spirit," which follows immediately upon baptism and leads directly to Eucharistic celebration.[119] The form of confir-

---

117. *CCC*, 1316 [367]. Cf. *CCT*, 221.

118. Jeremias II, *Reply of Ecumenical Patriarch* 1.3 (*CCFCT* 1:400).

119. Though a minority tradition among Baptists, some have advocated the laying on of hands immediately following baptism. For example, the Orthodox Creed (1678, British, General Baptist) states, "Prayer, with imposition of hands by the bishop, or elder, on baptized believers, as such, for the reception of the holy promised spirit of Christ, we believe is a principle of Christ's doctrine, and ought to be practiced and submitted to by every baptized believer in order to receive the promised spirit of the father and son" (Orthodox Creed, 32 [*BCF*, 320-21]). The Philadelphia Confession 31 (1742, American Baptist; *BCF*, 367), also affirms the "laying on of hands (with prayer) upon baptized believers," finding it to be "an ordinance of Christ" and something to which "all such persons that are admitted to partake of the Lord's Supper" should receive. Their practice, however, holds a slightly different meaning from the Orthodox Creed in that it was "not for the extraordinary gifts of the Spirit, but for (Eph 1:13-14) a farther reception of the Holy Spirit of promise, or for the additional graces of the Spirit, and the influences thereof; to confirm, strengthen, and comfort them in Christ Jesus." For a discussion of this practice among British Baptists in the late twentieth century, see Anthony R. Cross, *Baptism and the Baptists: Theology and Practice in Twentieth-Century Britain*, Paternoster Biblical and Theological Monographs (Waynesboro, GA: Paternoster, 2000), 447-48. Cf. Ernest Payne, "Baptists and the Laying on of Hands," *Baptist Quarterly* 15.5 (January 1954): 203-15; Ricky Primrose, "Thomas Grantham's Doctrine of the Imposition of

mation as a separate rite, then, is essentially the same in the baptism model (see ch. 2) and the prospective model; however, the context is different. The former grants confirmation or chrismation to an infant on the faith of the community, parents, and sponsors (i.e., a corporate or collective, alien faith). The latter grants confirmation in the context of a personal faith that has been confirmed as mature in baptism. Thus, the context of confirmation in the prospective model gives confirmation a more subjective quality than does the baptism model. Further, regarding the confirmation of personal faith, the prospective model freights baptism, not a rite of confirmation, with this function. In cases where confirmation appears as a separate rite within the prospective model, confirmation is, therefore, more objective in function than its retrospective-model counterpart.

PROJECTED VIEW OF THE CHURCH

The prospective model projects a view of the local church as an unmixed, regenerate body of confessors.[120] In placing catechesis before baptism and entrance, the prospective model is structured in such a way that great care is taken not to admit persons into the visible fellowship of the church apart from a personal faith that has adequately apprehended the irreducibly complex content of the gospel. Conversion is a present, visible reality manifested through baptism, not something anticipated in the future. As such, the prospective model *projects* the ideal of an unmixed body.

Additionally, the prospective model projects a view of the church as simultaneously a baptismal and eucharistic community. Here, baptism marks the fulfillment of the requirements for full-communicant status in the community. Those who are baptized are welcomed (immediately) to the Lord's Supper. Thus, the prospective model projects only one class of members within the church: full-communicant members.[121] No visible sign

---

Hands: Theological Implications for Baptist Ecclesiology" (PhD diss., Southwestern Baptist Theological Seminary, 2018).

120. This statement is made in the realm of the ideal, which is why the word "project" is employed. For example, saying the prospective model projects a view of the church as unmixed does not in fact mean that churches employing this model *are* unmixed entities composed only of those who have truly believed. Rather, this statement means that the prospective model reflects the ideal of an unmixed body.

121. Admittedly, the Catholic tradition considers catechumens to be members by intention: "Catechumens who, under the impulse of the Holy Spirit, expressly ask to be incorporated into the church are by this very desire joined to it, and Mother Church already embraces

of initiation has been given to anyone except those eligible for entrance. This means, as Kavanagh observes, that such a pattern "presupposes the presence of catechumens in local churches together with the evangelical and catechetical structures necessary to prepare them for baptism."[122] Consequently, this pattern cuts against the grain of the two-tier view of the retrospective model. If one receives the visible sign of baptism, one is also eligible for the Lord's Supper.

SUMMARY

This chapter has sketched the major contours of the prospective model. Regarding entrance, the prospective model, along with the retrospective model that preceded it, affirms credocommunion: only those who are able to examine and prepare themselves are admitted to the Lord's Supper.

Baptism is here given a subjective validity that is grounded in prebaptismal catechesis. The catechesis of the prospective model anticipates baptismal profession, baptismal administration, and baptismal life in the community. As discussed, baptismal administration in this context is a positive affirmation that, as far as can be discerned, the baptizand has manifested faith and repentance. Baptism is thus administered as a visible and mutual attestation of the baptizand and the church that personal faith and corporate faith have coalesced.

Catechesis in this model leads to an examination of the catechumen's faith prior to baptism. When confirmation is celebrated as a distinct right in this model it is not separated in time from baptism. Thus, in the prospective model confirmation holds an objective quality that differentiates it from that found in the retrospective model. The prospective model freights baptism, not confirmation, with the weight of confirming personal faith. Rather, in the prospective model confirmation as a sacrament is a separate rite from baptism that functions as an objective sign and seal of the Holy Spirit in a way similar to the baptism model.

Regardless of the particular manner in which conversion is connected to baptism—baptism either being the efficient cause (sacramental adult

---

them with love and care as its own" (Lumen Gentium 2.14 [*CCFCT* 3:586]). Nonetheless, the dismissal or sending out of catechumens from the mass makes the force of this affirmation proleptic, not actual: full entrance has still yet to occur.

122. Kavanagh, *Shape of Baptism*, 197.

baptism), instrumental cause (conversion-baptism), or the effect of conversion (credobaptism) — the prospective model projects a view of the church as a regenerate body. Members initiated after the pattern of the prospective model are, as far as the church can tell, converted. There is no anticipation of a future conversion.

Having developed the retrospective model and prospective model in chapters 3 and 4, I now turn attention to exploring how these models are related along with other insights that we may gain from them.

Before transitioning to the heuristic topics of the following chapters, it is important to pause and note that what has been written to this point has a standalone quality. The framework I have labored to construct — assuming it is sound — should hold explanatory value regardless of anything else we discuss. The dynamics I have traced in these four models should prove useful for readers across a variety of denominations. It is with the same spirit that I now want to transition to demonstrate the exploratory usefulness of this framework in the chapters that follow. As previously noted, I have given special attention to the development of the interdependent models to help fund further discussion of a catalytic question: Is there a discernible catalyst that gives rise to the existence of one interdependent model over another? If so, what is it? It is to this catalytic question that we will turn in the next chapter.

5
—

DISCERNING A THEOLOGICAL CATALYST

In chapter 2 I told you about our family trampoline purchase and construction. I likened the development of that chapter to the construction phase and chapters 3–4 to the completion phase, where one can begin to jump and enjoy. If we were to extend that metaphor to chapter 5, we might say that we are now pulling the trampoline up to the edge of our office building in order to drop a watermelon onto it to see what will happen. In other words, we are moving from the mode of explanation to the mode of exploration.

Thus far, this work has constructed an explanatory framework that accounts for the major varieties of logical-liturgical relationship between baptism and catechesis as entrance to the church. Chapter 2 introduced a framework consisting of four models. There, I sketched the two independent models (i.e., baptism and catechesis models) in order to introduce the dynamics of the framework, to map the poles of the objective-subjective continuum, and to demonstrate those models' contours and viability. Chapters three and four developed the interdependent models (i.e., retrospective and prospective models) in greater detail. The fuller development of the retrospective and prospective models stabilizes the framework and makes possible a heuristic analysis of the central seam that separates them. The present chapter takes up this task and seeks to discern a theological catalyst that, theoretically speaking, gives rise to one interdependent model over the other. The phrase "theoretically speaking" is important, as we need to recognize that this is an exploration of liturgical logic. In real-time situations there will be any number of pastoral pressures exerting influence on a particular church's or parish's practice.

Examining the catalyst question potentially illumines the decisive turns of practice and theology within an interdependent model's initiatory pattern. Discerning a catalyst holds practical value for understanding the theological stakes of relocating or redefining the catalytic element (whatever it is) within the initiatory structure. Chapter five will not focus on the practical ramifications of its conclusion. We will consider some of those ramifications along with other pastoral and ecclesial insights in chapter six. The three seams of the framework are particularly rich regions in which to mine, because a better understanding of the distinctions between models affords a greater understanding of the models themselves. For the sake of space, however, the present chapter confines itself to the central seam.

THE CENTRAL SEAM

Category	Independent	(A) Prerequisite(s) of entrance? Baptism or catechesis or both?	Interdependent			(C) Prerequisite(s) of entrance? Baptism or catechesis or both?	Independent
Model	Baptism		Retrospective	(B) Orientation of catechesis to baptism	Prospective		Catechesis
Sequence	Baptism ↓ Entrance ↓ Catechesis		Baptism ↓ Catechesis ↓ Entrance		Catechesis ↓ Baptism ↓ Entrance		Catechesis ↓ Entrance ↓ (Baptism)

◄——— OBJECTIVE   SUBJECTIVE ———►

Before proceeding further, we need to consider the layout of our framework and some of the relationships and groupings that it maps out. To this point we have not given much attention to the seams of the framework, but they are doing some work that needs to be noted. The three seams in the diagram above have been designated in this chapter as seam A, seam B, and seam C, moving left to right. Seam A separates the baptism and retrospective models, seam B separates the retrospective and prospective models, and seam C separates the prospective and catechesis models. Before focusing on the central seam between the retrospective model and prospective model—seam B—it is helpful to recall in brief the outer bounds of the larger interdependent category that these models share (i.e., seams A and C). Highlighting these boundaries will help clarify the parameters of the present chapter's explorations.

CATECHESIS SEAM (SEAM A)

Seam A may rightly be called the catechesis seam. All models to the right of this seam—retrospective, prospective, and catechesis models—make catechesis a prerequisite of entrance. This prerequisite is reflected in the shared practice of credocommunion (believers' Communion). The lone model to the left—baptism model—excludes catechesis from the entrance process, which is reflected in the practice of paedocommunion (infant or child Communion). Here, baptism alone is the prerequisite for entrance into the visible fellowship of the local church expressed at initial participation at the Communion Table.

BAPTISM SEAM (SEAM C)

Seam C may rightly be called the baptism seam. All models to the left of this seam—baptism, retrospective, and prospective models—make baptism a prerequisite of entrance. This prerequisite is reflected in the shared practice of closed membership, which only admits persons into membership who have been baptized. The lone model to the right—catechesis model—requires only catechesis for entrance. This exclusion of baptism from the process of entrance is reflected in the practice of open membership along with its concomitant practice of open Communion.[1]

ORIENTATION SEAM (SEAM B)

Seam B is titled "orientation of catechesis to baptism," and this seam is the focus of this chapter. This seam bisects the Interdependent category into the retrospective model and the prospective model. These interdependent models make baptism and catechesis a *tandem* means of entrance. Here, baptism and catechesis function together to render a candidate eligible for visible fellowship in the local church, specifically as expressed in the celebration of the Lord's Supper, Eucharist, or Communion (whatever the chosen designation of the tradition may be).[2]

---

1. As previously noted, open Communion as used in this study assumes discriminate administration to those with a credible profession of faith. Additionally, the term "membership" is used as a concept equivalent with "entrance." Entrance, as noted earlier, focuses on the inauguration of full, visible fellowship or membership through the sign of the Lord's Supper.

2. These terms will be used interchangeably in the ensuing discussion.

The wording "orientation of catechesis to baptism" privileges baptism. Baptism is the reference point of the relationship because of its status as an ordinance or sacrament (depending on the tradition) and its liturgical function as an initiatory rite. Simply stated, the catechesis required for entrance either looks back to baptism as its foundation (retrospective model) or anticipates baptism and grounds baptismal administration (prospective model). The orientation of catechesis to baptism is, therefore, the key indicator of the model's *nature*. However, the question pursued in this chapter is, What brings this orientation about? Theoretically and theologically speaking, what gives rise to this orientation?

NARROWING THE SEARCH

Chapter 1 listed several possible candidates for the catalyst question. The development of chapters 2-4, however, allows several of the candidates to be eliminated. Again, while other factors might exist on a practical level, I am here conducting a theoretical, exploratory exercise that examines the liturgical logic embedded in each model's pattern of initiation. Such an exercise is helpful because it sheds light on where practices may be cutting against the grain of confessional theology. One may of course come to understand that one's confessional theology needs to be changed in accordance with the Scriptures (see Protestantism's credo *reformata semper reformanda*: "reformed and always reforming"), but in all cases it seems that we want our practices to express our theology. The way one prays or worships shapes the way one believes (*lex orandi, lex credendi*).[3] Thus, what follows aims to aid pastors and other church leaders as they evaluate their initiation practices and the theology that the ordering and relationship of those practices communicates within the broader matrix of initiation.

ELIMINATING CATALYST CANDIDATES

First, the objective-subjective flexibility of the models eliminates the fault line between Catholic *ex opere operato* views and Reformation *sola fide* views of baptism as a viable catalyst candidate. First, the Roman Catholic Church's *ex opere operato* view of baptism understands grace to be conferred through the sacrament on the basis of the work done. The Catechism of the Council

---

3. I will discuss this key liturgical principle more in the next chapter.

of Trent describes the sacraments as "signs instituted not by man but by God, which we firmly believe *have in themselves the power of producing the sacred effects of which they are the signs.*"[4] Further, it describes baptism as "a sign which indicates the infusion of divine grace into our souls."[5]

The Reformed tradition, along with the larger Protestant tradition, rejects the *ex opere operato* view. Representatively, the Westminster Confession states, "Although it be a great sin to contemn or neglect this ordinance [of baptism], yet grace and salvation are not so inseparably annexed unto it, as that no person can be regenerated, or saved, without it; or, that all that are baptized are undoubtedly regenerated."[6] Similarly, even though the Lutheran tradition relates faith to infant baptism differently from the Reformed tradition, an *ex opere operato* view is explicitly denied. For example, commenting on the use of sacraments, the Augsburg Confession states, "Therefore they [i.e., Lutheran churches] also condemn those who teach that the sacraments justify *ex opere operato* and do not teach that faith, which believes that sins are forgiven, is required in the use of sacraments."[7]

As demonstrated in chapter 3, both the Roman Catholic and Reformed traditions exemplify the retrospective model, especially in their deployment of infant baptism. Though they hold opposing views on *ex opere operato* theology, they each manifest the retrospective model when administering baptism to infants. Therefore, the affirmation or denial of *ex opere operato* sacramental theology does not give rise to one model over the other.

Second, the fault line created by baptismal regeneration is also a weak catalyst candidate. Views on both sides of this issue were shown to be compatible with the prospective model in chapter 4. For example, the Catechism of the Catholic Church articulates a baptismal-regeneration view: "Through Baptism we are freed from sin and reborn as sons of God; we become members of Christ, are incorporated into the Church and made sharers in her mission: 'Baptism is the sacrament of regeneration through water in the word.'"[8] In contrast, Baptist Faith and Message 2000 states,

---

4. *CCT*, 152, emphasis added.

5. *CCT*, 154.

6. Westminster Confession 28.5 (*CCFCT* 2:642).

7. Augsburg Confession 13 (*BC*, 47.3; cf. 70.29).

8. *CCC*, 1213 [342].

"[Baptism] is an act of obedience *symbolizing* the believer's faith in a cru-
cified, buried, and risen Saviour, the believer's death to sin, the burial of
the old life, and the resurrection to walk in newness of life in Christ Jesus.
It is a testimony to his faith in the final resurrection of the dead."[9] Baptist
Faith and Message calls baptism a symbolic act and a "testimony to ... faith."
Baptism does not cause faith, but rather is a sign of faith. Nonetheless, the
catechesis-baptism-Eucharist pattern of the Catholic Rite of Christian
Initiation of Adults is rightly classified alongside the Southern Baptist
Convention's Baptist Faith and Message as examples of the prospective
model.[10] Thus, the issue of baptismal regeneration is not a satisfying theo-
logical catalyst either.

Finally, the possibility of two models operating within a single tradition rules out a large number of catalyst candidates related to views of
sacramental validity, efficacy, or nature. For example, the Roman Catholic
Church's view of infant baptism is compatible with the retrospective-
model pattern, and its view of adult baptism is compatible with the
prospective-model pattern. The Roman Catholic view of sacramental validity, efficacy, and nature remains constant for both infant and adult baptism.
Thus, these catalyst candidates may be set aside as well.

KEY DELIMITING FACTORS

The outer bounds of the interdependent models draw attention to two features that help to further delimit the search for a theological catalyst. First,
both interdependent models require baptism prior to entrance (i.e., closed
membership). Second, both interdependent models require a credible confession of faith prior to entrance (credocommunion). These prerequisites
form the common core of the interdependent category.

The interdependent models require a credible profession of faith prior
to entrance. The resultant practice is credocommunion. Credocommunion
was discussed in chapter 3 as the practice of reserving the Lord's Supper

---

9. Baptist Faith and Message 7 (2000; *BCF*, 516), emphasis added.

10. Baptist Faith and Message makes faith with specific content (i.e., "faith in a crucified,
buried, and risen Saviour ... [and] in the final resurrection of the dead") prerequisite to
baptism and thereby presupposing catechesis. It further makes baptism prerequisite to the
Lord's Supper (Baptist Faith and Message 7 [2000; *BCF*, 516]). Taken together, these elements
result in the practice of credocommunion.

for those who have a credible profession of faith as well as certain capacities and dispositions. The importance of and capacity for self-examination, personal confession, desire to partake of the elements, and ability to remember Christ's death—*inter alia*—are foundation stones of the credocommunion position.

Baptism is also a shared prerequisite between the retrospective and prospective models. Before one can enter the visible fellowship of the church, one must receive baptism. However, the practices of paedobaptism and credobaptism project different patterns of relationship between baptism, catechesis, and entrance. Most naturally, the retrospective model is associated with paedobaptism, and the prospective model is associated with credobaptism.

The Scottish Confession of Faith (1560) suffices to recall what was earlier developed regarding credocommunion and to illustrate the practical distinction between paedo- and credobaptism. First, this confession holds a classic paedobaptist position, affirming that baptism "applies as much to the children of the faithful as to those who are of age and discretion."[11] Thus, on baptism, the Scottish Confession of Faith affirms both paedobaptism and credobaptism.[12] Sinclair Ferguson summarizes, "Paedobaptists baptize believers and their children, including infants (*infantes*, literally those who do not speak)."[13]

Second, with the majority of Western traditions (paedo- and credobaptist alike), the Scottish Confession of Faith articulates a credocommunion position. It states, "The supper of the Lord is only for those who are of the household of faith and can try and examine themselves both in their faith and their duty to their neighbors. Those who eat and drink at that holy table without faith, or without peace and goodwill to their brethren, eat unworthily."[14] Thus, though the Scottish Confession of Faith considers infants and small children members of "the household of faith," it defers their participation in the Supper until such time as their capacities and

---

11. Scottish Confession of Faith 23 (1560; *RC*, 182).

12. To recall, the practice of credobaptism is to be distinguished from credobaptists. Credobaptism is the baptizing of an individual on the basis of a personal confession of faith. Credobaptists are those who *only* baptize persons on the basis of a personal confession of faith.

13. Sinclair Ferguson, "Infant Baptism View," in Wright, *Baptism: Three Views*, 78.

14. Scots Confession 23 (1560; *CCFCT* 2:403).

dispositions meet these criteria.[15] This practice is in line with the pattern of the retrospective model. However, by inference, those who have these capacities and dispositions at the time of their baptism—conditions presupposed by adult baptism—are immediately eligible for fellowship at the Communion Table. Thus, on the logic evident within the Scottish Confession of Faith, when credobaptism is administered, the pattern of the prospective model obtains: catechesis leads to baptism, which leads to entrance.

This leads to an observation. Anytime a credible profession of faith is required for admission to the Lord's Supper a corporate confirmation of personal faith is presupposed. This fact remains unchanged regardless of a tradition's position on the acceptable age for baptism. This observation paired with the differing patterns of baptism and instruction created by paedo- and credobaptism potentially reduces the catalytic question we are pursuing in this chapter to one of mere practicality. Simply put, is the line separating the retrospective and prospective models nothing other than the line separating paedobaptism and credobaptism? Is the answer to the catalyst question simply one of practicality?

A PRACTICAL ANSWER

On a practical level, the answer to the catalyst question may appear to be merely the life stage of the person baptized. When an infant is baptized, baptism is followed by catechesis, which leads to a confirmation of personal faith and entrance into the visible fellowship of the church as expressed by first Communion. Here, catechesis and confirmation of faith necessarily follow baptism because an infant is unable to receive instruction and articulate personal faith prior to baptism. Thus, instruction, examination, and profession, all of which are prerequisite to first Communion, follow baptism.

Conversely, when someone who has reached an age of discretion and discernment is baptized ("adult baptism"), catechesis (informal or formal) precedes baptism and a confirmation of personal faith (whether explicit or implicit) is conjoined with the baptismal event. For these individuals,

---

15. Cf. ch. 3 for a fuller discussion of credocommunion's biblical foundation and historical expression within both the Catholic and Protestant traditions.

catechesis, examination, and profession, all of which are prerequisite to first Communion, culminate in baptism. In most cases, therefore, the *life stage* of the baptizand—infant or adult—determines in a practical sense the sequence of the initiatory elements of baptism, catechesis, and entrance.

With infant baptism, the retrospective orientation of catechesis to baptism is uncontested. Baptism is the reference point for subsequent personal faith. Even Luther's infant-faith (*fides infantium*) view of faith's relation to baptism, which in effect makes baptism itself the chief catechetical lesson, gives logical priority to baptism, not catechesis. Though some of the Lutheran prebaptismal interrogations are directed at infants, John Mueller, a Lutheran dogmatician, finds these anticipatory of the faith that is wrought in the moment of baptism.[16] Baptism, after all, is the sacrament, not the human ceremonies that precede it. "Baptism," Mueller writes, "is indeed a *medium iustificationis*, or the means of regeneration, by which faith is engendered."[17] Here, the word of God in baptism is logically prior to infant faith. Further, the Lutheran tradition, in keeping with Luther, affirms credocommunion, delaying Table eligibility until the age at which discretion is attained.[18] Thus, a corporate confirma-

---

16. For an example of this, see Luther's *Baptismal Booklet*, which is appended to his *Small Catechism* (1529; BC, 371-75, esp. 374-75).

17. John Mueller, *Christian Dogmatics*, 503.

18. Frank Senn rightly notes that Luther discarded the sacrament of confirmation. See Senn, "Confirmation and First Communion: A Reappraisal," *Lutheran Quarterly* 23.2 (1971): 185; cf. Luther, *Babylonian Captivity of the Church*, in *Three Treatises*, 218-19. For his purposes, Senn abandons Luther in favor of other Reformers (e.g., Melancthon and Bucer) who retained the rite and were influential on the Lutheran tradition. However, it should be noted that Luther maintained the functionality of confirming personal faith via the practice of confession. By confession, Luther includes both the confession of sin and confession of the Christian faith. He contends that confession in both these aspects (properly understood; i.e., confession of sin is not *ad infinitum*) should precede admission to the Lord's Supper. Regarding youth who have been brought up under Christian nurture, Luther writes, "For such Confession does not go on only for their recounting of sins, but also one should listen to them concerning whether or not they understand the Lord's Prayer, the Creed, the Ten Commandments and whatever else the Catechism gives them." He continues, expanding the scope of this application to both youth and adults: "For we have come to know quite well how little the *common crowd* and the youth learn from the sermon, unless they are individually questioned or examined." He then concludes, "Where better [than Confession] would one want to do this and where is it more needed than for those who should go to the Sacrament?" Indeed, if any refuse to learn the Christian faith as summarized in the catechism, "they may not come to the Sacrament [of the Altar]." See Martin Luther, "An Open Letter to Those in Frankfurt on the Main, 1533," trans. Jon D. Vieker, *Concordia Journal* 16.4 (1990): 343, emphasis added.

tion of faith leading to full entrance is separated in time from baptism. Consequently, even the infant-faith view manifests the pattern of the retrospective model.

If the answer to the catalyst question is determined by the life stage of the baptizand, then the theological component of the catalyst is relegated to the doctrine underlying the practice of infant or adult baptism respectively. If such is the case, the model of entrance is simply the sum of the life stage at which baptism is administered—infant or adult—in coordination with credocommunion. On this answer, infant baptism plus credocommunion equals the retrospective model, and adult baptism plus credocommunion equals the prospective model. However, the notion of competing baptismal norms raises questions about the sufficiency of the life-stage answer surveyed above.

DIFFERING NORMS OF BAPTISM

In chapter 1, I introduced the concept of a baptismal norm. This concept offers a way for traditions practicing both infant and adult baptism to view one type of baptism as foundational or definitive of the other. The Roman Catholic liturgist Aidan Kavanagh draws attention to the competition of norms and polities between infant and adult baptism within his tradition. Kavanagh makes a distinction between a baptismal "norm" and "normal" (or "usual") baptism. A baptismal "norm" is a standard or key whereby all forms of the rite are understood. A "normal" or "usual" baptism is simply the form of baptism that is most often administered. "A *norm*," Kavanagh writes, "has nothing to do with the number of times a thing is done, but it has everything to do with the standard according to which a thing is done."[19] "Norm," therefore, is qualitative, whereas, "normal" or "usual" is quantitative.

ADULT BAPTISM AS NORMATIVE

Kavanagh believes that the return to a robust adult catechumenate, as signaled in the post-Vatican II document Rite of Christian Initiation of Adults, makes adult baptism the normative baptism.[20] Kavanagh com-

---

19. Kavanagh, *Shape of Baptism*, 108–9, emphasis original; Aidan Kavanagh, "Norm of Baptism: The New Rite of Christian Initiation of Adults," *Worship* 48.3 (1974): 143–52.

20. He admits that this conclusion is not explicitly stated. "The [*RCIA*]'s purpose is less to give liturgical recipes than to shift the Church's initiatory polity from one conventional norm

ments, "The norm of baptism was stated by the [Vatican II] Council ... to be solemn sacramental initiation done especially at the paschal vigil and preceded by a catechumenate of serious content and considerable duration." He concludes, "This implies strongly, even if it does not require, that the initiate be an adult or at least a child well advanced in years."[21]

While the Rite of Christian Initiation of Adults makes adult baptism normative, Kavanagh does not interpret it as illegitimating the practice of infant baptism. He writes,

> The notion that infant baptism must be regarded as something less than normal cannot set easily with many Catholics, lay as well as clerical, who have never known anything else. But its abnormality does not require one to conclude that it is illegitimate: tradition clearly seems to know the baptism of infants from the beginning. But tradition with equal clarity does *not* know one thing often implied by the conventional frequency of infant baptism, namely, that baptism in infancy is the normal manner in which one becomes a Catholic Christian.[22]

Infant baptism in Kavanagh's estimation is therefore better viewed as "abnormal."[23]

Infant baptism here represents an abnormality that may be either "benign" or "malign." Kavanagh views infant baptism as a benign abnormality (1) when infant baptism is administered discriminately with pastoral "prudence" and conservatively out of "pastoral necessity," and (2) when adult initiation is firmly established as the norm and practice of

---

centering on infant baptism to the more traditional norm centering on adults. Nowhere does the document say this in so many words. If this is not the case, however, then the document not only makes no sense but is vain and fatuous. Its extensive and sensitive dispositions for gradually incorporating adult converts into communities of faith nowhere suggest that this process should be regarded as the rare exception. On the contrary, from deep within the Roman tradition it speaks of the process presumptively as normative" (Kavanagh, *Shape of Baptism*, 106). The length, intensity, and sensitivity to each catechumen's growth as evinced in the *RCIA* lends support to Kavanagh's assertion (cf. *RCIA*, 76 [38]).

21. Kavanagh, *Shape of Baptism*, 109.

22. Kavanagh, *Shape of Baptism*, 109.

23. For more on "abnormal" sacramental practice, see Kavanagh's discussion of the "Norm of Eucharist" (*Shape of Baptism*, 106–9). Writing of the Eucharist as performed in nonnormative contexts, he writes, "No event that may occur apart from this norm, no matter how usual or frequent, can be anything but abnormal to some degree" (108).

the church. First, infant baptism should be administered discriminately and conservatively. He writes,

> Tradition's witness to the baptism of adults as the norm throws infant baptism into perspective as a benign abnormality so long as it is practiced with prudence as an unavoidable pastoral necessity—in situations such as the frail health of the infant, or in response to the earnest desire of Christian parents whose faith is vigorous and whose way of life gives clear promise that their child will develop in the faith of the Church.[24]

Apart from discriminate administration, infant baptism is an example of "pastoral malfeasance." Unfortunately, Kavanagh fails to provide clear pastoral insight into what is or is not "unavoidable pastoral necessity," especially when he qualifies that such necessity may be generated "in response to the earnest desire of Christian parents whose faith is vigorous and whose way of life gives clear promise that their child will develop in the faith of the Church."[25] It would seem that a paedobaptist definition of "discriminate administration" and application of this principle would make infant baptism more frequent ("normal") than adult baptism. Nonetheless, the implication seems to be that infant baptism should be avoided unless demanded by parents whose consciences are troubled by delaying baptism and enrolling their children as catechumens. Thus, Kavanagh argues that for infant baptism to be a benign abnormality, it must be both discriminately and conservatively administered.

Second, according to Kavanagh infant baptism is a benign abnormality when adult initiation is firmly established as the norm and practice of the church. He writes,

> Tradition's witness to adult baptism as the norm provides a solid counterbalance against infant baptism's becoming a malign abnormality due to pastoral malfeasance, theological obsession, or the decline of faith among Christian parents into some degree of merely social conformity. The data of neither scripture nor tradition can be made to support infant baptism as the pastoral norm.

---

24. Kavanagh, *Shape of Baptism*, 110.
25. Kavanagh, *Shape of Baptism*, 110.

But those same data clearly support the practice as a benign abnormality in the life of a community whose ministry regularly focuses upon the evangelization, catechesis, and initiation of adults of faith into its midst. Initiatory normality in this sense provides the richest pastoral and theological milieu within which infant baptism can be ascertained for what it really ought to be in the life of the Church—not an unremembered substitute for conversion in faith, but a modest manifestation of God's love for all ages and of the stunning liberality of his grace, especially in difficult circumstances.[26]

According to Kavanagh, infant baptism is a *malign* abnormality when it replaces adult sacramental initiation in the Easter celebration within the remembered memory of the church. In Kavanagh's estimation, so long as the fullest expression of adult initiation is regularly on display and infant baptism is administered conservatively and discriminately, infant baptism can be understood as a *benign* abnormality.

When infant baptism is practiced in these ways, Kavanagh argues that it is normed by adult baptism. William Harmless helpfully draws out the implications of Kavanagh's position.

Set against such a norm [of adult baptism], infant baptism will seem a mere "piano reduction" compared to the *RCIA*'s "symphonic orchestration": the key melodies may all be there, but scarcely with their proper richness and full-voiced tonality. In other words, the *RCIA* should, over time, quietly but profoundly challenge the standards and presuppositions that undergird our long-standing habit of infant baptism.[27]

Thus, on Kavanagh and Harmless's interpretation, the Rite of Christian Initiation of Adults makes adult baptism normative for infant baptism in such a way that observers can see infant baptism as adult baptism in miniature. As Kavanagh puts it, it allows infant baptism to function as

---

26. Kavanagh, *Shape of Baptism*, 110.
27. Harmless, *Augustine and the Catechumenate*, 14.

"a modest manifestation of God's love for all ages and of the stunning liberality of his grace, especially in difficult circumstances."[28]

Such a view has practical implications for the catechesis and examination of parents and sponsors, and, when allowed to have its proper effect, leads to the postponement of infant baptism when the parents and sponsors are not deemed spiritually competent. Viewing adult baptism as normative may also lead to allowing an infant to attain discernment in order to receive personal catechesis and profess personal faith.

Practically speaking, however, even where this norm is operative for infant baptisms, the situation for the baptizand is *unchanged*. While baptism is only administered to infants of catechized parents and sponsors, the infant is still incapable of prebaptismal catechesis and professing his or her faith. Thus, the result of infant baptism, even when normed by adult baptism, is still the same: *the baptizand is only enrolled into the process of initiation and given a noncommunicant status*. This means that of the two interdependent models, infant baptism (even if normed by adult baptism as Kavanaugh advocates) is only compatible with the retrospective model. The situation changes, however, when infant baptism is made normative for adult baptism.

INFANT BAPTISM AS NORMATIVE

While Kavanagh's interpretation of the Rite of Christian Initiation of Adults offers an example in which adult baptism is normative, the reverse can also occur: infant baptism may be understood to norm adult baptism. Two notable examples in which infant baptism functions as the normative baptism are found in the Lutheran tradition, namely, in the theology of Martin Luther and Oscar Cullmann. In what follows I will examine Luther's articulation of baptism in his treatise *Concerning Rebaptism* (1528) and his 1529 catechisms as well as Oscar Cullmann's discussion of baptism in *Baptism in the New Testament*.[29]

---

28. Kavanagh, *Shape of Baptism*, 110.

29. Luther, *Concerning Baptism* (1528; LW 40:227–62); *Small Catechism* and *Large Catechism* (1529; BC, 345–480); Cullmann, *Baptism in the New Testament*.

Example 1: Martin Luther

Martin Luther views infant baptism as normative for all baptisms.[30] In his treatise *Concerning Rebaptism* (1528) Luther writes a response to two pastors concerning the "heresy" of the Anabaptists.[31] In a key section of this treatise, Luther examines the Anabaptist usage of Mark 16:16 ("He who believes and is baptized will be saved"). He argues that baptism based on humanity's faith is uncertain. Indeed, unless one becomes God, one cannot discern the hearts of people.

For Luther the logical conclusion of the Anabaptist position is to not baptize anyone, since one can never be sure one is baptizing a true believer. He writes, "For whoever bases baptism on faith and baptizes on chance and not on certainty that faith is present does nothing better than he who baptizes him who has no faith." Further, he distinguishes confession and belief, stating that the former does not necessarily indicate the latter. Commenting on Mark 16:16 ("He who believes and is baptized will be saved"), Luther writes, "This verse 'Whoever believes,' does not compel us to determine who has faith or not. Rather, it makes it a matter of every man's conscience to realize that if he is to be saved he must believe and not pretend that it is sufficient for a Christian to be baptized."[32] The basis for administering baptism and the grounds for its legitimacy are, therefore, not the faith of the baptizand. Personal faith

---

30. For an excellent examination of the development and contours of Luther's baptismal theology, see Trigg, *Baptism in the Theology*. Trigg persuasively argues that Luther viewed baptism as the trysting place of God and humanity. As such, baptism is the starting point to which the believer must continually return. This pattern gives baptism a "present tense" in the life of a believer. Mervyn Wagner, drawing on this idea, notes that progress in the Christian life is always marked by a return to the baptismal dying and rising, and, while there may be growth, one never exits the cycle prior to death. Wagner cites Luther, "Therefore you are always in motion and at the beginning" (*LW* 10:53). See Mervyn A. Wagner, "Luther's Baptismal Theology: Implications for Catechesis," *Lutheran Theological Journal* 31.3 (1997): 105–14.

31. Luther admits that he has had limited interaction with the Anabaptists, and because the two pastors who had approached him failed to provide much information about the beliefs of the Anabaptists of whom they wrote, his answer is general. On Luther's appreciation of the differences between the various sectors of Anabaptism, see Lorenz Grönvik, *Die Taufe in der Theologie Martin Luthers* (Åbo: Åbo Akademi, 1968), 149.

32. Luther, *Concerning Baptism* (*LW* 40:239–41). Trigg observes that Luther takes "whoever believes" here to be directed not to the church as a measuring stick for determining upon whom to administer the sacrament but rather as a guide to the recipients so that they would know how to "grasp" God's word in this sign (*Baptism in the Theology*, 88; cf. 106).

is what makes baptism effective, not what makes it valid. This has implications for which form of baptism is normative.

Luther views infant baptism as the most certain form of baptism. Heiko Oberman explains, "Infant baptism revealed the meaning of baptism. From Luther's standpoint one could not genuinely preserve baptism while repudiating infant baptism, for it was in the child to be baptized that the meaning of Evangelical faith became visible: trusting only in the 'alien' justification granted by God; acting out of the 'alien,' the new conscience; and living on the intercession of others."[33] After discussing passages he finds supportive of infant baptism, Luther concludes, "I maintain ... that the most certain form of baptism is child baptism. For an adult might deceive and come to Christ as Judas and have himself baptized. But a child cannot deceive."[34] Infants do not bring their own works, reasons Luther, but rather come to Christ "that his Word and work might be effective in them, move them, and make them holy, because his Word and work cannot be without fruit. ... Were [his Word and work] to fail here it would fail everywhere and be in vain, which is impossible."[35]

In saying that infant baptism is more certain than adult baptism, Luther does not seek to cast doubt on the certainty of adult baptism. For Luther, personal faith or lack thereof does not affect the validity of baptism. Commenting in his *Large Catechism* (1529), Luther writes, "We do not put the main emphasis on whether the person baptized believes or not, for in the latter case baptism does not become invalid. Everything depends upon the Word and commandment of God."[36] Thus, Luther's words about the greater certainty of infant baptism should be understood rhetorically. Against those who say adult baptism is more certain because of the possibility of personal faith, Luther counters that framing baptism in this way makes it *less certain*. Baptism for Luther is not about the recipient's action but God's. Thus, Luther claims that infant baptism is normative for all

---

33. Heiko Oberman, *Luther: Man between God and the Devil*, trans. Eileen Walliser-Schwarzbart (New Haven: Yale University Press, 1982), 230.

34. Luther, *Concerning Baptism* (LW 40:244).

35. Luther, *Concerning Baptism* (LW 40:244); cf. statement in his postil in LW 40:229.

36. Luther, *Large Catechism* 4 (BC, 463.52).

baptisms because it shows most clearly what happens in baptism, namely, that *God* speaks and *God* baptizes.

Luther's grounding of baptism in the word and work of God projects a view of adult baptism that is normed by infant baptism. If one wants a clear picture of what God is doing in adult baptism, one should consider what happens in infant baptism. In light of the divine and objective grounding of baptism (it is "not our work, but God's work") as well as its incredible saving benefits, Luther exhorts, "Thus, we must regard baptism and put it to use in such a way that we may draw strength and comfort from it when our sins or conscience oppress us, and say: 'But I am baptized! [*Ego tamen Baptizatus sum!*] And if I have been baptized, I have the promise that I shall be saved and have eternal life, both in soul and body.' "[37] Thus, on Luther's view baptism for adults is no less God's work than it is in the case of infants. As such, baptism is a rock of safety and solace when terrors of conscience come.

Example 2: Oscar Cullmann

Oscar Cullmann in *Baptism in the New Testament* also articulates a view of baptism that holds infant baptism as normative for adult baptism.[38] For Cullmann, the personal faith of the baptizand in adult baptism is separated into two acts. The first act of faith precedes baptism and is a sign of election, giving the church an appropriate reason to administer baptism. Speaking of the conditions on which adult converts from Judaism or paganism are received for baptism, Cullmann writes,

> In such cases, it is required that their reception into the Christian Church should take place only if at least the appropriate intention is already present on the basis of faith, to make the response demanded in the time that follows Baptism. The faith of the candidate is thus not a condition of the possibility of the divine action;

---

37. Luther, *Large Catechism* 4 (BC, 460–461.35; 462.44). "Now, here in baptism there is brought, free of charge, to every person's door just such a treasure and medicine that swallows up death and keeps all people alive" (*Large Catechism* 4 [BC, 462.43]).

38. Cullmann's book is a response to Karl Barth's *The Teaching of the Church Regarding Baptism* (London: SCM, 1948). Cullmann calls Barth's work "the most serious challenge to infant Baptism which has ever been offered" (*Baptism in the New Testament*, 8).

nor is it a guarantee of the future perseverance of the person baptized. It is a sign for the Church as a criterion to baptized adults
of their being chosen.[39]

Thus, prebaptismal faith for adults plays an analogous role to that of
Christian parentage for infants, but prebaptismal faith is not the ground
for divine action in baptism or baptismal validity.

The second act of personal faith follows baptism. This faith is not the
faith in the moment of baptism, but rather the faith that follows the baptismal event. "Just as the possession by a child of Christian parentage is
indeed no guarantee of later faith, though indeed it is a *divine indication*
of it, so too the faith confessed at the moment of Baptism by the adult heathen or Jew is no guarantee, though it is a divine indication of that *later
faith* which is decisive."[40] The "later faith" spoken of here is the second
act of faith, and it is this act of faith that is primary.

Because the later act of faith is primary or decisive, Cullmann draws
only a minor distinction between infant and adult baptism. He concludes,

Adult Baptism can therefore be held to be distinct from infant
Baptism only in so far as prior confession of faith is demanded
in the case of adults coming over from Judaism or heathenism.
The doctrine of what happens in Baptism is nevertheless in both
cases the same, since even with adults the faith that is to be confessed *after* Baptism [*nach der Taufe*] by mouth and deed is decisive
[*entscheidend ist*]. Faith thus essentially belongs to the second and
not to the first act of the event of Baptism.[41]

---

39. Cullmann, *Baptism in the New Testament*, 50. Regarding the function of prebaptismal
faith, Cullmann writes, "In the case of an adult candidate coming over from heathenism or
Judaism, the natural sign of birth is lacking. But his affirmation of faith has an analogous
function to perform for the Church, and is for this reason indispensable: it shows the Church
that God will operate within the Church of Christ, and by the Spirit baptizes a man into it.
The Church requires such a sign in order to avoid arbitrariness in the selection of persons
to be baptized. This sign is provided for the Church by the birth of the child into a Christian
family in the one case, and in the other by the faith of the adult" (51).

40. Cullmann, *Baptism in the New Testament*, 52, emphasis original.

41. Cullmann, *Baptism in the New Testament*, 52; Oscar Cullmann, *Die Tauflehre des Neuen
Testaments: Erwachsenen- und Kindertaufe* (Zürich: Zingli-Verlag, 1948), 46.

Importantly, the "decisive" faith is that which *follows* baptism. Baptism, whether administered discriminately to a believing adult or to an infant of Christian parents, works the same way. In both cases, God's action in baptism precedes the decisive human response of faith. In both infant and adult baptism, "The faith that is to be confessed *after* Baptism by mouth and deed is decisive."[42]

For Cullmann, the faith leading to baptism and the faith following baptism are bisected by the faith in or during baptism. The decisive faith *during* baptism is not the faith of the baptizand, but rather *the faith of the baptizing community.* "*During* the baptismal act, faith is demanded of the praying *congregation.*" The congregation "prays that God may complete the miracle of Baptism in the baptized person, whether adult or infant."[43] It is this faith that makes baptism valid. The faith of the congregation contextualizes the administration of baptism within the sphere of the Holy Spirit. It is this pneumatic context of corporate faith, according to Cullmann, that makes baptism valid, not the personal faith of the baptizand. Cullman writes, "If faith were lacking in the congregation assembled for Baptism, it would not be a congregation; and then the Holy Spirit would be absent. But where the believing congregation is, there the Holy Spirit, operating within it and knowing not limitations, has the power to draw an infant into his sphere, just as in the case of all baptized persons who, according to Paul, are 'by one Spirit ... baptized into one body' of Christ."[44]

In sum, Luther and Cullmann offer two notable examples of how infant baptism may be construed as normative for adult baptism. For both Luther and Cullmann, baptism is valid apart from personal faith, *and* baptism is the point of sacramental reference for all postbaptismal faith and assurance. This design is the same for those baptized in infancy as well as those baptized who have attained discretion. Luther and Cullmann thus illustrate the possibility of adult baptism that is normed by infant baptism.

---

42. Cullmann, *Baptism in the New Testament*, 52.

43. Cullmann, *Baptism in the New Testament*, 54–55, emphasis original.

44. Cullmann, *Baptism in the New Testament*, 43.

IMPLICATIONS

Within the works surveyed above, while neither Luther nor Cullmann takes up the question pursued in this chapter, their respective positions have implications for the answer. Both men ground baptismal validity in the objective word and work of God. This understanding is expressed in their corresponding positions that adult baptism works the same way that infant baptism does (i.e., infant baptism norms adult baptism). When infant baptism is understood to norm adult baptism, a logical distinction is made between baptism and the confirmation of faith required for entrance. For here, baptism is not a confirmation of personal faith; it is an objective sign of God's grace. In some sense baptism still functions as a sign that personal faith has been evinced, because faith was demanded prior to baptism. However, the way in which baptism is framed theologically as a sign of divine action and cause of future faith, at minimum, diminishes the confirmatory aspect of baptism. In such cases, baptism functions primarily as a symbol of divine action and corporate faith. Whatever personal faith was found prior to baptism is relegated to a secondary or provisional status. As Cullmann puts it, "Even with adults the faith that is to be confessed *after* Baptism by mouth and deed is decisive."[45]

Further, as with infant baptism, adult baptism is seen here as causative of personal faith and a source of assurance (e.g., Luther's dictum "*Ego tamen Baptizatus sum!*" [I am baptized!]).[46] When these moves are made, the confirmation of personal faith required for entrance into the visible communion of the church is distinguished from the baptismal event and made logically secondary and subsequent to it. While it may still occur within the baptismal complex, there is no logical reason why it could not follow it in time or be accomplished in some other way (e.g., a rite of confirmation).[47] If such were to occur, the pattern of the retrospective model

---

45. Cullmann, *Baptism in the New Testament*, 52, emphasis original.

46. Luther, *Large Catechism* 4 (BC, 462.44).

47. Traces of this are evident in Luther's discussion of pre-Communion confession in "An Open Letter," 333–51. See previous note, in which Luther contends that confession (both of sin and of the Christian faith) should precede admission to the Lord's Supper. He concludes, "Where better [than confession] would one want to do this [examine a candidate's comprehension of the catechetical heads] and where is it more needed than for those who should go to the Sacrament?" ("Open Letter," 343, emphasis added). The connection between baptism and confession of the faith is not here in view. Further, it is not clear whether Luther is intending to freight a secondary rite of confession with the full weight of the confirmatory

would obtain, and a merely practical answer to the catalyst question would be shown to be insufficient for accounting for all the data.

AN ADULT EXAMPLE OF THE
RETROSPECTIVE MODEL

Several Methodists join Luther and Cullmann in arguing that infant baptism is the normative form of baptism. Grady Hardin, Joseph Quillian, and James White in their work *The Celebration of the Gospel* define baptism in a way that emphasizes the divine action of the sacrament: "Baptism is an action of God through his church. It is an action of God that is specific and personal, an action by which God claims a particular person into his victory through Jesus Christ."[48] These authors affirm that the divine "claiming" of baptism extends equally to infants and adults, indeed, "When *a person of whatever age* is baptized by whatever mode[49] [in the triune formula] ... he

---

function involved in bringing persons into the visible Communion of the church. Nonetheless, it is clear that Luther envisions such confession as universally prerequisite to reception of the Lord's Supper even if it were to occur in the context of baptism. These observations combined with Luther's insistence that baptism is to be understood as a divine action leave the theoretical door wide open to the possibility that the confirmation of personal faith that matters for reception to the Lord's Supper is properly distinct from baptism itself. A clearer example, however, will be discussed in the following section.

48. H. Grady Hardin, Joseph D. Quillian Jr., and James F. White, *The Celebration of the Gospel: A Study in Christian Worship* (New York: Abingdon, 1964), 111. The primary sources of this study to this point have been confessions and catechisms. It must be noted, here, that *Celebration of the Gospel* is a manual of church worship. As such, Steve McKinion's qualification of such materials in the patristic era offers a helpful caution regarding such works as purely descriptive of contemporary practice: "Church manuals such as the *Apostolic Constitutions* and its constituent documents indicate both contemporary church practice and *what their authors wished to be standard practice*." See McKinion, "Baptism in the Patristic Writings," in Schreiner and Wright, *Believer's Baptism*, 182, emphasis added. Examining this material is appropriate at this juncture as the catalyst question is a deeply theoretical one. Even if *Celebration of the Gospel* does not represent a majority position among Methodists, (to borrow from McKinion) it at minimum expresses "*what [its] authors wished to be standard practice*." As such it offers a way to pursue the catalyst question.

49. While the mode of immersion is primary, aspersion and affusion are affirmed and admitted by the authors to be more common within the Methodist tradition (Hardin, Quillian, and White, *Celebration of the Gospel*, 111–12). According to Tucker, architecture has played a role in the persistent preference of Methodists for modes other than immersion. She writes, "The addition of a rubric urging the performance of the rites in the company of the congregation and in the church building in effect demonstrated, for many of the episcopal Methodist branches, the preference for sprinkling and pouring, since few buildings had baptisteries to accommodate either immersion or submersion." See Karen B. Westerfield Tucker, *American Methodist Worship* (New York: Oxford University Press, 2001), 102; cf. 301n63. For a helpful brief overview of worship in the Methodist tradition, see Tucker, "Methodist Worship," in Bradshaw, *New SCM Dictionary*, 316–18.

is claimed by God as his child of redemption." Baptism, therefore, visibly delimits the church in the world.[50]

Infant baptism, here, is the norm for all baptisms. As Hardin, Quillian, and White put it, "Infant baptism is definitive of all baptism." They explain, "This is true because every person, whether seventy years or seven weeks, is an infant in Christ when he is baptized. Every baptized person always is growing up in the meaning of his baptism. For each of us, baptism 'ended the way to Christ, and began the life in Christ.' "[51]

The notion of infant baptism as the "definitive baptism" functions as a first principle for initiatory theology in *Celebration of the Gospel*, and this principle has several practical implications for its construal of adult baptism. First, as is the case with other sacramental traditions, baptism is understood to be unrepeatable. "Baptism is the once-and-for-all reminder of the gracious love of God that precedes any response we may make."[52] The unrepeatability of baptism is sometimes explained in other ways, but *Celebration of the Gospel* connects this trait to the principle that infant baptism is the definitive baptism. In grounding the sacrament in God's action rather than the baptizand's response, baptismal validity takes its shape from the prevenient grace pattern of infant baptism. Thus, baptism is an emblem of divine grace that goes before salvation, not personal faith.

Second, viewing infant baptism as the "definitive baptism" leads to the affirmation in *Celebration of the Gospel* that all baptizands—infant and adult—should have sponsors.

> The whole church and this congregation in particular, is godparent or sponsor at every baptism. ... When an adult is baptized, a member of the church ... may be asked to stand with the person to be baptized as a representative sponsor for the church. The presence of the sponsor undergirds the understanding that every person is baptized as an "infant in Christ," and is in need of growing up in the Christian faith.[53]

---

50. Hardin, Quillian, and White, *Celebration of the Gospel*, 112–13.

51. Hardin, Quillian, and White, *Celebration of the Gospel*, 113–14, quoting P. T. Forsyth, *The Church and the Sacraments* (Naperville, IL: Allenson, 1949), 203.

52. Hardin, Quillian, and White, *Celebration of the Gospel*, 114.

53. Hardin, Quillian, and White, *Celebration of the Gospel*, 115.

The use of sponsors not only reflects a practice typically associated with the baptism of infants; it suggests that a confirmation of personal faith is still to come and is *not* accomplished in the event of adult baptism.[54] Similar to Cullmann, the faith emphasized in the baptismal event is the faith of the praying sponsors and congregation, not the faith of the baptizand. For example, *Celebration of the Gospel* describes the actions of the baptismal event in corporate terms rather than personal ones. The authors write, "It is the minister who places water on the head of a baptized person and who says the words of blessing. It is a congregation of people who proclaim the Christian faith in this act of baptism, and take the responsibility of nurturing the one baptized in the Christian life."[55]

Third, *Celebration of the Gospel* expresses that if infant baptism were not the norming norm for all baptisms, "the assurance of ultimate security" as conveyed through baptism would be lost.[56] In language drawn from Luther, the authors assert that baptism's divine action and free grace are uncertain if the sacrament is grounded on personal faith.[57] When afflicted with doubts, the one baptized as an infant may take solace in one's baptism. According to *Celebration of the Gospel*, this is the case not only for those baptized temporally as infants but also for adults baptized *qualitatively* as new infants in Christ.

ADULTS BAPTIZED AS INFANTS?

"How can an adult be baptized as if he were an infant?" "What of a person who is not baptized as an infant? How can he receive infant baptism?" To these questions, *Celebration of the Gospel* responds that one can be qualitatively baptized as an infant "by spirit and intention."[58] It explains,

---

54. More will be said about this in what follows.

55. Hardin, Quillian, and White, *Celebration of the Gospel*, 111.

56. "Yet another *reason* for pressing infant baptism as definitive of all baptism is the primal need each of us has for the assurance of ultimate security. For Christians, this can mean only the certainty of God's love" (Hardin, Quillian, and White, *Celebration of the Gospel*, 115).

57. Hardin, Quillian, and White, *Celebration of the Gospel*, 115. Luther's statement, "I am baptized! [*Ego tamen Baptizatus sum!*]" is cited in support of this point; cf. Luther, *Large Catechism* 4 (BC, 462.44–45).

58. Hardin, Quillian, and White, *Celebration of the Gospel*, 116.

If we are clear that baptism is a God-initiated beginning of life in Christ, then an adult can be baptized as a "babe in Christ." He may say in effect, "I know that I cannot save myself and I throw myself upon the mercy of God. I am as dependent upon him for salvation as a baby is upon parents for food and care. I do not pretend to know all about the Christian faith and life, but I want to know it and to live it."[59]

The case is unchanged even for those who have received catechesis prior to baptism.

If the adult happens to be a person of inquiring mind who is insistent upon learning all he can about the Christian faith before he is baptized, and he does so, then surely his baptism is clear to him primarily as a gracious act of God rather than primarily a result of his own knowledge and decision. He appropriates by earnest the meaning of an infant baptism in which he has not been reared but wishes that he had. There is, then only *one* baptism for persons of all ages. It is the baptism that is the act of God through his church to initiate a person into membership in Jesus Christ.[60]

Thus, a qualitative infant baptism is held out to adults who seek to bring nothing to baptism. Even where one "insists" on catechesis prior to baptism, one must understand that the divine action of baptism supersedes one's knowledge and faith. In fact, the implication is that prebaptismal catechesis would involve instruction to this end.

"CONFIRMATION: AN ESSENTIAL SEQUEL TO INFANT BAPTISM"

As noted above, infant baptism's status as the definitive baptism serves as a first principle for the initiatory theology and structure in *Celebration of the Gospel*. This move has interesting implications for its construal of the "ordinance" of confirmation.[61]

---

59. Hardin, Quillian, and White, *Celebration of the Gospel*, 116.
60. Hardin, Quillian, and White, *Celebration of the Gospel*, 116–17.
61. Hardin, Quillian, and White, *Celebration of the Gospel*, 119.

The title for *Celebration of the Gospel's* section on confirmation is "Confirmation: An Essential Sequel to Infant Baptism." The section clarifies that confirmation is not a sacrament in a proper sense.[62] Echoing the Methodist tradition from which it hails, *Celebration of the Gospel* affirms only the sacraments of baptism and the Lord's Supper.[63]

Celebration of the Gospel defines confirmation as follows: "Confirmation is the action of a baptized person in confirming in the presence of the church the acceptance of his baptism in an act of personal commitment, and the action of God through his church in confirming and blessing him in his commitment to this baptismal faith."[64] Having construed baptism wholly in terms of divine action, confirmation is now freighted with the weight of human response.

At face value, it may appear that *Celebration of the Gospel* has narrowed its focus from infant baptism as the definitive baptism to infant baptism proper. However, this is not so. Since infant baptism is normative of all baptisms, the term "infant baptism" stands in place of all baptisms. The authors write,

> When a person, *regardless of the age at which he was baptized,* has been instructed in the meaning of baptism and of the Christian faith, he then is called upon to acknowledge and affirm the faith in which he has been reared and taught. At confirmation a person in effect says: "I give thanks for what was done for me by God and his church that I could not do for myself. *I now consciously affirm the meaning of my baptism, and seriously and gratefully take upon myself the duties and privileges of being a member of the church of Jesus Christ.*"[65]

---

62. According to Tucker, "confirmation" as a rite by this name was fairly unknown within early Methodism. However, rites of reception into local church membership closely followed it in function. The term "confirmation" was introduced in 1965 (the year after *Celebration of the Gospel* was published—this is a note of correspondence, not influence; see Tucker, *American Methodist Worship,* 115).

63. "Baptism is the initiating sacrament; Holy Communion is the nurturing sacrament" (Hardin, Quillian, and White, *Celebration of the Gospel,* 110–11; cf. Thirty-Nine Articles 25, in Schaff, *Creeds of Christendom* 3:502).

64. Hardin, Quillian, and White, *Celebration of the Gospel,* 118.

65. Hardin, Quillian, and White, *Celebration of the Gospel,* 118; emphasis added.

As with baptism,[66] age is not a consideration in determining the function and meaning of confirmation. Regardless of whether one is baptized in infancy *or adulthood*, confirmation is in all cases a maturity rite that marks conscious affirmation of one's baptism.[67] Confirmation is then by definition a distinct and subsequent rite to baptism. Importantly, confirmation, not baptism, is determinative for "the duties and privileges" of membership.[68]

The division of labor between baptism and confirmation is punctuated by a delay between baptism and confirmation. *Celebration of the Gospel* advocates a clear temporal separation between these elements as a best practice even for adult initiation. "It is important," *Celebration of the Gospel* states, "for a person *of whatever age* to be baptized at one time and to be confirmed and received into membership at another. This is the best way to keep clear the respective meanings of these acts."[69] The separation advocated here has an interesting effect on the orientation between catechesis and baptism.

As noted in previous chapters, the separation of confirmation from baptism creates a liminal space in which the baptized person is initiated in some sense but has not fully entered the visible fellowship of the church. This dynamic is created by the structure of *Celebration of the Gospel* as well. According to *Celebration of the Gospel*, "The normal procedure is for a person to be instructed in the meaning of the Christian faith and life *between the time that he is baptized and the time that he is confirmed*. The time of instruction may be several years in the instance of a person's being baptized in infancy, *or it may be only several months, or even weeks*."[70] Importantly, it clarifies, "Even if an adult has been thoroughly instructed prior to his baptism, it may be well to wait at least until the next Sunday before he is confirmed. This timing of baptism and confirmation keeps us aware of the relationship between God's grace and our faith."[71]

---

66. Baptism and Holy Communion are understood to be sacraments, whereas confirmation is called an ordinance (Hardin, Quillian, and White, *Celebration of the Gospel*, 119).

67. This corresponds with the maturity form in the discussion of confirmation in ch. 3; cf. Turner, "Confusion over Confirmation."

68. Hardin, Quillian, and White, *Celebration of the Gospel*, 118.

69. Hardin, Quillian, and White, *Celebration of the Gospel*, 118, emphasis added.

70. Hardin, Quillian, and White, *Celebration of the Gospel*, 118–19, emphasis added.

71. Hardin, Quillian, and White, *Celebration of the Gospel*, 119. The authors summarize their conception of the initiatory pattern as follows: "So it is that we are claimed, called, and branded by God through baptism as his child in Christ; we are nurtured in God's love by

Once again baptism is placed in the sphere of divine action, and confirmation is placed in the sphere of human response. Moreover, placing the point of personal response and ratification of baptismal vows subsequent to the baptismal event effectively enfolds baptism into the catechesis that leads to entrance. The implication of the pattern articulated in *Celebration of the Gospel* is that for one to fully appreciate and respond to the grace of God, one must first experience it in the sacrament of baptism. The catechesis leading to entrance is thereby given a mystagogical quality, and baptism forms a necessary existential grounding for its later completion.[72]

The moves made by *Celebration of the Gospel* place catechesis in primary relation to the rite of *confirmation*, not baptism. In structuring initiation in this way, confirmation, not baptism, ratifies the reception of catechesis and inaugurates full visible fellowship with the local church. The separation between baptism and confirmation combined with the economy of functions between the two rites (e.g., divine initiative and human response) are primarily responsible for this shift. The shift is underscored by the use of sponsors even for adults, a practice that indicates that the faith grounding the baptismal event is located in the baptizing congregation, not the baptizand. The specific causes aside, the final effect is that personal affirmation of one's baptism as well as the corporate recognition of one's faith as formed through catechesis are reserved for the ordinance of confirmation *subsequent* to baptism.

IMPLICATIONS FOR THE CATALYST QUESTION

The initiatory logic of *Celebration of the Gospel* offers a fully formed example of adult baptism that is explicitly normed by infant baptism. This section examines *Celebration of the Gospel* to see whether its brand of *adult* baptism matches the interdependent, retrospective-model pattern. If so, the

---

being reared in his church; in due time we are enabled by God's grace to confirm by personal commitment his claim upon us and to assume our responsibility in joyful obedience to him; and we are blessed and affirmed by God in this confirmation."

72. To recall the discussion of ch. 3, "mystagogy" is the "study or explanation of mysteries." "Mystagogical catechesis" is a form of catechesis typically associated with the early church in which newly baptized persons were debriefed on their experience of the sacraments and rites of initiation. On this practice, the experience of the sacraments of initiation was necessary in order to grasp their meaning in fullness. See Baerwald, "Mystagogy"; Johnson, "Mystagogical Catechesis."

life-stage answer to the catalyst question proves wanting, and the search for a theological catalyst must push further in.

Before moving to consider the implications of the foregoing material, it is important to note that the structure proposed in *Celebration of the Gospel* fits within the broader interdependent category. Both baptism and catechesis, the latter of which culminates in confirmation, are prerequisite to entrance into the visible fellowship of the local church. While the issue of entrance is not taken up directly, the treatment of key elements in *Celebration of the Gospel* displays key markers of an interdependent model.

First, *Celebration of the Gospel* makes baptism integral to entrance into the visible fellowship of the local church. Baptism is here defined as "the act of God through his church to initiate a person into membership in Jesus Christ."[73] In the initiatory framework of *Celebration of the Gospel*, confirmation is prerequisite to initiation into the local church's visible fellowship; baptism is prerequisite to confirmation; and consequently, baptism is also prerequisite to initiation into the local church's visible fellowship.[74] Therefore, unlike the catechesis model, which places baptism outside the process of entrance, *Celebration of the Gospel* makes it integral to entrance.

Second, *Celebration of the Gospel* assumes as normative the practice of credocommunion on the basis of an examined faith. While Methodist worship standards of the twentieth century offer a broad invitation to the Lord's Supper,[75] *Celebration of the Gospel* views the New Testament pattern

---

73. Hardin, Quillian, and White, *Celebration of the Gospel*, 117.

74. The requirement of baptism for local church membership has a convoluted history within Methodism. Tucker writes, "In the early years, the disparate official statements regarding church membership were commonly reconciled by identifying baptism with general membership in 'Christ's holy Church,' taking Philip's baptism of the Ethiopian eunuch into no particular church (Acts 8:35–39) as the scriptural precedent and justification. Denominational affiliation was granted following the period of probation, ideally with, but also without, baptism. After 1836, membership in a local Methodist Episcopal congregation was contingent upon prior baptism" (*American Methodist Worship*, 111). *Celebration of the Gospel* falls in line with the post-1836 practice as described by Tucker.

75. The 1965 Book of Worship states, "All people who intend to lead a Christian life are invited to receive this holy Sacrament." See Methodist Church, *The Book of Worship for Church and Home* (Nashville: Methodist Publishing House, 1964–1965), 15; Methodist Church, *The Book of Worship for Church and Home* (Methodist Publishing House, 1944–1945), 377. The

for Table fellowship as reserved for believers. Speaking of this pattern, the authors write, "The Lord's Supper was celebrated for those who were already within the body of Christ. Thus, whenever it was celebrated, it was a sacrament of the unity which existed between the believers and their Lord."[76] *Celebration of the Gospel* reflects a similar pattern in its explanation of confirmation and of the Lord's Supper itself.

Celebration of the Gospel makes confirmation subsequent to baptism, even "an essential sequel" to baptism. While baptism may be "the act of God through his church to initiate a person into membership in Jesus Christ," it is only through *confirmation* that one takes up "the duties and privileges of being a member of the church of Jesus Christ."[77] One such privilege is the ongoing nurture of the Lord's Supper.[78] These statements hint toward the traditional sequence of baptism, confirmation, and first Communion,[79] but the explanation in *Celebration of the Gospel* of the meaning of the Lord's Supper makes this normative structure unmistakable.

Celebration of the Gospel construes the Lord's Supper as a renewal of the meanings of both baptism and confirmation. "The meaning of baptism

---

1992 United Methodist Book of Worship states, "Christ our Lord invites to his table all who love him, who earnestly repent of their sin and seek to live in peace with one another." See United Methodist Church, *The United Methodist Book of Worship* (Nashville: United Methodist Publishing House, 1992), 35. For a lucid summary of Methodist practice regarding admission to the Table, see Tucker, *American Methodist Worship*, 143–48. Tucker notes that early Methodism tended to fence the Table from the unbaptized or unexamined (*American Methodist Worship*, 144). However, Tucker also observes that the early policies loosened, and though subsequent attempts to restrict admission to the Supper were made periodically, each failed to succeed largely because of polemical concerns. For example, she writes, "Efforts during the mid-nineteenth century to establish a disciplinary rule delineating baptism as a precondition failed, primarily because Methodists, in polemical debates with the Baptists at the time, were reluctant to concede either the necessity of baptism prior to Communion or the validity of a restricted, 'close Communion' " (*American Methodist Worship*, 145).

76. Hardin, Quillian, and White, *Celebration of the Gospel*, 43. The authors state that they wrote the book in response to "the need for a brief basic study which treats Christian worship under a unifying motif, and which intentionally is in accord with the doctrinal standards of Methodism" (8). However, even if they join the twentieth-century standards noted above in offering Communion to seekers, they clearly view believers' Communion or credocommunion as the *normative* practice.

77. Hardin, Quillian, and White, *Celebration of the Gospel*, 43, 118, emphasis added.

78. Baptism is explicitly called "the initiating sacrament," and Holy Communion is identified as "the nurturing sacrament" (Hardin, Quillian, and White, *Celebration of the Gospel*, 110–11; cf. 119). *Celebration of the Gospel's* implicit, normative sequence follows the traditional baptism-confirmation-first Communion sequence.

79. See ch. 3 for discussion of the normative sequence of the sacraments of initiation, especially "Reordering the Sacraments of Initiation: Soft Paedocommunion."

is recapitulated in confirmation in a new dimension of conscious commitment. The meaning of both baptism and confirmation is increased throughout our lives. ... Among the most important means of maturing as Christians ... is the Holy Communion." In the liturgical vision of *Celebration of the Gospel*, the Lord's Supper takes up the meaning of *both baptism and confirmation*. The authors write, "Whereas baptism and confirmation are a once-and-for-all sacrament and a once-and-for-all ordinance, Holy Communion is the repeated sacrament in which *we are renewed in our baptism and confirmation every time we participate in it.*"[80] If such a renewal is integral to the sacrament of the Lord's Supper, then both baptism and confirmation are clearly normative to its celebration. Baptism and catechesis, which culminates in confirmation, work in tandem to accomplish entrance into the visible fellowship of the local church.

So where should we place *Celebration of the Gospel* on our framework of models? On the one hand, the practice of credocommunion places the initiatory pattern of *Celebration of the Gospel* to the right of the baptism model. On the other hand, the integration of baptism into the process of entrance places it to the left of the catechesis model. Thus, while the authors do not take up the question of independence or interdependence directly, their statements manifest the key marks of an interdependent model. In the pattern of entrance in *Celebration of the Gospel*, baptism and catechesis work in tandem to effect entrance into the visible fellowship of the local church.

THE CELEBRATION OF THE GOSPEL ADULT BAPTISM:

A RETROSPECTIVE-MODEL EXEMPLAR

As discussed in chapter 3, the retrospective model is an interdependent model in which baptism and catechesis are both prerequisites for entrance. Catechetical preparation, whether formal or informal, prior to entrance is a key mark of this model. In this model catechesis is grounded on and looks back to baptism. The catechetical process is concluded with examination of some sort (e.g., a rite of confirmation), which is prerequisite to first Communion. In the retrospective model, baptism functions as an *existential* grounding for the catechesis that leads to entrance. With the

---

80. Hardin, Quillian, and White, *Celebration of the Gospel*, 119, emphasis added.

retrospective model clearly defined, the question arises: Does *Celebration of the Gospel* follow the initiatory pattern of the retrospective model?

Like the retrospective model, *Celebration of the Gospel* separates the confirmation of personal faith required for entrance from the event of baptism and places it after baptism. The effect of this structure is that the baptizand is placed in a liminal, noncommunicant category (even if only for a brief time). Here, "the duties and privileges" of membership are reserved for the confirmed. For *Celebration of the Gospel*, the confirmation of personal faith that matters for entrance takes place subsequent to baptism.

As noted earlier, placing the point of personal response and ratification of baptism after the baptismal event enfolds baptism into the catechesis that leads to entrance. On the pattern articulated in *Celebration of the Gospel*, for one fully to appreciate and respond to the grace of God one must first experience it through the sacrament of baptism. The catechesis leading to entrance is thereby given a mystagogical quality, and baptism forms a necessary existential grounding for its completion. These features lead to the conclusion that the version of *adult* initiation in *Celebration of the Gospel* exemplifies the retrospective-model pattern of entrance into the visible fellowship of the local church.

OBJECTION: ADULT BAPTISM IN *THE CELEBRATION OF THE GOSPEL* IS DISCRIMINATE

At this point, a potential objection may be raised about classifying any form of discriminate adult baptism, *Celebration of the Gospel* or otherwise, as an example of the retrospective model. Discriminate adult baptism by definition involves catechesis and examination *prior* to the baptismal event. If catechesis and examination were not prior to baptism, then the baptism would cease to be discriminate, for the church would have no grounds on which to administer it. In what way, then, can the brand of adult baptism in *Celebration of the Gospel* be placed into this category?

As noted in chapter 4, the administration of discriminate adult baptism is in some sense a confirmation of personal faith, for a demonstration of personal faith is required prior to baptism. Further, an "adult" (i.e., a person of discernment) expresses personal faith through the actions of requesting and receiving baptism. In many cases there is also an accompanying verbal profession that is made in the baptismal event as well.

The key question, however, is whether the confirmation of faith performed in baptism is decisive for entrance. Even where adult baptism is administered discriminately, if the baptizand is not yet eligible for entrance into the visible fellowship of the church, the decisive confirmation of personal faith has yet to occur. This has a profound implication for the function of prebaptismal catechesis.

For example, in the case of *Celebration of the Gospel*'s construal of adult baptism, the function of prebaptismal catechesis is changed. No longer is this catechesis primarily an anticipation of baptism, but rather it, along with baptism, anticipates confirmation. In this pattern, baptism is enfolded into the catechetical process leading to entrance. Baptism here is itself the chief catechetical lesson of God's grace toward the baptizand. As such it forms the existential grounding for subsequent catechesis as well as the confession and commitment to Christ that *will later be* decisive for entrance. Importantly, however, the baptismal event is *not* the occasion for the confession and commitment to Christ that is decisive for entrance.

Thus, within the pattern of initiation in *Celebration of the Gospel* the faith required of adults prior to baptism becomes provisional, functioning merely as a sign of election and as a basis for the community to begin the initiation process responsibly.[81] The faith required for membership in the community and fellowship at its Table is that which has been formed by the divine action of baptism. That baptism does not immediately confer "the duties and privileges of being a member of the church of Jesus Christ"[82] signifies that the individual is not yet fully initiated. Adult baptism in *Celebration of the Gospel*, therefore, demonstrates the pattern of the retrospective model. Here, adult baptism functions as the existential grounds

---

81. The function of prebaptismal catechesis implied here is analogous to that of Oscar Cullmann, as discussed earlier in this chapter.

82. These "duties and privileges," according to *Celebration of the Gospel*, are officially conferred through confirmation (Hardin, Quillian, and White, *Celebration of the Gospel*, 118). Tucker writes, "Recovery of a unified sacramental initiation rite (water bath, invocation of the Holy Spirit and laying on of hands ['confirmation'], first Communion) using fourth-century models was the goal of the United Methodist Church's revisionary work from the 1970s through the 1990s, and the desire at the end of the twentieth century of other Christian churches as well" (*American Methodist Worship*, 115). Cf. *Report of the Commission on Worship: General Conference of the Methodist Church* (Nashville: Methodist Publishing House, 1960), 26–27. The continuity of *Celebration of the Gospel* with the broader Methodist tradition is of little import for the purpose of this chapter, as *Celebration of the Gospel* functions here as a theoretical, not historical, foil for the life-stage, catalyst candidate.

for the faith and commitment that will be ratified in a later ordinance of confirmation. This ratification of faith following baptism is the decisive confirmation for entrance into the visible fellowship and communion of the church. Whatever confirmatory function the act of baptism performs, this act is necessary but not sufficient for full entrance into the visible fellowship of the local church.

DISCERNING THE CATALYST

We are now ready to consider the implications of the preceding survey. The title of this section and the endeavor of this chapter may be judged to be misguided and quixotic. Is it possible to locate not just *a* theological catalyst but *the* theological catalyst that gives rise between the retrospective and prospective models? The answer depends on the definition of "theological catalyst." If by this phrase we meant something along the lines of "the unique mixture of theological commitments that gives rise to one interdependent model or the other," then the search for a specific, unique catalyst would be impossible. The matrix of issues, *both practical and theological*, that factor into and shape a particular tradition's practices is too complicated for us to provide a singular answer that would apply across denominations and even local contexts. However, if by this phrase we simply mean "the unique theological-liturgical move that gives rise to one interdependent model or the other," then the task is within reach. While differing rationales may exist, a unique theological-liturgical move can be identified that catalyzes or gives rise to one interdependent model or the other (i.e., retrospective model or prospective model).

The model of adult initiation in *Celebration of the Gospel* helps isolate the key theological-liturgical move that catalyzes the interdependent models' respective orientations of catechesis to baptism. In light of the foregoing examination of evidence, we can reach several conclusions. First, in demonstrating that *adult* baptism in *Celebration of the Gospel* manifests the key marks of the retrospective model, the life-stage candidate proves an inadequate explanation. Here, adults with full powers of discernment are *not* given full entrance to visible fellowship in the Lord's Supper upon baptism. Thus, the answer to our question is not merely how old one is when one is baptized.

Second, the way in which *Celebration of the Gospel* defines and relates confirmation both to baptism and entrance illumines the key issue, namely, the connection and placement of the decisive confirmation of faith that leads to entrance. By "decisive confirmation of faith" we are acknowledging the fact that in discriminate adult baptism there is at minimum a *provisional* affirmation of faith. If this were not so, then the baptism would be administered indiscriminately. The confirmation of faith becomes *decisive* for entrance when it becomes the basis on which one is rendered eligible for the Lord's Supper. The separation of the decisive confirmation of faith from adult baptism in *Celebration of the Gospel* is a logical result of making infant baptism the definitive baptism. For both infants and adults, "regardless of the age at which he was baptized," baptism is the mark of the beginning of an initiatory sequence that will lead to personal commitment. Great pains are taken in *Celebration of the Gospel* to frame baptism wholly in terms of divine action, not human response. Personal commitment is, therefore, strained out of the baptismal waters and transferred into confirmation. In fact, the personal response of confirmation is a response to the grace of God in baptism.

Third, while *Celebration of the Gospel* argues that adults can be given a baptism that is an infant baptism in quality,[83] what this essentially means is that the decisive confirmation of personal faith that leads to entrance is separated from the baptismal event. On the account in *Celebration of the Gospel*, the type of baptism—infant or adult—may be put forward as a catalyst candidate. However, the key issue is whether or not baptism functions as the decisive confirmation of faith for entrance, regardless of how a tradition formally classifies the nature of the baptism it administers to adults. It seems, then, wiser to focus attention on the point at which faith is confirmed and its relative connection to baptism rather than on the peculiar definition of adult-infant baptism proffered by *Celebration of the Gospel*. The role of normative baptism, as we have discussed in previous chapters, is a significant issue that may be overlooked by many on the pastoral level.

---

83. In making infant baptism the definitive baptism, *Celebration of the Gospel* offers some explanation as to why the life-stage answer has so much correspondence with the overwhelming majority of infant-baptism examples that illustrate the retrospective-model pattern. Nonetheless, in providing an example of an *adult* baptism that manifests the retrospective model, *Celebration of the Gospel* demonstrates that the infant-baptism versus adult-baptism divide is not the root issue.

Focusing on the nature of baptism illumines potential rationales for connecting baptism with or separating baptism from the decisive confirmation of faith. The problem with putting this forward as *the* catalyst is that it operates at a depth that is beyond clear detection.[84] I believe we are on firmer ground if we confine our conclusion to the theological moves evident in the liturgy of the process. Thus, more visibly the issue is where the structure places the decisive confirmation of faith required for entrance.

Therefore, while somewhat tentative, I suggest that logically and liturgically speaking the theological catalyst that gives rise to one interdependent model over the other is *the way in which the decisive confirmation of faith for entrance is connected to baptism*. On the one hand, when entrance-defining confirmation temporally coincides with the baptismal event, the prospective model obtains. Catechesis has anticipated baptism, and baptism has rendered one eligible for entrance into the local church, as evidenced through first Communion.

On the other hand, when entrance-defining confirmation is separated from and subsequent to the baptismal event, then the retrospective model obtains. As shown in this chapter, infant baptism can be construed as definitive of adult baptism. If and when this occurs, baptism functions primarily as an emblem of divine action and grace, and only secondarily or provisionally of personal faith. Consequently, the decisive confirmation of personal faith for entrance occurs subsequent to the baptismal event. For *Celebration of the Gospel* this occurs in the ordinance of confirmation. Such a confirmation could just as well be accomplished through some other rite (e.g., personal confession with the priest or bishop). Regardless of how it is fleshed out in liturgical practice, the way in which the decisive confirmation of faith for entrance is connected to baptism serves as the catalyst between the interdependent models.

SUMMARY

Building on the development of the retrospective and prospective models (chapters 3–4), the present chapter has conducted a heuristic analysis of the central seam that separates them. Specifically, it has sought to discern

---

84. In this way, I am conceding that the catalyst answer we are putting forward here is good as far as it goes (liturgically speaking). The underlying reasons for making this liturgical move will likely be varied and complex, not singular and simple.

the theological catalyst that gives rise to one interdependent model over the other. In final analysis, I argue that the theological catalyst that gives rise to one interdependent model over the other is the way in which the decisive confirmation of faith for entrance is connected to baptism.

The heuristic thesis heightens the implications of the interconnectedness between baptism, catechesis, and entrance noted in chapter 1 and brings ecclesiology into interplay with soteriology. As shown above, the restructuring of the relationship between baptism, catechesis, and entrance by moving the catalytic element changes the initiatory pattern in a substantive way. The analysis of the construal of the baptism-catechesis-entrance relationship in *Celebration of the Gospel* demonstrates that the liturgical logic it deploys in adult baptism differs in kind from that of the prospective model. Theologically, the effect is that baptism is objectified and enfolded into the catechesis that leads to entrance. The adoption of a retrospective-model pattern for adults in *Celebration of the Gospel* implies that God through the sacramental action of the local church implants the seed of the gospel into an individual so that the individual might later respond to it savingly and be visibly included in the fellowship of that church. Baptism is framed, therefore, neither as a personal response to the gospel nor a congregation's confirmation of an individual's faith. Instead, baptismal administration is enfolded into the evangelization of the baptizand and the baptizand's catechesis in the gospel.

As stated in the introduction to this chapter, examining the catalyst question has potential for illumining the decisive turns of practice and theology within an interdependent model's initiatory pattern. Discerning a catalyst holds practical value for understanding the theological stakes of relocating or redefining the catalytic element (i.e., the connection of the decisive confirmation of faith for entrance to baptism) within the initiatory structure. I will examine key points of significance of both the catalyst thesis as well as the study as a whole in brief in the following, final chapter.

6
—
PASTORAL AND ECCLESIAL IMPLICATIONS

If this study has demonstrated anything, I hope it is that the ordinances or sacraments of initiation are inextricably linked within the process of entrance into the visible community of the church. Importantly, the link between baptism, catechesis, and Communion is not limited to the process of entrance. It extends like a ray from entrance forward. I illustrated this link in my examination of Hardin, Quillian, and White's model of initiation in *Celebration of the Gospel* in the previous chapter. There we saw that *Celebration of the Gospel* construes the Lord's Supper as a renewal of the meanings of both baptism and confirmation. "The meaning of baptism is recapitulated in confirmation in a new dimension of conscious commitment. The meaning of both baptism and confirmation is increased throughout our lives. ... Among the most important means of maturing as Christians ... is the Holy Communion." In the liturgical vision of *Celebration of the Gospel*, the Lord's Supper takes up the meaning of *both baptism and confirmation*. The authors write, "Whereas baptism and confirmation are a once-and-for-all sacrament and a once-and-for-all ordinance, Holy Communion is the repeated sacrament in which *we are renewed in our baptism and confirmation every time we participate in it.*"[1]

While the model of *Celebration of the Gospel* is unique in many respects, Hardin, Quillian, and White's explanation of the Lord's Supper as a renewal of the other sacraments of initiation rightly applies to all the models of our framework. If the Lord's Supper is the only *repeatable* ordinance or sacrament of initiation, then it stands to reason that the Lord's Supper (discriminately administered) is the ongoing sign of initiation that renews

---

1. Hardin, Quillian, and White, *Celebration of the Gospel*, 119, emphasis added.

everything that was symbolized and accomplished in and through initiation and its attendant ordinances or sacraments. As such, the Lord's Supper becomes a synecdoche standing in place of baptism and the confirmation of faith that led to entrance (in whatever form it took). For this reason, observances of the Lord's Supper are an ongoing reminder and symbol of baptismal theology.

Theology involves two basic modes of operation: summary and explanation.[2] Over time, explanation without summary leaves the Christian faith disorganized and disjointed. Similarly, repeated summary without explanation leads to an evaporation of the understanding and meaning of the Christian faith. The ordinances or sacraments of baptism and the Lord's Supper are symbols that summarize the entirety of Christian theology. The catechesis that follows entrance into the church forms a dialogical relationship with the Lord's Supper. As the Lord's Supper is celebrated and the church catechizes its members through its ongoing teaching ministry, a rhythm of summary and explanation forms. Further, as we will see, as others are brought into the visible fellowship of the church through baptism, the members of the congregation function as witnesses to the initiate's inclusion even as they renew their own baptismal vows and personal faith. Thus, the ongoing catechesis of the church in the faith (*fides quae creditor*; objective faith; Jude 3) via sermons and its teaching ministry informs the summaries and confessions of that faith by its members (*fides qua creditor*; personal faith) through the ordinances of baptism and the Lord's Supper. And, importantly, the way in which the ordinances are sequenced and framed says something. The economy of entrance exerts formative pressure on the shape and theology conveyed both through the ordinances or sacraments themselves as well as the catechesis that explains those ordinances or sacraments.

Prosper of Aquitaine (ca. 390–ca. 463) offered a basic liturgical principle that is worth mentioning at this point: *lex orandi, lex credendi* ("the law of prayer and worship is the law of faith"). The Catechism of the Catholic Church summarizes the principle and its relation to the sacraments as follows:

---

2. I owe this insight to Steve McKinion.

The purpose of the sacraments is to sanctify men, to build up the Body of Christ and, finally, to give worship to God. Because they are signs they also instruct. They not only presuppose faith, but by words and objects they also nourish, strengthen, and express it. That is why they are called "sacraments of faith."

The Church's faith precedes the faith of the believer who is invited to adhere to it. When the Church celebrates the sacraments, she confesses the faith received from the apostles—whence the ancient saying: *lex orandi, lex credendi* (or: *legem credendi lex statuat supplicandi*, according to Prosper of Aquitaine). The law of prayer is the law of faith: the Church believes as she prays. Liturgy is a constitutive element of the holy and living Tradition.[3]

While Protestant readers will wince at the notion of a "living Tradition,"[4] the *lex orandi, lex credendi* principle should receive a warm welcome. The idea that the way we pray and worship is an expression of the faith we confess, and its converse, that the way we believe shapes the way we pray and worship, should be beyond dispute. In other words, there is an inextricable link between the two.[5]

As our development of each model has sought to demonstrate, the liturgical logic on display projects various understandings of faith, baptism, confirmation, the Lord's Supper, the church, and so on. Thus, the ordering and connection of baptism, catechesis, and Communion within a model is saying something: it is performing a kind of catechesis itself. Simply put, the model of entrance we deploy speaks. We do well, then, to consider what it is saying.

---

3. *CCC*, 1123-24 [318].

4. This is not to say that Protestants reject tradition altogether, but rather the two-source model of tradition embraced by the Roman Catholic Church. See Heiko A. Oberman, "Quo Vadis Patre? Tradition from Irenaeus to *Humani Generis*," in *The Dawn of the Reformation: Essays in the Late Medieval and Early Reformation Thought* (Edinburgh: T&T Clark, 1986), 269-96.

5. For a nuanced discussion of this principle see Jaroslav Pelikan, "Chapter 6: The Rule of Prayer and the Rule of Faith," in *Credo*, 158-85. It seems that whatever theology is expressed in prayer and worship tends to gain ascendancy if or when it is in conflict with formal statements of theology. This observation corresponds with the fact that Pelikan's chapter contains multiple examples in which credal theology lagged behind the theology expressed in liturgy and prayer. Further, the discussion of the tension between the Anglican Thirty-Nine Articles and the Book of Common Prayer, and the latter's ascendency over the former, offers another poignant example (see *Credo*, 177-78). The way we pray and worship shapes the way we believe.

The previous chapters have been strongly analytical and at points technical. Nonetheless, a number of theological and pastoral insights have surfaced along the way that need to be highlighted and developed. In some cases, I have already teased out the heart of the implications, but in other instances the insight was more implied than stated. The remainder of this chapter will seek to pull together and make explicit some of the more interesting and important of these insights. The process of writing this work has proven fruitful for my own thinking on these issues, and I hope that it fosters similar fruit for you the reader.

DISCRIMINATE ADMINISTRATION
AS FAITHFUL WITNESS

In chapter 3 of Langston Hughes's biography, *The Big Sea*, he recounts his "salvation" experience.[6] Unfortunately, this was at once a "conversion" and a deconversion as the experience ultimately turned him away from belief in Christ. As he describes, "I was saved from sin when I was going on thirteen. But not really saved." He goes on to describe a revival service he attended in which he and other children were "escorted to the front row and placed on the mourners' bench with all the other young sinners, who had not yet been brought to Jesus." The service and sermon were animated and drew to the climactic altar call at the end: " 'Won't you come? Won't you come to Jesus? Young lambs, won't you come?' And [the minister] held out his arms to all us young sinners there on the mourners' bench. And the little girls cried. And some of them jumped up and went to Jesus right away. But most of us just sat there."[7]

Young Langston had been told by his aunt that when you converted "you could see and hear and feel Jesus in your soul,"[8] and he was eagerly waiting for this sensory experience. Unfortunately, it never came. Nonetheless, the longer he waited for the experience the more the pressure mounted. As it grew apparent that the service wouldn't end until they converted (or at

---

6. I am grateful to my Charleston Southern University colleague Scott Yarbrough for putting me on to this account.

7. Langston Hughes, "Salvation," in *The Big Sea* (New York: Hill and Wang, 1940, 1993), 18–19.

8. Hughes, "Salvation," 19.

least would end much quicker if they did), his friend Westley finally gave in. Langston continued to wait. He writes,

> I heard the songs and the minister saying: "Why don't you come? My dear child, why don't you come to Jesus? Jesus is waiting for you. He wants you. Why don't you come? Sister Reed, what is this child's name?"
> "Langston," my aunt sobbed.
> "Langston, why don't you come? Why don't you come and be saved? Oh, Lamb of God! Why don't you come?"[9]

Hughes continues,

> Now it was really getting late. I began to be ashamed of myself, holding everything up so long. I began to wonder what God thought about Westley, who certainly hadn't seen Jesus either, but who was now sitting proudly on the platform, swinging his knickerbockered legs and grinning down at me, surrounded by deacons and old women on their knees praying. God had not struck Westley dead for taking his name in vain or for lying in the temple. So I decided that maybe to save further trouble, I'd better lie, too, and say that Jesus had come, and get up and be saved.
> So I got up.
> Suddenly the whole room broke into a sea of shouting, as they saw me rise. Waves of rejoicing swept the place. Women leaped in the air. My aunt threw her arms around me. The minister took me by the hand and led me to the platform.
> When things quieted down, in a hushed silence, punctuated by a few ecstatic "Amens," all the new young lambs were blessed in the name of God. Then joyous singing filled the room.[10]

The effect on Langston's faith was tragic.

> That night, for the first time in my life but one for I was a big boy twelve years old—I cried. I cried, in bed alone, and couldn't stop. I buried my head under the quilts, but my aunt heard me. She woke

---

9. Hughes, "Salvation," 20.
10. Hughes, "Salvation," 20–21.

up and told my uncle I was crying because the Holy Ghost had come into my life, and because I had seen Jesus. But I was really crying because I couldn't bear to tell her that I had lied, that I had deceived everybody in the church, that I hadn't seen Jesus, and that now I didn't believe there was a Jesus anymore, since he didn't come to help me.[11]

Though neither baptism nor the Lord's Supper are mentioned in Hughes's memoir, his account offers a lamentable example of indiscriminate conversionism. Assuming the normal course of initiation for one converted from outside the covenant community, Langston and these other young converts would be baptized on their profession of faith and welcomed into its visible fellowship. For our purposes, this anecdote illustrates the wreckage that can result from such pastoral malfeasance and the importance of discernment in the process of initiation into the church's visible fellowship.

In chapter 2 I noted that the models of this study were constructed with the assumption of discriminate administration of baptism and the Lord's Supper. This presupposition was important because it protected the liturgical logic of each model and (practically speaking) narrowed the scope of inquiry. With the models now constructed, we are in a better position to appreciate how discriminate administration of these ordinances or sacraments protects the liturgical logic of the models, or, put differently, how the indiscriminate administration of these rites undermines the liturgical logic of these models. However, Hughes's experience reminds us that beyond the notion of liturgical logic much is at stake in this issue pastorally. Here we will briefly review why discriminate administration of baptism and the Lord's Supper is so important, but we will do so with an eye toward how we might best ensure such administration.

BAPTISM

In brief, the discriminate administration of baptism involves the examination either of the candidate or of the parents and sponsors of the baptizand. As noted in chapter 2, the liturgical logic of both credobaptism

---

11. Hughes, "Salvation," 21.

and paedobaptism is undermined by indiscriminate baptism. For example, indiscriminate baptismal administration subverts the credobaptist conviction that that a personal profession of faith is part of the nature of baptism. Similarly, indiscriminate baptismal administration subverts the paedobaptist understanding that baptism is a covenant sign given to the children of believing parents. Likewise, the catechesis associated with baptism is undermined by indiscriminate baptism because it fails to examine either the baptizand or the parents and sponsors prior to baptism. Importantly, as we have developed to some degree in chapters 2–5, the church is speaking in and through its administration of baptism. Through baptism, the church is declaring God's grace, confirming the faith of the baptizand or the parents and sponsors or both, and renewing its own confession of the faith once for all delivered to the saints that is signed herein. All of these are acts of proclamation. As such the church must speak truthfully through its administrations of baptism.

THE LORD'S SUPPER

In like manner, as a sign of fellowship in the gospel, the Lord's Supper functions not merely as a profession of faith on the part of the communicant but also as a statement of affirmation by the church body that administers it. The church is speaking when it administers this meal. As people saved by the truth (John 8:32), sanctified by the truth (John 17:17), and witnesses to the truth (Acts 1:8), the church must speak the truth at all times (Eph 4:15, 25): even and especially when she administers the Lord's Supper (a meal that proclaims the truth about Christ; 1 Cor 11:26). The Lord's Supper not only marks the fullness of one's entrance into the visible fellowship, but in its repeated administration it functions as the ongoing renewal of this fellowship. Thus, "as often as" the local community celebrates this meal together it "proclaim[s] the Lord's death until He comes" (1 Cor 11:25–26), and in so doing it marks off its visible community and fellowship before the world. It effectively affirms each communicant as part of its fellowship and declares its participation and unity to those who observe its celebration. Indiscriminate administration of this meal is at minimum negligent and at worst hypocritical and deceptive.

The concept of entrance as we have developed it also serves to highlight the importance of administering the Lord's Supper discriminately. This administration should be grounded on a discernable response to the gospel and identification with Christ.[12] This affirmation is especially emphasized in the catechesis model of Bunyan and others. While advocates of the other three models would take issue with the spiritualizing of baptism in which baptism is cast as merely "a sign to the person baptized, and a help to his own faith,"[13] there is an admirable emphasis on examination and responsible administration of the Lord's Supper in Bunyan's theology. This is interestingly illustrated in Bunyan's classic *Pilgrim's Progress*.

In part 1, stage 3, of his allegory *Pilgrim's Progress*, Bunyan reflects the great care given to the admission of new members into the local church. The main character, called Christian, approaches the house called Beautiful and seeks lodging for the night. The house represents the church and is "built by the Lord of the Hill … for the relief and security of Pilgrims." Before being admitted to the house, the porter who keeps the gate questions him about his name and why he is so late in coming. After these preliminary questions, the porter beckons one of the daughters of the house, Discretion. When asked why she was called, he explains that it is so that she "mayest do as seemeth thee good, even according to the Law of the house." Discretion is soon joined by three others, Prudence, Piety, and Charity. Christian is then questioned about where he has been and where he is now going, how he came to be in the narrow way, and what things he has experienced in his journey. With his testimony established on the examination of these witnesses, we then read that "after a little more discourse with him, [that they] had him into the Family" and that many others then welcomed him at the "Threshold of the House."[14]

While they are waiting on the meal, the other sisters (Piety, Prudence, and Charity) continue to interview Christian about his experience. While Discretion was concerned to discover the legitimacy of Christian's identity and journey (how he came to be in the way, where he is going, what he has seen and met with in his journey, and what his name is), the other sisters probe into aspects of his experience in more detail.

---

12. Discriminate administration of the Supper within a paedocommunion framework requires discernable faith on the part of the parents and sponsors.

13. Bunyan, *Confession of My Faith* (*MWJB*, 4:172; Offor 2:610).

14. Bunyan, *Pilgrim's Progress*, 47. Note that capitalizations are irregular in the source text.

Each sister takes her turn in asking Christian questions. They ask questions such as: "What moved you at first to betake yourself to a Pilgrim's Life?" "How did it happen that you came out of your Country this Way?" "Did you not come by the House of the Interpreter?" "Do you not think sometimes of the Country from whence you came?" "Do you not yet bear away with you some of the things that then you were conversant withal?" (I.e., Do you still think about the fleshly things you used to think about and delight in?) "Do you not find sometimes as if those things were vanquished, which at other times are your Perplexity?" (I.e., Do you find that sometimes you struggle with sins in areas you thought you had conquered?) "What is it that makes you so desirous to go to Mount Zion?" They also ask him about his family and why he failed to bring them with him.[15]

Bunyan narrates this dialogue up until the point when "supper was ready." He then narrates that "when they had made ready, they sat down to meat. Now the Table was furnished with fat Things, and with Wine that was well refined; and all their talk at the Table was about the Lord of the Hill; as, namely, about what He had done, and wherefore He did what He did, and why He had built that House."[16]

This section of the book describes the careful process of admission to the Lord's Supper that Bunyan envisions. For our purposes it is important to note that this careful admission to the Table began with interrogations by the porter and Discretion. Christian was not admitted without good reason by those of the house, and Discretion led the way.

Even though there has been no point along the way that Christian has done anything that can readily be interpreted as baptism, he is nonetheless admitted to the house called Beautiful, and this on the basis of his answers to Discretion, Piety, Prudence, and Charity. In these allegorical terms Bunyan is suggesting that this interview process was motivated and guided by discretion (discernment), piety, prudence, and charity. Harry Poe observes that in this section Bunyan "presented his understanding of how one gained entry to the church. He based it solely on discovery of one as a 'visible saint' by virtue of faith in Christ as revealed in the gospel. This understanding of the basis for fellowship in the church and

---

15. See Bunyan, *Pilgrim's Progress*, 47–53.

16. Bunyan, *Pilgrim's Progress*, 53.

the conspicuous absence of baptism as a rite of entry in his theology set Bunyan at odds with many Baptists who held strict Communion views."[17]

Before moving on, one more note seems prudent. If we consider the other end of our framework and continuum, we can see that affirming the importance of discriminate administration of the Lord's Supper is true even for the baptism model, which practices paedocommunion. In giving entrance to an infant of believing parents (or sponsors), the baptism model is saying on its own terms that its community has been formed by a discernible response to the gospel and identification with Christ *by the believing parents (or sponsors)* who have brought their infant to the font and who commit to raising this child in the faith. As such, the practice of indiscriminately administering the Lord's Supper undermines a coherent understanding of visible fellowship, because the persons communing together visibly are not (even in pretense) manifesting union with Christ or each other.

HEARING THE THREE-VOICE HARMONY OF THE ORDINANCES

Most churches today have sophisticated sound equipment, including microphones and mixing boards. I once was on a praise team in which I was fairly certain that the person running the sound board had a low view of my singing ability. I surmised this because week after week I could barely hear my voice in the monitors or over the main speakers. The soundboard tech had kindly and quietly turned down the volume on my mic. Thus, all my efforts to harmonize with the lead vocalist were not being heard (or appreciated!) by the congregation.[18]

Our exploration of baptism, catechesis, and entrance has highlighted multiple voices that are speaking in and through the administration of the ordinances or sacraments of baptism and the Lord's Supper. More specifically, three voices have been heard: (1) the divine voice, (2) the initiate's voice, and (3) the congregation's voice. In their healthiest expressions all four models attend to each of these voices to one degree or another. Nonetheless, each model mixes the voices differently.

---

17. Poe, "John Bunyan," 38.
18. In all honesty that was probably the right call.

THE DIVINE VOICE

The baptism and retrospective models have turned up the volume on the divine voice. God speaks a word in and through baptism that reverberates beyond the baptismal moment. Representing the baptism model (see ch. 2), the Joint Federal Vision Statement affirms that "*God* formally unites a person to Christ and to His covenant people through baptism into the triune Name, and that this baptism obligates such a one to lifelong covenant loyalty to the triune God, each baptized person repenting of his sins and trusting in Christ alone for his salvation."[19] Note that the key actor in baptism is God, not the baptizand or the baptizing community. One should also observe that within the baptism model as it relates to the process of entrance the voice of the initiate has effectively been put on mute. While there is a hope and even expectation that the initiate will be schooled in the faith and later come to profess it personally, the initiate is given entrance into the visible community via paedocommunion apart from any expression of personal faith. As he or she learns to sing their confession (quite literally in the Eastern Orthodox tradition), the volume level will be turned up. The initiate's confession will grow as he or she grows and develops in understanding and capacity to articulate a faith that is personal.

Before continuing, it is important to remember that the models are not an attempt to flatten out the differences that exist between denominations. In any given application of a model a number of theological issues are interacting even as they are broadly following a similar pattern. That is, there is an interplay of a number of theological issues, such as views of divine sovereignty and human responsibility, the nature of personal faith and its expression, and the nature of the church and its role in initiation. For example, though unique theologies of divine sovereignty and human responsibility exist between the monergistic federal vision and the synergistic Eastern Orthodox, the baptism model (in both cases) places emphasis on the divine voice. The Eastern Orthodox and federal vision manifest diversity on a variety of issues such as *ex opere operato*, the use and nature of chrismation, the bestowal of the Holy Spirit, the polity and role of the

---

19. "Joint Federal Vision Statement" (2007), Peter Leithart et al., under "The Sacrament of Baptism," https://federal-vision.com/ecclesiology/joint-federal-vision-statement, emphasis added.

bishop, and the nature of Christ's presence in the Supper—to name some of the most obvious.[20] Nonetheless, the emphasis on the divine voice in this model of entrance is still observable in the common practices of infant baptism combined with paedocommunion. The variety of theological differences will no doubt give each instance a different equalizer setting (to stick with the audio metaphor), but the volume level on the divine voice remains emphasized in each.

The emphasis on the divine voice was also evident in chapter 3 with the retrospective model. Even Luther's view of infant faith places the emphasis on the divine voice in baptism. Recall that Luther defined baptism as "[1] water enclosed in [2] God's command and connected with [3] God's Word."[21] It is God's word that makes the sacrament.[22] God's command to baptize (Matt 28:19) gives baptism a "divine origin" and makes baptism a divine action. "To be baptized in God's name," he writes, "is to be baptized not by human beings but by God himself. Although it is performed by human hands, it is nevertheless truly God's own act."[23]

We also noted this emphasis on the divine voice in chapter 5. There we considered Hardin, Quillian, and White's *Celebration of the Gospel* and its presentation of adult baptism as normed by infant baptism. On their view the divine voice is clearly the loudest voice, especially in baptism: "Baptism is the once-and-for-all reminder of the gracious love of God that precedes any response we may make."[24] As we saw, baptism here is cast as a sign of divine grace that precedes the personal profession that is decisive for entrance. In this way the volume on the divine mic has been elevated above the others. Here, however, the initiate's voice is mixed in since the initiate must give a personal profession of faith *prior to entrance* (i.e., credocommunion). This expresses the pattern of the retrospective model and its use of confirmation as a completion or fulfillment of baptism. The divine voice

---

20. For a helpful overview of Eastern Orthodoxy's understanding of the sacraments see Karmiris, "Concerning the Sacraments," 21–31.

21. Luther, *Small Catechism* (1529; BC, 359.1–2). A similar definition appears in his Smalcald Articles (1537): "Baptism is nothing other than God's Word in the water, commanded by God's institution, or, as Paul says, 'washing by the Word' " (BC 319:5.1).

22. Luther, *Small Catechism* (1529; BC, 359.1–2); "On the Freedom of a Christian," in *Three Treatises*, 279; Althaus, *Theology of Martin Luther*, 345.

23. Luther, *Large Catechism* (1529; BC, 457.6, 9–10).

24. Hardin, Quillian, and White, *Celebration of the Gospel*, 114.

is primary in the process of entrance, but we can hear the initiate's voice giving an antiphonal response as well. However, the next two models of our framework invert this emphasis.

THE INITIATE'S VOICE

The prospective and baptism models emphasize to greater degree the voice of the initiate. Representing the catechesis model, Bunyan's emphasis on the theology of baptism over the sign of baptism demonstrates this emphasis (see ch. 2). On Bunyan's view, the richness of baptism is found in what baptism signifies, not the baptism itself. The doctrine of baptism is none other than the gospel truths of Jesus' death, burial, and resurrection and the initiate's identification with Jesus in his saving activity (buried with and raised with Christ *by faith*). Though the outward sign of water baptism may be lacking, Bunyan argues that one's faith is visible in other ways. Bunyan holds, "By the word of faith, and of good works; moral duties Gospellized, we ought to judge the fitness of members by, by which we ought also to receive them into fellowship."[25] In other words, a personal profession of faith in the gospel and a pattern of godly living that is consistent with it are the marks of a true Christian.[26] If a person bears these marks of fellowship with God (i.e., if God has received that person), then fellowship in the local church should and must be extended. Thus, the loudest voice in this process of entrance is the voice of the initiate even and apart from the sign of water baptism.

The prospective model (model 3 in our framework), with its placement of catechesis prior to baptism and framing of baptism as an act of personal profession, also emphasizes the initiate's voice. Here the volume is louder than the retrospective model but less isolated from the other voices than the baptism model. In chapter 4 we examined the catechesis of the prospective model and concluded that it anticipates the profession of baptism, preparing the baptizand, at minimum, to understand the confessional significance of the approaching event, and, in a fuller sense, to prepare the baptizand to give an explicit, verbal profession of faith both in the moment of baptism and beyond. Here personal faith (*fides qua creditur*) coalesces

---

25. Bunyan, *Confession of My Faith* (*MWJB* 4:165; Offor 2:607).
26. Bunyan, *Confession of My Faith* (*MWJB* 4:167; Offor 2:607).

with the corporate faith of the church (*fides quae creditur*) via profession in the baptismal waters. We made this point by noting the close association of baptism and creed within Christian history.[27] The illustration of our point here needs no further elaboration. Both the prospective and catechesis models clearly emphasize the voice of the baptizand. But what of the final voice, the voice of the congregation?

THE CONGREGATION'S VOICE

As it relates to the voice of the congregation, we can begin by simply noting what we have said already about discriminate administration of the ordinances. The volume level of this mic is directly determined by the extent to which the congregation has been faithful on its own confessional terms to administer both baptism and the Lord's Supper in a responsible and discerning way. When congregations have sufficiently catechized and examined either the initiates or at minimum their parents and sponsors, the act of administration functions as an ecclesial witness to the appropriateness of entrance. When and where discriminate administration falters or fails, so too does the voice of the congregation.

Discriminate administration of the ordinances makes the congregation's voice implicit. However, this voice is heard explicitly in some traditions. For example, the Anglican Book of Common Prayer contains the following baptismal liturgy:

> *After all have been presented, the Celebrant addresses the congregation, saying*
> "Will you who witness these vows do all in your power to support these persons in their life in Christ?"
> *People:* "We will."
> *The Celebrant then says these or similar words*
> "Let us join with *those* who *are* committing themselves to Christ and renew our own baptismal covenant."[28]

---

27. Lietzmann states, "It is indisputable that the root of all creeds [*Regulae fide*] is the formula of belief [*Glaubensformel*] pronounced by the baptizand, or pronounced in his hearing and assented to by him, before his baptism" (Lietzmann, "Die Anfänge des Glaubensbekenntnisses," 226); cf. Pelikan, "Introduction," CCFCT 1:15; Leith, "Creeds and Their Role," 6.

28. *The Book of Common Prayer: And Administration of the Sacraments and Other Rites and Ceremonies of the Church; Together with the Psalter or Psalms of David* (New York: Church Hymnal

The baptismal vows of belief in the articles of the Apostles' Creed, resolve to continue in the apostles' teachings, resistance of evil, repentance, proclamation of the gospel, and Christlike service are then all affirmed *together* (i.e., candidates and congregation all at once).[29] In this way, each baptismal service calls forth both a congregational reaffirmation of baptismal vows and also a congregational commitment to walk with those who are baptized, encouraging them to live in accordance with everything signified therein. The Anglican tradition thus offers a shining example of how the congregation's voice can be made explicit in baptismal practice.[30]

LEARNING BY LISTENING TO OTHER MODELS

As each model has a voice that it emphasizes, it stands to reason that churches may benefit from observing how the other models mix the three voices differently. For example, churches using the prospective model may benefit from considering how the catechesis of the retrospective model draws on and returns to the voice of God in baptism. Recall what we discussed in chapter 3. Martin Luther illustrates a retrospective focus on baptism itself when he writes,

> In baptism ... every Christian has enough to study and practice all his or her life. Christians always have enough to do to believe firmly what baptism promises and brings—victory over death and the devil, forgiveness of sin, God's grace, the entire Christ, and the Holy Spirit with his gifts. In short, the blessings of baptism are so

---

Corporation and the Seabury Press, 1977), 303.

29. *Book of Common Prayer*, 304–5. Walsh, commenting on the relation between the celebrant and the congregation, writes, "The presiding celebrant acts not so much for, or on behalf of, a passive congregation, but with them. He or she leads the people in prayer, in listening to and assimilating the word, in response and offering, encourages the participation of all and co-ordinates it into one harmonious action." See Christopher Walsh, "Celebrant," in Bradshaw, *New SCM Dictionary*.

30. This point connects with Oscar Cullmann's position, discussed in ch. 5, regarding the faith of the congregation in the baptismal moment. It also connects with the affirmation in *Celebration of the Gospel* that "the whole church and this congregation in particular, is godparent or sponsor at every baptism" (Hardin, Quillian, and White, *Celebration of the Gospel*, 115). Cullmann and *Celebration of the Gospel* say more here than most credobaptists are comfortable with (i.e., Cullmann and *Celebration of the Gospel* ground baptismal validity not on personal faith but on the faith of the congregation). Nonetheless, even a strict credobaptist should be able to acknowledge the importance of the congregation's confession of the gospel as the proper, pneumatic context for administration. Borrowing language from our discussion of Cullman's view: the faith of the congregation contextualizes the administration of baptism within the sphere of the Holy Spirit (see ch. 5).

boundless that if our timid nature considers them, it may well doubt whether they could all be true.[31]

Despite points of disagreement that some traditions would have with Luther's baptismal theology (e.g., baptismal regeneration), traditions across the denominational spectrum will agree with Luther that the theological mysteries signed in baptism (even in the variety of ways in which they are understood) are inexhaustible. That is, the ongoing use of baptism is not simply a remembrance of one's identification with Jesus as his disciple, it is a remembrance of the entirety of the Christian faith and all that God has done for one in salvation. There is a theological depth to baptism that suits it for its ongoing pedagogical function.[32] While the prospective model will not apply this to its process of entrance in the form of paedobaptism, there is no reason why this insight should not inform postentrance catechesis.

Similarly, the notion of improving one's baptism seems compatible with ongoing catechesis subsequent to entrance. The Westminster Larger Catechism, question 167, asks, "How is our baptism to be improved by us?" It responds,

The needful but much neglected duty of improving our baptism, is to be performed by us all our life long, especially in the time of temptation, and when we are present at the administration of it to others; by serious and thankful consideration of the nature of it [i.e., baptism], and of the ends for which Christ instituted it, the privileges and benefits conferred and sealed thereby, and our solemn vow made therein; by being humbled for our sinful defilement, our falling short of, and walking contrary to, the grace of baptism, and our engagements; by growing up to assurance of

---

31. Luther, *Large Catechism* (1529; BC, 461). A similar example is found in the Roman tradition, "Baptism is justly called by us the Sacrament of faith, by the Greeks, the mystery of faith, because it embraces the entire profession of the Christian faith" (CCT, 240).

32. In ch. 3 we developed this depth more extensively, showing how it symbolizes major heads of doctrine such as the Trinity, Christology (person and work), salvation (i.e., conversion, cleaning, union with Christ, and glorious exchange), the Christian life and Christian ethics, ecclesiology (e.g., incorporation into the church), and eschatology (resurrection hope).

pardon of sin, and of all other blessings sealed to us in that sacrament; by drawing strength from the death and resurrection of
Christ, into whom we are baptized, for the mortifying of sin, and
quickening of grace; and by endeavouring to live by faith, to have
our conversation in holiness and righteousness, as those that have
therein given up their names to Christ; and to walk in brotherly
love, as being baptized by the same Spirit into one body.[33]

By "improving" baptism, the catechism does not mean adding new things
to baptism, but rather, it intends that the individual live out more fully
the grace benefits signified and sealed in baptism. To do so, this baptism
must be recalled "by serious and thankful consideration."[34] This recollection is specific, not generic; for the believer is to recall its "nature," "ends,"
"privileges and benefits," and "solemn vow made therein." Baptism and all
it represents is here portrayed as a resource for living the Christian life.

The improvement of baptism envisioned within the Westminster
Larger Catechism is not specific to the process of initiation, for it "is
to be performed by us all our life long." There is, therefore, a sense in
which all models of the conceptual framework are compatible with this
notion *following entrance*. Our sketch here demonstrates that churches
that reflect the prospective model's pattern of entrance stand to gain by
observing some of the dynamics of the other models. Even where for any
number of reasons direct application to the process of entrance cannot be
achieved, key insights for ongoing catechesis and liturgy may be applicable. In this case, the divine voice in baptism may be given greater volume
by appreciating the retrospective aspects of catechesis on display within
the retrospective model.

Similarly, churches using the retrospective model in their process of
entrance may benefit from observing how the prospective model emphasizes the voice of the initiate in giving witness to their participation in
the gospel. As we noted in chapter 4, the catechesis of the prospective
model anticipates baptismal profession and subsequent life as a confessor. Personal faith (*fides qua creditur*) must coincide with corporate faith

---

33. Westminster Larger Catechism, q. 167 (RC, 217, 219).
34. Westminster Larger Catechism, q. 167 (RC, 217, 219).

(*fides quae creditur*; "the faith that was once for all *time* handed down to the saints," Jude 3) if it is to be Christian faith. Catechesis seeks to hand down this faith to those who would follow after the risen Christ so that they might know and obey all that he commands (Matt 28:18–20).

As it relates to the retrospective model, there seems to be two key areas in which benefit could come from appreciating the dynamics of the prospective model. First, churches using the retrospective model are pressed to consider how well they are equipping parents and sponsors in their personal profession of faith in the Christian faith as well as in how to hand down this faith to the children whom they are covenanting to raise in it. These parents and sponsors are committing to shepherd these little ones to see and savor Christ. How well is this commitment being conveyed, and in what ways is it being resourced?

Second, in the liminal space between baptism as an infant and confirmation and first Communion, how intentional is the church being in its catechizing of these catechumens? Further, where a catechism class is administered, is the transition from the class to confirmation automatic, or is there a careful pastoral process that charges catechumens to count the cost of discipleship and places the onus for requesting confirmation and first Communion (i.e., entrance) on the catechumens? Does this process involve careful examination that listens for personal trust in the Christian faith from the candidates? Careful answers to these questions may help those using the retrospective model better hear the voice of the initiate.[35]

The above paragraphs are just two examples of how models might listen to and learn from one another even if the insights must be adjusted for the models' own pattern of initiatory liturgical logic and unique theological distinctives (polity, theology of presence, etc.). In so doing a better mix of voices heard in the process of initiation and beyond may be achieved.

---

35. To be clear, I am not suggesting that many of these same questions should not be answered by those who argue for an exclusively prospective model approach. From my own experience, sometimes those within the credobaptist tradition do a poor job in answering these questions in their own contexts.

EVALUATING INTERNAL CONSISTENCY
AND THEOLOGICAL PROJECTIONS

A potential benefit of the framework of this book is that it offers a way to consider the internal consistency of a church's theology and practice of initiation. This is especially important for those of the low-church or free-church tradition who may not have considered the implications of their initiation practices, but this applicability is not limited to this segment of the Christian church. As we have sought to show, the various models of relating baptism, catechesis, and entrance project different views of the nature of baptism, faith's relation to baptism, the timing and nature of confirmation, and a particular view of the church. As such, reviewing how a church's sequence of the key elements of initiation and comparing it with what the church formally confesses about these things may help eliminate dissonance between confessional theology and pastoral practice.

For example, I attended a Baptist church once in which the standard practice was to baptize new believers soon after their profession of faith.[36] The church elders were careful to disciple and examine the baptismal candidate prior to administering baptism. At the appointed service, the candidate would give his or her testimony of conversion and then receive baptism. After this, however, the elders would have the newly baptized come to the next regularly scheduled members' meeting to once again give their testimony and allow the members to provide their approval or reservation about admitting the person into membership.

Some of the church's core theological values should be noted. First, the church placed a strong emphasis on discriminate credobaptism. On this view, personal faith needs to precede baptism, and this particular church did its best to ensure this was the case. Second, the church sought to embody the notion of "regenerate church membership." This is the conviction that only those who express personal faith through baptism should be admitted to the church. Finally, the church, though it had a plurality of elders, practiced a congregational polity (i.e., elder led with

---

36. The following example will feel foreign to those outside a congregational context, but it serves to show the impact that sequence has on the meaning of key initiatory elements.

congregational involvement). As it related to its initiatory structure, the church congregation was responsible to decide who was admitted to the visible local body by examination and vote. Interestingly, what this congregation did not realize for some time was that the structure of initiation was projecting several theological views that they would formally deny.

First, the structure projected a view of baptism that said believer's baptism was a baptism into the universal church but not the local church. After all, the new member was not yet a member until the members' meeting, where the faith necessary for entrance was confirmed by the body. Given the church's commitment to discriminate believers' baptism, it was saying conflicting things. On the one hand, through the careful process of catechesis and examination, the church was saying, "We baptize you as a believer." On the other hand, because the baptizand was not made a member through baptism, it was effectively saying, "We are not sure whether you are a believer, so tell us your testimony again so we can deliberate."

Second, and extending the previous point, this structure projected the view that it was the elder(s) and not the church who had authorized and administered baptism to this person. This cut against the church's congregational polity and its confessed view that baptism was a church ordinance. In practice, the church's practice was projecting a polity of baptism that muted the congregation's voice in baptismal administration.

The church later came to realize the dissonance that this structure was causing. As a result, it inverted the structure, having persons come to a members' meeting to give a personal testimony and request to become a candidate for baptism. The membership would then vote on whether to proceed with administering baptism. Once the candidate was baptized, he or she became a full-communicant member with voting rights in the church.

Our discussion in chapter 5 exemplifies the importance of sequence. Where does the decisive confirmation of faith required for entrance take place? Does the confirmation of faith take place *in* baptism, when the confession is given by the parents and sponsors (baptism model) or by the baptizand (prospective model)? If it does not occur in baptism, does it take place *after* baptism in confirmation and first Communion (retrospective model), or is it *separated from baptism altogether* and accomplished merely through a verbal profession of faith (catechesis model)? Each of the models of our study represents different economies of entrance, and each model projects unique theologies of baptism, catechesis, entrance, the church, and so on. Becoming more aware of the impacts of these issues will only serve toward the end of clearer internal consistency between a local church's theology and practice.

CONCLUSION

As we, like the early church, continue to add people to our number through baptism, catechesis, and Communion, we do well to recognize that the way we do so both forms and reforms the church. The way people are initiated shapes their understanding of the church's nature, their place within it, and their life together within its communion. As such we do well to consider the sermons our initiatory pattern (or patterns!) is preaching to our people. Over time, these sermons will bear fruit. My prayer is that this book helps us hear that sermon better than before. Where there is dissonance with God's word, may he grant us grace to reform our patterns and practice.

APPENDIX 1

—

The following illustration and chart are intended to summarize the final outcome of the book's framework and discussion. Chapters 2–5 contain a visual illustration of the study's proposed framework. Minor developments occur over the course of presentation. The short-form illustration from chapter 5 appears below.

Category	Independent	Prerequisite(s) of entrance? Baptism or catechesis or both?	Interdependent			Prerequisite(s) of entrance? Baptism or catechesis or both?	Independent
Model	Baptism		Retrospective	Orientation of catechesis to baptism	Prospective		Catechesis
Sequence	Baptism ↓ **Entrance** ↓ Catechesis		Baptism ↓ Catechesis ↓ **Entrance**		Catechesis ↓ Baptism ↓ **Entrance**		Catechesis ↓ **Entrance** ↓ (Baptism)

← OBJECTIVE   SUBJECTIVE →

The illustration above has been expanded into a chart, which follows on the next page. The chart spans two pages, but it should be understood as comprising one chart. The "sequence" row seeks to account for some of the nuances of the preceding discussion by use of slashes and parentheses. Slashes indicate that two elements occur together; parentheses indicate that the element is sometimes practiced and sometimes not. Charts of this nature are inherently reductionistic, so the reader is referred to the main body of text for the final word on a matter. My hope, however, is that this helps bring greater clarity to the preceding presentation.

APPENDIX – LONG-FORM ILLUSTRATION

Category	Independent	A	Interdependent	B		C	Independent
Model	Baptism		Retrospective		Prospective		Catechesis
Description	Baptism is sole prerequisite for entrance. Catechesis is subsequent to entrance and grounded upon baptism and Lord's Supper.	Seam (A): Prerequisite(s) of Entrance: Baptism or Catechesis or Both?	Baptism and catechesis are both prerequisites for entrance. Catechesis is grounded upon and looks back to baptism. It forms/grows the seed of faith implanted in baptism. Faith that matters follows baptism. Confirmation of faith is a prerequisite to entrance.	Seam (B): Orientation of Catechesis to Baptism?	Baptism and catechesis are both prerequisites for entrance. Catechesis grounds and looks forward to baptism. Faith that matters precedes baptism and is confirmed in the baptismal event prior to entrance.	Seam (C): Prerequisite(s) of Entrance: Baptism or Catechesis or Both?	Catechesis along with its concomitant examination is sole prerequisite for entrance. Baptism is subsequent to entrance.
Sequence	Baptism/ (Chrismation)/ Entrance-Catechesis-Faith		Baptism-Catechesis-Faith-Confirmation-Entrance		Catechesis-Faith-Baptism/ (Confirmation)-Entrance		Catechesis-Faith-Entrance-(Baptism)
Projected View of Baptism	Paedobaptism; covenant sign of election		Paedobaptism; covenant sign of election		Conversion and credobaptism; sign of identification and decisive profession of faith for entrance		Se-baptism, private, or no baptism; rite of personal growth; separate from entrance
Projected View of Baptismal Faith	Objective gift mediated through community and sacrament. Before: parents/ sponsors; during: community; after: baptizand		Objective gift mediated through community and sacrament. Before: parents/ sponsors; during: community; after: baptizand		Subjective response manifested through baptism and con. Baptizand's faith in the corporate faith is emphasized throughout.		Preexisting faith previously confirmed visibly via admittance to fellowship at Table. Baptizand's faith is emphasized, even on what is a valid baptism.
Exemplars	Paedocommunion (e.g., Eastern Orthodox [EO]; pockets among Reformed)		Roman Catholic and Protestant paedobaptism; adult-infant baptism (CG)		Sacramental adult baptism; conversion-baptism; credobaptism		Credocommunion with open membership

OBJECTIVE ◄───► SUBJECTIVE

APPENDIX – LONG-FORM ILLUSTRATION (CONT)

Category	Independent		Interdependent				Independent
Model	Baptism	(A)	Retrospective	(B)	Prospective	(C)	Catechesis
Confirmation	Initiation form (form 1). Connected in time to event of baptism. Objective conferral of Holy Spirit. Subjective affirmation of content of faith is absent (not counting proxy) and is not prerequisite to entrance.	Seam (A): Catechesis Seam	Maturity-rite form (form 2). Separated in time from event of baptism. Primarily cognitive in nature, confirming understanding of content of faith and subjective affirmation of it. Prerequisite to entrance.	Seam (B): Orientation Seam	Initiation form (form 1) when separated from function of baptism. As a separated rite, typically viewed as sealing of Holy Spirit. Conjoined to event of baptism. Given in the context of a personal faith that has been previously examined.	Seam (C): Baptism Seam	Reception to the Lord's Supper functions as a kind of confirmation. Water baptism (if practiced) is projected to be "mere profession," not confirmation of faith. Entrance is grounded on evidence of Spirit baptism.
Projected View of Church	Christendom view; *corpus permixteum*		Christendom view; *corpus permixteum*		Believers' church; regenerate church		Believer's church; regenerate church

OBJECTIVE ◄————————————————————————————————————► SUBJECTIVE

APPENDIX 2

—

Questions for Reflection

1. Which model of this study most closely aligns with your church's or parish's process of initiation?

2. Would you describe your local church's or parish's practice of baptism as discriminate? Why or why not?

3. Would you describe your local church's or parish's practice of the Lord's Supper or Eucharist as discriminate? Why or why not?

4. Do you see the interviewing of prospective members as important? Do you agree with Bunyan that such an interview can be discerning, spiritually authentic, wise, and loving, or is it none of the church's business (ch. 6)?

5. If you implemented an interview process, what questions would you ask?

6. What obstacles would prevent you from strengthening perceived areas of weakness in your local church's or parish's discriminate administration of the ordinances?

7. Does the divine voice or the initiate's voice receive the strongest emphasis in your church's or parish's process of entrance? How might you strengthen the weaker of the two?

8. How well is the congregation's voice being heard in this process? Are there any ways it might be helpfully strengthened?

9. How might this study's discussion of the theological depth of baptism (see ch. 3) inform a connection between catechesis and baptism (both before and after baptismal administration)?

10. Do you agree or disagree with the notion of an ongoing use of baptism (ch. 4)? How might this be worked out in preaching and in discipleship?

11. In light of chapter 5, where is the decisive confirmation of faith placed liturgically in your church or parish's process of entrance? What is being projected by this placement? Does this projection align with your confessed theology (e.g., the nature of the church, the nature of baptism and the Lord's Supper, the relation of faith to these sacraments or ordinances, the role of the church in confirming faith, covenant and church membership, church discipline, etc.)?

BIBLIOGRAPHY

—

CREEDS, CONFESSIONS, CATECHISMS, LITURGIES, AND CHURCH MANUALS

Anglican Catechism [1549, 1662]. Pages 517–23 in vol. 3 of *The Creeds of Christendom*, 6th rev and enl. ed. Edited by Philip Schaff. New York: Harper & Brothers, 1877.

Apology of the Augsburg Confession [1531]. Pages 107–294 in *The Book of Concord: The Confessions of the Evangelical Lutheran Church*. Edited by Robert Kolb and Timothy J. Wengert. Minneapolis: Fortress, 2000.

Apostles' Creed: Textus Receptus [ca. 753]. Page 669 in vol. 1 of *Creeds and Confessions of Faith in the Christian Tradition*. Edited by Jaroslav Pelikan and Valerie R. Hotchkiss. New Haven: Yale University Press, 2003.

Apostolic Tradition. Page 61 in vol. 1 of *Creeds and Confessions of Faith in the Christian Tradition*. Edited by Jaroslav Pelikan and Valerie R. Hotchkiss. New Haven: Yale University Press, 2003.

Augsburg Confession [1530]. Pages 27–106 in *The Book of Concord: The Confessions of the Evangelical Lutheran Church*. Edited by Robert Kolb and Timothy J. Wengert. Minneapolis: Fortress, 2000.

Augustine. *On the Catechising of the Uninstructed*. In vol. 3 of *Nicene and Post-Nicene Fathers*, series 1. Edited by Philip Schaff. 14 vols. 1886–1889. Repr., Grand Rapids: Eerdmans, 1994.

Baptism, Eucharist and Ministry: The Lima Report. Faith and Order Paper 111. Geneva: World Council of Churches, 1982.

Baptist Faith and Message [1925]. Pages 343–54 in *Creeds of the Churches: A Reader in Christian Doctrine from the Bible to the Present*, 3rd ed. Edited by John H. Leith. Louisville: Westminster John Knox, 1982.

Baptist Faith and Message [1963]. Pages 410–17 in *Baptist Confessions of Faith*, 2nd rev. ed. Edited by William L. Lumpkin and Bill J. Leonard. Valley Forge, PA: Judson, 2011.

Baptist Faith and Message [2000]. Pages 510–19 in *Baptist Confessions of Faith*, 2nd rev. ed. Edited by William L. Lumpkin and Bill J. Leonard. Valley Forge, PA: Judson, 2011.

Barclay, Robert. *An Apology for the True Christian Divinity: Being an Explanation and Vindication of the Principles and Doctrines of the People Called Quakers*. New York: S. Wood and Sons for the Trustees of Obadiah Brown's Benevolent Fund, 1827.

———. *Barclay's Apology in Modern English*. Edited by Dean Freiday. Newberg, OR: Barclay, 1991.

———. *A Catechism and Confession of Faith*. Philadelphia: Friends' Book Store, 1673.

———. *Theses Theologicae*. Pages 789–98 in vol. 3 of *The Creeds of Christendom*, 6th rev and enl. ed. Edited by Philip Schaff. New York: Harper & Brothers, 1877.

Basil of Caesarea. *The Treatise De Spiritu Sancto*. In vol. 8 of *Nicene and Post-Nicene Fathers*, series 2. Edited by Philip Schaff and Henry Wace. 14 vols. 1890–1900. Repr., Peabody, MA: Hendrickson, 1994.

Beeke, Joel R., and Sinclair B. Ferguson, eds. *Reformed Confessions: Harmonized*. Grand Rapids: Baker, 1999.

Belgic Confession [1561]. Pages 185–219 in *Reformed Confessions of the Sixteenth Century*. Edited by Arthur C. Cochrane. Louisville: Westminster John Knox, 2003.

Book of Common Prayer and Other Rites and Ceremonies of the Church, According to the Use of the Church of England. London: John Bill, Thomas Newcomb, and Henry Hills, 1681.

"Book of Order of the Federation of Reformed Churches" [11th rev.
	ed., 2013]. The Federation of Reformed Churches. http://www.
	federationorc.org/.

The Book of Worship for Church and Home. Nashville: Methodist Publishing
	House, 1964–1965.

Bradshaw, Paul F., Maxwell E. Johnson, L. Edward Phillips, and Harold W.
	Attridge. *The Apostolic Tradition: A Commentary.* Minneapolis:
	Fortress, 2002.

Bull of Union with the Armenians [1439]. Pages 755–65 in vol. 1 of *Creeds
	and Confessions of Faith in the Christian Tradition.* Edited by Jaroslav
	Pelikan and Valerie R. Hotchkiss. New Haven: Yale University Press,
	2003.

Bunyan, John. *A Confession of My Faith, and a Reason of My Practice* [1672].
	Pages 593–616 in vol. 2 of *The Works of John Bunyan.* Edited by
	George Offor. London: Blackie and Son, 1861.

———. *Differences in Judgment about Water-Baptism, No Bar to Communion*
	[1673]. Pages 189–264 in vol. 4 of *The Miscellaneous Works of John
	Bunyan.* Edited by T. L. Underwood and Roger Sharrock. New York:
	Oxford University Press, 1989.

———. *Peaceable Principles and True* [1674]. Pages 269–90 in vol. 4 of *The
	Miscellaneous Works of John Bunyan.* Edited by T. L. Underwood and
	Roger Sharrock. New York: Oxford University Press, 1989.

———. *Some Gospel-Truth Opened* [1656]. Pages 7–116 in vol. 1 of *The
	Miscellaneous Works of John Bunyan.* Edited by T. L. Underwood and
	Roger Sharrock. Oxford: Clarendon, 1980.

———. *A Vindication of Gospel Truths Opened* [1657]. Pages 122–220 in
	vol. 1 of *The Miscellaneous Works of John Bunyan.* Edited by T. L.
	Underwood and Roger Sharrock. Oxford: Clarendon, 1980.

Campbell, Thomas. *Propositions from Declaration and Address* [1809].
	Pages 220–22 in vol. 3 of *Creeds and Confessions of Faith in the
	Christian Tradition.* Edited by Jaroslav Pelikan and Valerie R.
	Hotchkiss. New Haven: Yale University Press, 2003.

Canons and Decrees of the Council of Trent. Translated by Henry Joseph Schroeder. Rockford, IL: Tan Books, 1978.

Catechism of the Catholic Church: With Modifications from the Editio Typica. New York: Doubleday, 1997.

Catechism of the Council of Trent: For Parish Priests. Translated with notes by John A. McHugh and Charles J. Callan. Charlotte: TAN Books, 1982.

Cochrane, Arthur, ed. *Reformed Confessions of the Sixteenth Century.* Louisville: Westminster John Knox, 2003.

The Code of Canon Law: In English Translation. Translated by the Canon Law Society of Great Britain and Ireland. Grand Rapids: Eerdmans, 1983.

Confession of Faith Containing XXIII Articles [1673]. Pages 127–48 in vol. 3 of *Creeds and Confessions of Faith in the Christian Tradition.* Edited by Jaroslav Pelikan and Valerie R. Hotchkiss. New Haven: Yale University Press, 2003.

Confession of the Free-Will Baptists [1834, 1868]. Pages 749–56 in vol. 3 of *The Creeds of Christendom*, 6th rev. and enl. ed. Edited by Philip Schaff. New York: Harper & Brothers, 1877.

"Constitution and Canons" of the Episcopal Church [2012]. Title I, Canon 17, Sec. 7 (page 59). Archives of the Episcopal Church. http://www.episcopalarchives.org/sites/default/files/publications/2012_CandC.pdf.

Creed of Marcellus [340]. Page 23 in *Creeds of the Churches: A Reader in Christian Doctrine from the Bible to the Present*, 3rd ed. Edited by John H. Leith. Louisville: Westminster John Knox, 1982.

Cyril of Jerusalem. *The Catechetical Lectures of S. Cyril.* In vol. 7 of *Nicene and Post-Nicene Fathers*, series 2. Edited by Philip Schaff and Henry Wace. 1890–1900. 14 vols. Repr., Peabody, MA: Hendrickson, 1994.

Didache. Page 42 in vol. 1 of *Creeds and Confessions of Faith in the Christian Tradition.* Edited by Jaroslav Pelikan and Valerie R. Hotchkiss. New Haven: Yale University Press, 2003.

Divine Liturgy of St. John Chrysostomos. Pages 269–95 in vol. 1 of *Creeds and Confessions of Faith in the Christian Tradition*. Edited by Jaroslav Pelikan and Valerie R. Hotchkiss. New Haven: Yale University Press, 2003.

Doctrinal Basis of the Baptist Union of Victoria, Australia [1888]. Pages 434–37 in *Baptist Confessions of Faith*, 2nd rev. ed. Edited by William L. Lumpkin and Bill J. Leonard. Valley Forge, PA: Judson, 2011.

Dogmatic Decrees of the Council of Trent [1545–1563]. Pages 819–71 in vol. 2 of *Creeds and Confessions of Faith in the Christian Tradition*. Edited by Jaroslav Pelikan and Valerie R. Hotchkiss. New Haven: Yale University Press, 2003.

Dordrecht Confession [1632]. Pages 61–73 in *Baptist Confessions of Faith*, 2nd rev. ed. Edited by William L. Lumpkin and Bill J. Leonard. Valley Forge, PA: Judson, 2011.

Dositheus and the Synod of Jerusalem. Confession [1672]. Pages 615–35 in vol. 1 of *Creeds and Confessions of Faith in the Christian Tradition*. Edited by Jaroslav Pelikan and Valerie R. Hotchkiss. New Haven: Yale University Press, 2003.

English Declaration at Amsterdam [1611]. Pages 106–13 in *Baptist Confessions of Faith*, 2nd rev. ed. Edited by William L. Lumpkin and Bill J. Leonard. Valley Forge, PA: Judson, 2011.

Formula of Concord [1577]. Pages 481–660 in *The Book of Concord: The Confessions of the Evangelical Lutheran Church*. Edited by Robert Kolb and Timothy J. Wengert. Minneapolis: Fortress, 2000.

Geneva Catechism [1541/42]. Pages 320–63 in vol. 2 of *Creeds and Confessions of Faith in the Christian Tradition*. Edited by Jaroslav Pelikan and Valerie R. Hotchkiss. New Haven: Yale University Press, 2003.

Heidelberg Catechism [1563]. Pages 305–31 in *Reformed Confessions of the Sixteenth Century*. Edited by Arthur C. Cochrane. Louisville: Westminster John Knox, 2003.

Hubmaier, Balthasar. "A Christian Catechism." Pages 339–65 in *Balthasar Hubmaier: Theologian of Anabaptism*. Edited by H. Wayne Pipkin and John H. Yoder. Classics of the Radical Reformation 5. Scottdale, PA: Herald, 1989.

"Instruction on Infant Baptism *(Pastoralis actio)*" [1980]. Congregation for the Doctrine of the Faith. http://www.vatican.va/roman_curia /congregations/cfaith/documents/rc_con_cfaith_doc_19801020 _pastoralis_actio_en.html.

Interrogatory Creed of Hippolytus [ca. 215]. Page 23 in *Creeds of the Churches: A Reader in Christian Doctrine from the Bible to the Present*, 3rd ed. Edited by John H. Leith. Louisville: Westminster John Knox, 1982.

Jeremias II. *The Reply of Ecumenical Patriarch Jeremias II to the Augsburg Confession* [1576]. Pages 392–474 in vol. 1 of *Creeds and Confessions of Faith in the Christian Tradition*. Edited by Jaroslav Pelikan and Valerie R. Hotchkiss. New Haven: Yale University Press, 2003.

Justin Martyr. *First Apology*. Pages 45–47 in vol. 1 of *Creeds and Confessions of Faith in the Christian Tradition*. Edited by Jaroslav Pelikan and Valerie R. Hotchkiss. New Haven: Yale University Press, 2003.

Kolb, Robert, and Timothy J. Wengert, eds. *The Book of Concord: The Confessions of the Evangelical Lutheran Church*. Translated by Robert Kolb, Charles Arand, Eric Gritsch, William Russell, James Schaaf, and Jane Strohl. Minneapolis: Fortress, 2000.

Leith, John H., ed. *Creeds of the Churches: A Reader in Christian Doctrine from the Bible to the Present*. 3rd ed. Louisville: Westminster John Knox, 1982.

Longer Catechism of the Orthodox, Catholic, Eastern Church. Pages 445–542 in vol. 2 of *The Creeds of Christendom*, 6th rev. and enl. ed. Edited by Philip Schaff. New York: Harper & Brothers, 1877.

Lumen Gentium: Dogmatic Constitution on the Church [1964]. Pages 572–634 in vol. 3 of *Creeds and Confessions of Faith in the Christian Tradition*. Edited by Jaroslav Pelikan and Valerie R. Hotchkiss. New Haven: Yale University Press, 2003.

Lumpkin, William L., and Bill J. Leonard, eds. *Baptist Confessions of Faith*. 2nd rev. ed. Valley Forge, PA: Judson, 2011.

Migne, Jacques-Paul, ed. *Patrologia Graeca* [= *Patrologiae Cursus Completus: Series Graeca*]. 162 vols. Paris: 1857–1886.

Moglia, Peter. *The Orthodox Confession of the Catholic and Apostolic Eastern Church* [1638/42]. Pages 561–612 in vol. 1 of *Creeds and Confessions of Faith in the Christian Tradition*. Edited by Jaroslav Pelikan and Valerie R. Hotchkiss. New Haven: Yale University Press, 2003.

Nettles, Tom J. *Teaching Truth, Changing Hearts: The Study of Catechisms in Baptist Life*. Amityville, NY: Calvary, 1998.

New Hampshire Confession [1833]. Pages 376–83 in *Baptist Confessions of Faith*, 2nd rev. ed. Edited by William L. Lumpkin and Bill J. Leonard. Valley Forge, PA: Judson, 2011.

Niceno-Constantinopolitan Creed [381]. Pages 160–63 in vol. 1 of *Creeds and Confessions of Faith in the Christian Tradition*. Edited by Jaroslav Pelikan and Valerie R. Hotchkiss. New Haven: Yale University Press, 2003.

Orthodox Creed [1678]. Pages 298–347 in *Baptist Confessions of Faith*, 2nd rev. ed. Edited by William L. Lumpkin and Bill J. Leonard. Valley Forge, PA: Judson, 2011.

Pelikan, Jaroslav, and Valerie R. Hotchkiss, eds. *Creeds and Confessions of Faith in the Christian Tradition*. 3 vols. New Haven: Yale University Press, 2003.

Philadelphia Confession [1742]. Pages 363–69 in *Baptist Confessions of Faith*, 2nd rev. ed. Edited by William L. Lumpkin and Bill J. Leonard. Valley Forge, PA: Judson, 2011.

Religious Doctrine of the Evangelical Christians [Russian, 1884]. Pages 440–52 in *Baptist Confessions of Faith*, 2nd rev. ed. Edited by William L. Lumpkin and Bill J. Leonard. Valley Forge, PA: Judson, 2011.

Report of the Commission on Worship: General Conference of the Methodist Church. Nashville: Methodist Publishing House, 1960.

Rite of Christian Initiation of Adults [Ordo Initiationis Christianae Adultorum]: Prepared by International Commission on English in the Liturgy and Bishops' Committee on the Liturgy. Washington, DC: United States Catholic Conference, 1988.

Roman Symbol [second century]. Pages 681–82 in vol. 1 of *Creeds and Confessions of Faith in the Christian Tradition*. Edited by Jaroslav

Pelikan and Valerie R. Hotchkiss. New Haven: Yale University Press, 2003.

Schaff, Philip, ed. *The Creeds of Christendom*. 3 vols. 6th rev. and enl. ed. New York: Harper & Brothers, 1877.

Schleitheim Confession [1527]. Pages 22–30 in *Baptist Confessions of Faith*, 2nd rev. ed. Edited by William L. Lumpkin and Bill J. Leonard. Valley Forge, PA: Judson, 2011.

Scottish Confession of Faith [1560]. Pages 159–84 in *Reformed Confessions of the Sixteenth Century*. Edited by Arthur C. Cochrane. Louisville: Westminster John Knox, 2003.

Second Helvetic Confession [1566]. Pages 220–301 in *Reformed Confessions of the Sixteenth Century*. Edited by Arthur C. Cochrane. Louisville: Westminster John Knox, 2003.

Second London Confession [1677, 1688]. Pages 216–97 in *Baptist Confessions of Faith*, 2nd rev. ed. Edited by William L. Lumpkin and Bill J. Leonard. Valley Forge, PA: Judson, 2011.

Short Confession of Faith of Hans de Ries [1610]. Pages 755–67 in vol. 2 of *Creeds and Confessions of Faith in the Christian Tradition*. Edited by Jaroslav Pelikan and Valerie R. Hotchkiss. New Haven: Yale University Press, 2003.

Smalcald Articles [1537]. Pages 295–328 in *The Book of Concord: The Confessions of the Evangelical Lutheran Church*. Edited by Robert Kolb and Timothy J. Wengert. Minneapolis: Fortress, 2000.

Teaching of the Twelve Apostles, Commonly Called the Didache. Pages 171–180 in vol. 1 of *Early Christian Fathers*. Edited and translated by Cyril C. Richardson. Philadelphia: Westminster, 1953.

Thirty-Nine Articles [1562]. Pages 486–516 in vol. 3 of *The Creeds of Christendom*, 6th rev. and enl. ed. Edited by Philip Schaff. New York: Harper & Brothers, 1877.

Torrence, T. F. *The School of Faith: The Catechisms of the Reformed Church*. London: Clarke, 1959.

"*Unitatis redintegratio*: Decree on Ecumenism." Doctrinal Decrees of the Second Vatican Council (1962-65), 5.3. Pages 635-50 in vol. 3 of *Creeds and Confessions of Faith in the Christian Tradition*. Edited by Jaroslav Pelikan and Valerie R. Hotchkiss. New Haven: Yale University Press, 2003.

The United Methodist Book of Worship. Nashville: United Methodist Publishing House, 1992.

Waterland Confession [1580]. Pages 42-60 in *Baptist Confessions of Faith*, 2nd rev. ed. Edited by William L. Lumpkin and Bill J. Leonard. Valley Forge, PA: Judson, 2011.

Westminster Larger Catechism [1647]. In *Reformed Confessions: Harmonized*. Edited by Joel R. Beeke and Sinclair B. Ferguson. Grand Rapids: Baker, 1999.

Westminster Shorter Catechism [1646]. In *Reformed Confessions: Harmonized*. Edited by Joel R. Beeke and Sinclair B. Ferguson. Grand Rapids: Baker, 1999.

Whitaker, E. C., and Maxwell E. Johnson. *Documents of the Baptismal Liturgy*. Rev. and exp. ed. Collegeville, MN: Liturgical, 2003.

BOOKS AND MONOGRAPHS

Aland, Kurt. *Did the Early Church Baptise Infants?* London: SCM, 1963.

———. *Die Stellung der Kinder in der frühen christlichen Gemeinden und ihre Taufe*. Munich: Kaiser, 1967.

———. *Taufe und Kindertaufe: 40 Sätze zur Aussage des Neuen Testaments und dem historichen Befund, zur modernen Debatte darüber*. Gütersloh: Gütersloher Verlagshaus Gerd Mohn, 1971.

Allison, Gregg R. *Historical Theology: An Introduction to Christian Doctrine*. Grand Rapids: Zondervan, 2011.

———. *Sojourners and Strangers: The Doctrine of the Church*. Foundations of Evangelical Theology 5. Wheaton, IL: Crossway, 2012.

Althaus, Paul. *The Theology of Martin Luther*. Philadelphia: Fortress, 1966.

Barth, Karl. *The Teaching of the Church Regarding Baptism*. London: SCM, 1948.

Beasley-Murray, George R. *Baptism in the New Testament*. New York: St. Martin's, 1962.

———. *Baptism Today and Tomorrow*. New York: St. Martin's, 1966.

Behe, Michael. *Darwin's Black Box: The Biochemical Challenge to Evolution*. New York: Simon & Schuster, 1998.

Blomberg, Craig L. *Matthew*. New American Commentary 22. Nashville: Broadman, 1992.

Bruce, F. F. *The Epistle of Paul to the Galatians: A Commentary on the Greek Text*. New International Greek Testament Commentary. Exeter: Paternoster, 1982.

Bucer, Martin. "De Regno Christi." Pages 174–394, in *Melanchthon and Bucer*. Edited and translated by Wilhem Pauck. Louisville: Westminster John Knox, 1969.

Calvin, John. *Institutes of the Christian Religion*. Translated by Henry Beveridge. London: Clarke, 1957.

———. *Institutes of the Christian Religion*. Edited by John T. McNeill. Translated by Ford L. Battles. 2 vols. Library of Christian Classics 20–21. Louisville: Westminster John Knox, 1960.

Campbell, Alexander. *Christian Baptism, with Its Antecedents and Consequents*. Bethany, VA: 1851.

Cross, Anthony R. *Baptism and the Baptists: Theology and Practice in Twentieth-Century Britain*. Paternoster Biblical and Theological Monographs. Waynesboro, GA: Paternoster, 2000.

———. *Recovering the Evangelical Sacrament: Baptisma Semper Reformandum*. Eugene, OR: Pickwick, 2013.

Cross, F. L., and E. A. Livingstone, eds. *Oxford Dictionary of the Christian Church*. 3rd rev. ed. New York: Oxford University Press, 2005.

Cullmann, Oscar. *Baptism in the New Testament*. Studies in Biblical Theology 1/1. London: SCM, 1950.

———. *Die Tauflehre des Neuen Testaments: Erwachsenen- und Kindertaufe*. Zürich: Zingli-Verlag, 1948.

Davies, J. G. *The Architectural Setting of Baptism.* London: Barrie & Rockliff, 1962.

Dix, Gregory. *Confirmation, or Laying On of Hands.* London: Society for Promoting Christian Knowledge, 1936.

———. *The Theology of Confirmation in Relation to Baptism.* London: Dacre, 1946.

Dujarier, Michael. *A History of the Catechumenate: The First Six Centuries.* Translated by Edward J. Haasl. New York: Sadlier, 1979.

Dulles, Avery. *The Craft of Theology: From Symbol to System.* New exp. ed. New York: Crossroad, 1992.

———. *Models of Revelation.* Maryknoll, NY: Orbis Books, 1992.

———. *Models of the Church.* New York: Doubleday, 1978.

Dunn, James D. G. *Baptism in the Holy Spirit: A Re-examination of the New Testament Teaching on the Gift of the Spirit in Relation to Pentecostalism Today.* Philadelphia: Westminster, 1970.

Fairbairn, Donald. *Life in the Trinity: An Introduction to Theology with the Help of the Church Fathers.* Downers Grove, IL: IVP Academic, 2009.

Ferguson, Everett. *Baptism in the Early Church: History, Theology, and Liturgy in the First Five Centuries.* Grand Rapids: Eerdmans, 2009.

Fiddes, Paul S., and Bruce Matthews. *Conversations around the World 2000–2005: The Report of the International Conversations between the Anglican Communion and the Baptist World Alliance.* London: Anglican Communion Office, 2005.

Finn, Thomas M. *Early Christian Baptism and the Catechumenate: West and East Syria.* Edited by Thomas Halton. Message of the Fathers of the Church 5. Collegeville, MN: Liturgical, 1992.

Fisher, John D. C. *Christian Initiation: Baptism in the Medieval West; A Study in the Disintegration of the Primitive Rite of Initiation.* London: SPCK, 1965.

Flemington, W. F. *The New Testament Doctrine of Baptism.* London: SPCK, 1948.

Forsyth, P. T. *The Church and the Sacraments*. Naperville, IL: Allenson, 1949.

Fox, George. *The Journal of George Fox*. 8th ed. Vol. 2. London: Friend's Bookstop, 1902.

Freeman, Curtis W. *Contesting Catholicity: Theology for Other Baptists*. Waco: Baylor University Press, 2014.

Fuller, Andrew. *Baptism and the Terms of Communion: An Argument*. 3rd ed. Charleston, SC: Southern Baptist Publication Society, 1854. Repr., Paris, AR: Baptist Standard Bearer, 2006.

Gallant, Tim. *Feed My Lambs*. Grande Prairie, AB: Pactum Reformanda, 2002.

Gantt, Susan Denise. "Catechetical Instruction of Children as an Educational Process for the Teaching of Doctrine to Children in Southern Baptist Churches." PhD diss., Southern Baptist Theological Seminary, 2004.

Garrett, James Leo. *Systematic Theology*. Vol. 2. Grand Rapids: Eerdmans, 1995.

George, Timothy. *Theology of the Reformers*. Nashville: Broadman & Holman, 1988.

Grönvik, Lorenz. *Die Taufe in der Theologie Martin Luthers*. Åbo: Åbo Akademi, 1968.

Guthrie, Donald. *New Testament Theology*. Leicester, UK: Inter-Varsity, 1981.

Hagner, Donald A. *Matthew 14–28*. Word Biblical Commentary 33B. Dallas: Word, 1995.

Hammett, John. *40 Questions about Baptism and the Lord's Supper*. Grand Rapids: Kregel, 2015.

Hammond, Peter, ed. *Towards a Church Architecture*. London: Architectural, 1962.

Hardin, H. Grady, Joseph D. Quillian Jr., and James F. White. *The Celebration of the Gospel: A Study in Christian Worship*. New York: Abingdon, 1964.

Harmless, William. *Augustine and the Catechumenate*. Collegeville, MN: Liturgical, 1995.

Hubbard, B. J. *The Matthean Redaction of a Primitive Apostolic Commissioning: An Exegesis of Matthew 28:16–20.* Society of Biblical Literature Dissertation Series 19. Missoula, MT: Scholars, 1974.

Jamieson, Bobby. *Going Public: Why Baptism Is Required for Church Membership.* Nashville: B&H Academic, 2015.

Jensen, Robin M. *Baptismal Imagery in Early Christianity.* Grand Rapids: Baker Academic, 2012.

Jeremias, Joachim. *Infant Baptism in the First Four Centuries.* London: SCM, 1960.

———. *The Origins of Infant Baptism.* London: SCM, 1963.

Johnson, Maxwell E. *The Rites of Christian Initiation: Their Evolution and Interpretation.* 2nd ed. Collegeville, MN: Liturgical, 2007.

Justification: Report of the Committee to Study the Doctrine of Justification. Willow Grove, PA: Committee on Christian Education of the Orthodox Presbyterian Church, 2007.

Karmiris, John. "Concerning the Sacraments." Pages 21–31 in *Eastern Orthodox Theology: A Contemporary Reader.* Edited by Daniel B. Clendenin. Grand Rapids: Baker Academic, 2003.

Kavanagh, Aidan. *Confirmation: Origins and Reform.* New York: Pueblo, 1988.

———. *The Shape of Baptism: The Rite of Christian Initiation.* New York: Pueblo, 1978.

Keuhn, Regina. *A Place for Baptism.* Chicago: Liturgy Training, 1992.

Kiffin, William. *A Sober Discourse of Right to Church-Communion.* Baptist Distinctives Series 31. London: Printed by Geo. Larkin for Enoch Prosser, 1681. Repr., Paris, AR: Baptist Standard Bearer, 2006.

Kittel, Gerhard, and Gerhard Friedrich, eds. *Theological Dictionary of the New Testament.* Translated by Geoffrey W. Bromily. 10 vols. Grand Rapids: Eerdmans, 1964–1976.

Lampe, G. W. H. *Seal of the Spirit: A Study in the Doctrine of Baptism and Confirmation in the New Testament and the Fathers.* 2nd ed. London: SPCK, 1967.

Lee, Jason K. *Theology of John Smyth*. Macon, GA: Mercer University Press, 2003.

Lohse, Bernhard. *Martin Luther's Theology: Its Historical and Systematic Development*. Edited and translated by Roy A. Harrisville. Minneapolis: Fortress, 1999.

Lossky, Vladimir. *The Mystical Theology of the Eastern Church*. Crestwood, NY: St. Vladimir's Seminary Press, 1976.

Luther, Martin. *Babylonian Captivity of the Church*. Pages 113–260 in *Three Treatises*. Translated by A. T. W. Steinhäuser. Edited by Frederick C. Ahrens and Abdel Ross Wentz. *LW* 36:3–126. Philadelphia: Fortress, 1970.

———. *Concerning Rebaptism*. *LW* 40:229–62. Edited by Helmut T. Lehmann. Translated by Conrad Bergendoff. Philadelphia: Muhlenberg, 1958.

———. *Defense and Explanation of All Articles*. *LW* 32:3–100. Edited by George W. Forell. Translated by Charles M. Jacobs. Philadelphia: Muhlenberg, 1958.

———. *On the Freedom of a Christian*. Pages 261–315 in *Three Treatises*. Translated by W. A. Lambert and Harold J. Grimm. *LW* 31:327–77. Philadelphia: Fortress, 1970.

Luz, Ulrich. *Matthew 21–28: A Commentary*. Edited by Helmut Koester. Translated by James E. Crouch. Hermeneia. Minneapolis: Fortress, 2005.

Mason, Arthur J. *The Relation of Confirmation to Baptism: As Taught in Holy Scripture and the Fathers*. London: Longmans, Green, 1891.

Mastrantonis, George. *Augsburg and Constantinople: The Correspondence between the Tübingen Theologians and Patriarch Jeremiah II of Constantinople on the Augsburg Confession*. Brookline, MA: Holy Cross Orthodox, 1982.

Mayer, F. E., and Arthur Carl Piepkorn. *The Religious Bodies of America*. 4th rev. ed. St. Louis: Concordia, 1961.

McKim, Donald. *Westminster Dictionary of Theological Terms*. Louisville: Westminster John Knox, 1996.

Melanchthon, Philip. *Loci Communes* [1543]. Translated by J. A. O. Preus. St. Louis: Concordia, 1992.

Metzger, Bruce M. *A Textual Commentary on the Greek New Testament*. 2nd ed. Stuttgart: Deutsche Bibelgesellschaft, 1994.

Miller, Samuel. *The Utility and Importance of Creeds and Confessions: An Introductory Lecture, Delivered at the Opening of the Summer Session of the Theological Seminary of the Presbyterian Church, Princeton, July 2, 1824*. Princeton, NJ: D. A. Borrenstein, 1824. Repr., Lexington, KY: Forgotten Books, 2012.

Moo, Douglas J. *The Epistle to the Romans*. New International Commentary on the New Testament. Grand Rapids: Eerdmans, 1996.

Mueller, John. *Christian Dogmatics: A Handbook of Doctrinal Theology for Pastors, Teachers, and Laymen*. St. Louis: Concordia, 1934.

Naylor, Peter. *Calvinism, Communion and the Baptists: A Study of English Calvinistic Baptists from the Late 1600s to the Early 1800s*. Milton Keynes: Paternoster, 2004.

Niebuhr, H. Richard. *Christ and Culture*. New York: HarperCollins, 2001.

Oberman, Heiko. *Luther: Man between God and the Devil*. Translated by Eileen Walliser-Schwarzbart. New Haven: Yale University Press, 1982.

Oden, Thomas C. *Systematic Theology*. 3 vols. San Francisco: HarperSanFrancisco, 1987–1992.

Packer, J. I. *Concise Theology: A Guide to Historic Christian Beliefs*. Wheaton: Tyndale House, 1993.

——. *Evangelism and the Sovereignty of God*. Downers Grove, IL: InterVarsity, 1961.

Packer, J. I., and Gary A. Parrett. *Grounded in the Gospel: Building Believers the Old-Fashioned Way*. Grand Rapids: Baker, 2010.

Pelikan, Jaroslav. *Credo: Historical and Theological Guide to Creeds and Confessions of Faith in the Christian Tradition*. New Haven: Yale University Press, 2003.

———. *Luther the Expositor: Introduction to the Reformer's Exegetical Writings.* Companion Volume to *Luther's Works.* St. Louis: Concordia, 1959.

Pelikan, Jaroslav, and Helmutt T. Lehmann, eds. *Luther's Works.* 55 vols. St. Louis: Concordia [vols. 1–30]; Philadelphia, PA: Muhlenberg, 1955–86, [vols. 31–55].

Pomazansky, Michael. *Orthodox Dogmatic Theology: A Concise Exposition.* Platina, CA: Saint Herman of Alaska Brotherhood, 1997.

Primrose, Ricky. "Thomas Grantham's Doctrine of the Imposition of Hands: Theological Implications for Baptist Ecclesiology." PhD diss., Southwestern Baptist Theological Seminary, 2018.

Ratzinger, Joseph Cardinal. *Introduction to the Catechism of the Catholic Church.* San Francisco: Ignatius, 1994.

Regan, Jane E. *Exploring the Catechism.* Collegeville, MN: Liturgical, 1994.

Ristow, Sebastian. *Frühchristliche Baptisterien.* Jahrbuch für Antike und Christentum, Egänzungsband 27. Münster: Aschendorff, 1998.

Sandlin, Andrew, ed. *Backbone of the Bible: Covenant in Contemporary Perspective.* Nacogdoches, TX: Covenant Media, 2004.

Schaberg, Jane. *The Father, the Son, and the Holy Spirit: The Triadic Phrase in Matthew 18:19b.* Society of Biblical Literature Dissertation Series 61. Chico, CA: Scholars, 1982.

Schaeffer, Francis A. *Two Contents, Two Realities.* Downers Grove, IL: InterVarsity, 1975.

Schenck, Lewis Bevens. *The Presbyterian Doctrine of Children in the Covenant.* Yale Studies in Theology 12. New Haven: Yale University Press, 1940.

Schlatter, Adolf. *The Theology of the Apostles.* Translated by Andreas J. Köstenberger. Grand Rapids: Baker, 1999.

Schlink, Edmund. *Die Lehre von der Taufe.* Kassell: J. Stauda Verlag, 1969.

Schmemann, Alexander. *Introduction to Liturgical Theology.* Crestwood, NY: St. Vladimir's Seminary Press, 1986.

Strawbridge, Gregg, ed. *The Case for Covenant Communion.* Monroe, LA: Athanasius, 2006.

Taft, Robert F. *The Diptychs*. Vol. 4. A History of the Liturgy of St.
   John Chrysostom. Rome: Pontificium Institutum Studiorum
   Orientalium, 1991.

Thomas Aquinas. *Summa Theologica: Complete English Edition*. 5 vols.
   Translated by Fathers of the English Dominican Province. Allen,
   TX: Christian Classics, 1981.

Trigg, Jonathan D. *Baptism in the Theology of Martin Luther*. New York:
   Brill, 1994.

Trueman, Carl. *The Creedal Imperative*. Wheaton, IL: Crossway, 2012.

Tucker, Karen B. Westerfield. *American Methodist Worship*. New York:
   Oxford University Press, 2001.

Turner, Paul. *Sources of Confirmation: From the Fathers through the
   Reformers*. Collegeville, MN: Liturgical, 1993.

Ursinus, Zacharias. *The Commentary of Dr. Zacharias Ursinus on the
   Heidelberg Catechism*. 3rd American ed. Translated by G. W. Williard.
   Cincinnati: Bucher, 1851.

Venema, Cornelius P. *Children at the Lord's Table: Assessing the Case of
   Paedocommunion*. Grand Rapids: Reformation Heritage Books, 2009.

Walker, Michael. *Baptists at the Table: The Theology of the Lord's Supper
   amongst English Baptists in the Nineteenth Century*. Didcot: Baptist
   Historical Society, 1992.

Ware, Timothy. *The Orthodox Way*. Crestwood, NY: St. Vladimir's
   Seminary Press, 1986.

Waters, Guy Prentiss. *The Federal Vision and Covenant Theology:
   A Comparative Analysis*. Phillipsburg, NJ: P&R, 2006.

White, R. E. O. *The Biblical Doctrine of Initiation*. London: Hodder &
   Stoughton, 1960.

Wilkins, Steve, and Duane Garner, eds. *The Federal Vision*. Monroe, LA:
   Athanasius, 2004.

Wright, David F. *Sacraments as God's Self-Giving*. Nashville: Abingdon, 1983.

Yarnell, Malcolm B., III. *The Formation of Christian Doctrine*. Nashville:
   B&H Academic, 2007.

Yarnold, Edward. *The Awe-Inspiring Rites of Initiation: The Origins of the R.C.I.A.* 2nd ed. Collegeville: Liturgical, 1994.

ARTICLES AND ESSAYS

Allen, David. " 'Dipped for Dead:' The Proper Mode of Baptism." Pages 81–106 in *Restoring Integrity in Baptist Churches*. Edited by Thomas White, Jason G. Duesing, and Malcolm B. Yarnell III. Grand Rapids: Kregel, 2008.

Allister, Donald. "Admitting Children to Holy Communion." *Churchman* 113.4 (1999): 295–306.

Baerwald, Jeffrey P. "Mystagogy." In *The New Dictionary of Sacramental Worship*, 2nd ed. Edited by Peter E. Fink. Collegeville, MN: Liturgical (1990): 881–83.

"Baptized Children and the Lord's Table" [1990]. Reformed Church in America Theological Commission. http://images.rca.org/docs /synod/BaptizedChildrenAtTable1990.pdf.

"Baptized Non-communicants and the Celebration of the Lord's Supper" [1977]. Reformed Church in America Theological Commission. http://images.rca.org/docs/synod/BaptizedNonComm1977.pdf.

"Baptized Non-communicants and the Celebration of the Lord's Supper" [1984]. Reformed Church in America Theological Commission. http://images.rca.org/docs/synod/BaptizedNonComm1984.pdf.

Beasley-Murray, George R. "The Authority and Justification for Believers' Baptism." *Review & Expositor* 77.1 (1980): 63–70.

——. "Baptism." Pages 60–66 in *Dictionary of Paul and His Letters*. Edited by Gerald F. Hawthorne, Ralph P. Martin, and Daniel G. Reid, 60–66. Downers Grove, IL: InterVarsity, 1993.

Bingham, Jeffrey. "The Relationship between Baptism and Doctrine in the Second Century." Day-Higginbotham Lectures, Southwestern Baptist Theological Seminary, 2012. http://swbts.edu/media /item/390/the-relationship-between-baptism-and-doctrine-in -the-second-century.

Braaten, Carl E. "Communion before Confirmation." *Dialog* 1.3 (1962): 61–62.

Bradshaw, Paul F. "The Gospel and the Catechumenate in the Third Century." *Journal of Theological Studies* 50.1 (1999): 143–52.

———. "The Profession of Faith in Early Christian Baptism." *Evangelical Quarterly* 78.2 (2006): 101–15.

Burnish, Raymond. "Baptismal Preparation under the Ministry of St John Chrysostom in Fourth-Century Antioch." Pages 370–401 in *Baptism, the New Testament, and the Church: Historical and Contemporary Studies in Honour of R. E. O. White*. Edited by Stanley E. Porter. Sheffield: Sheffield Academic, 1999.

Caneday, A. B. "Baptism in the Stone-Campbell Restoration Movement." Pages 284–328 in *Believer's Baptism*. Edited by Thomas R. Schreiner and Shawn D. Wright. Nashville: B&H Academic, 2006.

Charles, J. D. "Vice and Virtue Lists." Pages 1252–57 in *Dictionary of New Testament Background*. Edited by Stanley E. Porter and Craig A. Evans. Downers Grove, IL: IVP Academic, 2000.

"Children at the Table" [1988]. Reformed Church in America Theological Commission. http://images.rca.org/docs/synod/BaptizedChildrenAtTable1988.pdf.

Connolly, R. H. "On the Text of the Baptismal Creed of Hippolytus." *Journal of Theological Studies* 25 (1924): 131–39.

Covino, Paul F. X. "The Postconciliar Infant Baptism Debate in the American Catholic Church." *Worship* 56.3 (1982): 240–60.

Craycraft, Kenneth R. "Sign and Word: Martin Luther's Theology of the Sacraments." *Restoration Quarterly* 32.3 (1990): 143–64.

Cullmann, Oscar. "Traces of an Ancient Baptismal Formula in the New Testament." Pages 71–80 in *Baptism in the New Testament*. Studies in Biblical Theology 1/1. London: SCM, 1950.

Deweese, Charles W. "Believer's Baptism Is Covenant." Pages 103–11 in *Defining Baptist Convictions: Guidelines for the Twenty-First Century*. Edited by Charles W. Deweese. Franklin, TN: Providence House, 1996.

Dudley, Martin. "Baptistry." Pages 55–56 in *The New SCM Dictionary of Liturgy and Worship*. Edited by Paul F. Bradshaw. London: SCM 2013.

Durheim, Benjamin, and David Farina Turnbloom. "Having Patience with the Practice: A Response to Michael Tuck Regarding Communion without Baptism." *Worship* 87.3 (2013): 212–25.

Edmondson, Stephen. "Opening the Table." *Anglican Theological Review* 91 (2009): 213–34.

Farwell, James. "Baptism, Eucharist, and the Hospitality of Jesus: On the Practice of Open Communion." *Anglican Theological Review* 86 (2007): 215–38.

———. "A Brief Reflection on Kathryn Tanner's Response to 'Baptism, Eucharist, and the Hospitality of Jesus.'" *Anglican Theological Review* 87 (2007): 303–9.

Ferguson, Sinclair. "Infant Baptism View." Pages 77–111 in *Baptism: Three Views*. Edited by David F. Wright. Downers Grove, IL: IVP Academic, 2009.

Foster, Douglas A., Paul M. Blowers, and D. Newell Williams. "Baptism." Pages 56–67 in *The Encyclopedia of the Stone-Campbell Movement*. Edited by Douglas A. Foster, Paul M. Blowers, and D. Newell Williams. Grand Rapids: Eerdmans, 2004.

France, R. T. "Exegesis in Practice: Two Samples." Pages 252–81 in *New Testament Interpretation: Essays on Principles and Methods*. Edited by I. Howard Marshall. Carlisle: Paternoster, 1977.

———. "Jesus the Baptist?" Pages 94–111 in *Jesus of Nazareth: Lord and Christ*. Edited by J. B. Green and M. M. B. Turner. Carlisle: Paternoster, 1994.

Freudenberg, Matthias. "Catechisms." Pages 206–14 in *The Calvin Handbook*. Edited by Herman J. Selderhuis, translated by Judith J. Guder. Grand Rapids: Eerdmans, 2008.

Frost, Jerry William. "Dry Bones of Quaker Theology." *Church History* 39.4, (1970): 503–23.

Garrett, James Leo. "Should Baptist Churches Adopt Open Membership" [2010]. The Center for Theological Research, Southwestern Baptist Theological Seminary. http://www.baptisttheology.org/ baptisttheology/assets/File/ShouldBaptistChurchesadoptOpen Membership-Garrett.pdf.

George, Timothy. "The Southern Baptists." Pages 39-51 in *Baptism and Church*. Edited by Merle D. Strege. Grand Rapids: Sagamore Books, 1986.

Gustafson, James M. "Preface: An Appreciative Interpretation." Pages xxi-xxxv in *Christ and Culture*. New York: HarperCollins, 2001.

Hammett, John S. "Article VII: Baptism and the Lord's Supper." Pages 71-82 in *Baptist Faith and Message 2000: Critical Issues in America's Largest Protestant Denomination*. Edited by Douglas K. Blount and Joseph D. Wooddell. New York: Rowman & Littlefield, 2007.

Hendricks, William L. "Baptism: A Baptist Perspective." *Southwestern Journal of Theology* 31 (1989): 22-33.

Hicks, John Mark. "Stone-Campbell Sacramental Theology." *Restoration Quarterly* 50.1 (2008): 35-48.

Hoek, Annewies van den. "The 'Catechetical' School of Early Christian Alexandria and Its Philonic Heritage." *Harvard Theological Review* 90.1 (1997): 59-87.

Hughes, Langston. "Salvation." Pages 18-21 in *The Big Sea*. New York: Hill and Wang, 1940, 1993.

Johnson, Maxwell E. "From Three Weeks to Forty Days: Baptismal Preparation and the Origins of Lent." *Studia Liturgica* 20 (1990): 185-200.

———. "Mystagogical Catechesis." Pages 56-67 in *The New SCM Dictionary of Liturgy and Worship*. Edited by Paul F. Bradshaw. London: SCM, 2013.

Jordan, James B. "Children and the Religious Meals of the Old Creation." Pages 49-68 in *The Case for Covenant Communion*. Edited by Gregg Strawbridge. Monroe, LA: Athanasius, 2006.

Karmiris, John. "Concerning the Sacraments." Pages 21–31 in *Eastern Orthodox Theology: A Contemporary Reader*. Edited by Daniel B. Clendenin. Grand Rapids: Baker Academic, 2003.

Kavanagh, Aidan. "Norm of Baptism: The New Rite of Christian Initiation of Adults." *Worship* 48.3 (1974): 143–52.

Keidel, Christian L. "Is the Lord's Supper for Children." *Westminster Theological Journal* 37.3 (1975): 301–41.

Kenny, J. P. "The Age of Confirmation." *Worship* 35.1 (1960): 4–15.

Kolb, Robert. " 'What Benefit Does the Soul Receive from a Handful of Water?': Luther's Preaching on Baptism, 1528–1539." *Concordia Journal* 25.4 (1999): 346–63.

Kosmala, Hans. "The Conclusion of Matthew." *Annual of the Swedish Theological Institute* 4 (1965): 132–47.

Kreider, Alan. "Baptism, Catechism, and the Eclipse of Jesus' Teaching in Early Christianity." *The Mennonite Quarterly Review* 72.1 (1998): 5–30.

Küng, Hans. "Confirmation as the Completion of Baptism (I): To Edward Schillebeeckx on His 60th Birthday." *Colloquium* 8.1 (1975): 33–40.

———. "Confirmation as the Development, Re-affirmation and Completion of Baptism. II." *Colloquium* 8.2 (1976): 5–13.

Lane, Anthony N. S. "Dual-Practice Baptism View." Pages 139–71 in *Baptism: Three Views*. Edited by David F. Wright. Downers Grove, IL: IVP Academic, 2009.

Leith, John H. "Creeds and Their Role in the Church." Pages 1–11 in *Creeds of the Churches*, 3rd ed. Louisville: John Knox, 1982.

Leithart, Peter, et al. "Joint Federal Vision Statement" [2007]. https://federal-vision.com/ecclesiology/joint-federal-vision-statement/.

Lietzmann, Hans. "Die Anfänge des Glaubensbekenntnisses." Pages 226–42 in *Festgabe für D. Dr. A. von Harnack ... zum siebzigsten Geburtstag dargebracht von Fachgenossen und Freunden*. Tübingen: Mohr Siebeck, 1921.

Littler, Keith T., Leslie J. Francis, and T. Hugh Thomas. "The Admission of Children to Communion before Confirmation: A Survey among Church in Wales Clerics." *Contact* 139 (2002): 24–38.

Lorenzen, Thorwald. "Baptism and Church Membership: Some Baptist Positions and Their Ecumenical Implications." *Journal of Ecumenical Studies* 18.4 (1981): 561–74.

Luther, Martin. "An Open Letter to Those in Frankfurt on the Main, 1533." Translated by Jon D. Vieker. *Concordia Journal* 16.4 (1990): 333–51.

McKinion, Steve. "Baptism in the Patristic Writings." Pages 163–88 in *Believer's Baptism: Sign of the New Covenant in Christ*. Edited by Thomas R. Schreiner and Shawn D. Wright, NAC Studies in Bible and Theology. Nashville: B&H Academic, 2006.

Merrigan, Terrence. "Models in the Theology of Avery Dulles: A Critical Analysis." *Bijdrage, tijdschrisft voor filosofie en theologie* 54.2 (1993): 141–61.

Meyers, Jeffrey. "Presbyterian, Examine Thyself." Pages 19–34 in *The Case for Covenant Communion*. Edited by Gregg Strawbridge. Monroe, LA: Athanasius, 2006.

Mitchell, Nathan. "The Once and Future Child: Towards a Theology of Childhood." *Living Light* 12 (1975): 423–37.

Morozowich, Mark M. "Liturgical Changes in Russia and the Christian East? A Case Study: The Mysteries (Sacraments) of Initiation with the Eucharistic Liturgy." *Worship* 83.1 (2009): 30–47.

Needham, Nick. "Children at the Lord's Table in the Patristic Era." Pages 145–62 in *Children and the Lord's Supper*. Edited by Guy Water and Ligon Duncan. Ross-shire, UK: Christian Focus, 2011.

Nelson, Paul. "Lutheran Worship." Pages 293–94 in *The New SCM Dictionary of Liturgy and Worship*. Edited by Paul F. Bradshaw. London: SCM, 2013.

Niebuhr, H. Richard. "Introduction: Types of Christian Ethics." Pages xxxvii–lv in *Christ and Culture*. New York: HarperCollins, 2001.

Oberman, Heiko A. "Quo Vadis Patre? Tradition from Irenaeus to

Humani Generis." Pages 269–96 in *The Dawn of the Reformation: Essays in the Late Medieval and Early Reformation Thought.* Edinburgh: T&T Clark, 1986.

Payne, Ernest. "Baptists and the Laying on of Hands." *Baptist Quarterly* 15.5 (January 1954): 203–15.

Pipes, Carol. "Lord's Supper: LifeWay Surveys Churches' Practices, Frequency" [2012]. http://www.bpnews.net/38730.

Poe, Harry L. "John Bunyan." Pages 26–48 in *Baptist Theologians.* Edited by Timothy George and David S. Dockery. Nashville: Broadman, 1990.

———. "John Bunyan's Controversy with the Baptists." *Baptist History and Heritage* 23.2 (1988): 25–35.

Quinn, Frank C. "Confirmation Reconsidered: Rite and Meaning." Pages 219–37 in *Living Water, Sealing Spirit.* Edited by Maxwell E. Johnson. Collegeville, MN: Liturgical, 1995.

Rainbow, Jonathan H. " 'Confessor Baptism': The Baptismal Doctrine of the Early Anabaptists." *American Baptist Quarterly* 8.4 (1989): 276–90.

Ramsey, Patrick. "*Sola Fide* Compromised? Martin Luther and the Doctrine of Baptism." *Themelios* 34.2 (2009). http://themelios .thegospelcoalition.org/article/sola-fide-compromised-martin -luther-and-the-doctrine-of-baptism.

Rayburn, Robert. "A Presbyterian Defense of Paedocommunion." Pages 3–34 in *The Case for Covenant Communion.* Edited by Gregg Strawbridge. Monroe, LA: Athanasius, 2006.

Scaer, David P. "Luther, Baptism, and the Church Today." *Concordia Theological Quarterly* 62.4 (1998): 247–68.

Schaff, Philip. "§ 72. Catechetical Instruction and Confirmation." Pages 255–58 in *Ante-Nicene Christianity, A.D. 100–325.* History of the Christian Church 2. Grand Rapids: Eerdmans, 1910.

Schenk, Berthold von. "First Communion and Confirmation." *Concordia Theological Monthly* 42.6 (1971): 353–60.

Senn, Frank C. "Confirmation and First Communion: A Reappraisal."
    Lutheran Quarterly 23.2 (1971): 178–91.

Shriver, George H. "Southern Baptists Ponder Open Membership: An
    End of Re-baptism." *Journal of Ecumenical Studies* 6.3 (1969): 423–29.

Stancil, Bill. "Rebaptisms in the Southern Baptist Convention: A
    Theological and Pastoral Dilemma." *Perspectives in Religious Studies*
    21.2 (1994): 127–41.

Stein, Robert. "Baptism in Luke-Acts." Pages 35–66 in *Believer's Baptism*.
    Edited by Thomas R. Schreiner and Shawn D. Wright. Nashville:
    B&H Academic, 2006.

Strawbridge, Gregg. "The Polemics of Infant Communion." Pages 147–65
    in *The Case for Covenant Communion*. Edited by Gregg Strawbridge.
    Monroe, LA: Athanasius, 2006.

Tanner, Kathryn. "In Praise of Open Communion: A Rejoinder to James
    Farwell." *Anglican Theological Review* 86 (2009): 473–85.

Tuck, Michael. "Who Is Invited to the Feast? A Critique of the Practice of
    Communion without Baptism." *Worship* 86.6 (2012): 505–27.

Tucker, Karen B. Westerfield. "Methodist Worship." Pages 316–18 in
    The New SCM Dictionary of Liturgy and Worship. Edited by Paul F.
    Bradshaw. London: SCM 2013.

Turner, Paul. "Confusion over Confirmation." *Worship* 71.6 (1997): 537–45.

———. "The Origins of Confirmation: An Analysis of Aidan Kavanagh's
    Hypothesis (with Response by Aidan Kavanagh)." Pages 238–58 in
    Living Water, Sealing Spirit: Readings on Christian Initiation. Edited
    by Maxwell E. Johnson. Collegeville, MN: Liturgical, 1995.

Wagner, Mervyn A. "Luther's Baptismal Theology: Implications for
    Catechesis." *Lutheran Theological Journal* 31.3 (1997): 105–14.

Walsh, Christopher. "Celebrant." Page 101 in *The New SCM Dictionary of
    Liturgy and Worship*. Edited by Paul F. Bradshaw. London: SCM, 2013.

Ward, Alan. "Communion before Confirmation: A Response to
    'Admitting Children to Holy Communion' in Churchman 113/4
    (1999)." *Churchman* 114.4 (2000): 295–99.

White, James Emery. "Rebaptism in the Life of the Church." *Search* 19.2 (1989): 24–33.

Williams, Daniel H. "Considering Catechism for Suspicious Protestants." Pages 20–29 in *Christian Reflection*. Waco: Center for Christian Ethics at Baylor University, 2007. http://www.baylor.edu/ifl /christianreflection/Catechism.pdf.

Wills, Gregory A. "Sounds from Baptist History." Pages 285–312 in *The Lord's Supper: Remembering and Proclaiming Christ until He Comes*. Edited by Thomas R. Schreiner and Matthew R. Crawford, NAC Studies in Bible and Theology 10. Nashville: B&H Academic, 2010.

Wilson, Douglas. "Union with Christ: An Overview of the Federal Vision." Pages 1–8 in *The Auburn Avenue Theology, Pros and Cons: Debating the Federal Vision*. Edited by E. Calvin Beisner. Fort Lauderdale, FL: Knox Theological Seminary, 2004.

Yeager, D. M. "The View from Somewhere: The Meaning of Method in Christ and Culture." *Journal of the Society of Christian Ethics* 23 (2003): 101–20.

SUBJECT INDEX

—

SCRIPTURE INDEX

—

Old Testament

New Testament